A GOOD AND VALUABLE OFFICER

Daniel Morgan in the Revolutionary War

Michael Cecere

HERITAGE BOOKS
2016

HERITAGE BOOKS
AN IMPRINT OF HERITAGE BOOKS, INC.

Books, CDs, and more—Worldwide

For our listing of thousands of titles see our website
at
www.HeritageBooks.com

Published 2016 by
HERITAGE BOOKS, INC.
Publishing Division
5810 Ruatan Street
Berwyn Heights, Md. 20740

Copyright © 2016 Michael Cecere

All rights reserved. No part of this book may be reproduced or transmitted in any form or by any means, electronic or mechanical, including photocopying, recording or by any information storage and retrieval system without written permission from the author, except for the inclusion of brief quotations in a review.

International Standard Book Numbers
Paperbound: 978-0-7884-5748-7
Clothbound: 978-0-7884-5996-2

Contents

Ch. 1 "The Obscurity from Which He Rose"
       1736-1774..................1

Ch. 2 "Remarkably Stout and Hardy Men"
       1775.....................15

Ch. 3 "A Scene of Trouble to Go Through"
       Arnold's Expedition to Quebec: 1775........33

Ch. 4 "Betwixt Every Peal [of Gunfire] the Awful
       Voice of Morgan is Heard"
       Quebec: 1775...................57

Ch. 5 Captivity, Promotion, Morgan's Rifle Corps
       1776-1777......................79

Ch. 6 "Morgan...Poured Down Like a Torrent
       from a Hill"
       Saratoga: 1777..................101

Ch. 7 "[Morgan] is a Brave Officer, and
a Well Meaning Man"
1778-1780……..…..…137

Ch. 8 "Morgan's Character as a Soldier is Well
Known in America"
Morgan Returns to the Army: 1780.….171

Ch. 9 "I Have Given [Tarleton] a
Devil of a Whipping"
Cowpens: 1781...……..…...191

Ch. 10 "Nothing Will Help Me But Rest"
1781……...……....213

Appendix………………………………………..225

Bibliography………………………………….255

Index…………………………...………………...269

Acknowledgements

This work is the result of several years of research that really began with other projects (biographies of Charles Porterfield and Thomas Posey, an account of American riflemen in the Revolutionary War and an account of Maine's role in the Revolution) to name a few. As always, I am grateful for the support and comradeship of my fellow Revolutionary War reenactors, both in my unit, the 7th Virginia Regiment, and outside my unit among the various Continental and Crown forces. One such reenactor (and national park historian at Saratoga) is Eric Schnitzer. Eric was most generous with his research and his time and I enjoyed my visits to the battlefield immensely thanks to him. Debbie Riley, an editor with Heritage Books helped me tackle the maps and images in the book, a task I have yet to master. Two institutions in particular, the Simpson Library at the University of Mary Washington in Fredericksburg and the Rockefeller Library at Colonial Williamsburg were tremendous resources for my research. Lastly, my wife Susan deserves my appreciation for allowing me to turn our romantic visits to Quebec and family visits to Maine into research visits as well. Thanks for indulging me Sue.

About the Author

Michael Cecere Sr. teaches American History in Virginia. An avid Revolutionary War re-enactor, he currently is the commander of the 7th Virginia Regiment and participates in numerous living history events throughout the country.

Other books by Michael Cecere

They Behaved Like Soldiers: Captain John Chilton and the Third Virginia Regiment, 1776-1778 (2004)

An Officer of Very Extraordinary Merit: Charles Porterfield and the American War for Independence, 1775-1780 (2004)

Captain Thomas Posey and the 7th Virginia Regiment (2005)

They Are Indeed a Very Useful Corps: American Riflemen in the Revolutionary War (2006)

In This Time of Extreme Danger: Northern Virginia in the American Revolution (2006)

Great Things Are Expected from the Virginians: Virginia in the American Revolution (2008)

To Hazard Our Own Security: Maine's Role in the American Revolution (2010)

Wedded to My Sword: The Revolutionary War Service of Light Horse Harry Lee (2012)

Cast Off the British Yoke: The Old Dominion and American Independence, 1763-1776 (2014)

A Universal Appearance of War: The Revolutionary War in Virginia, 1775-1781 (2014)

Second to No Man But the Commander in Chief: Hugh Mercer, American Patriot (2015)

Chapter One

"The Obscurity From Which He Rose"

1736 - 1774

General Daniel Morgan is a revered figure to many Revolutionary War enthusiasts and scholars. Few soldiers contributed more to American victory in the Revolutionary War than the rugged rifle commander from the Virginia frontier who served heroically at Quebec, was instrumental in America's victory at Saratoga, and who destroyed "Bloody" Banastre Tarleton at Cowpens, (lifting American morale at a critical time in the war). Accounts of Morgan's exploits and accomplishments are numerous and he represents to those familiar with his story the quintessential American hero; one who rose from poverty and obscurity to become one of America's greatest Revolutionary War commanders. Perhaps no one captured Morgan's legacy to the Revolutionary War better than General Morgan's minister and friend, the Reverend William Hill in his 1802 eulogy of Morgan.

> *When we consider the obscurity from which he rose; the honour and power to which he ascended; the great services which he has rendered his country, we may say he had few, very few equals.... I think we may venture to assert, that he has not left another behind him to whom we are so much indebted for our Independence and Liberty.*[1]

---

[1] Reverend William Hill, "Sketch of Daniel Morgan, Notes and Sermon," Virginia Historical Society (Henceforth referred to as William Hill Notes)

Northwestern Virginia Map
Adapted from Library of Congress

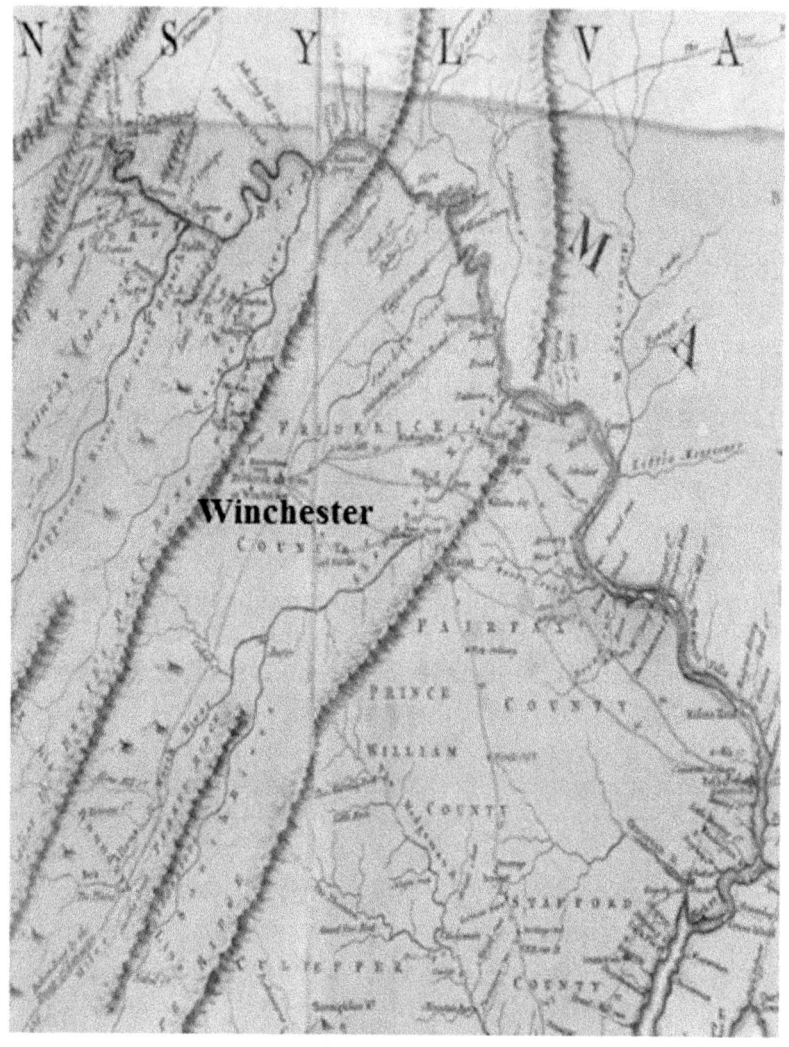

Frederick & Berkley County Virginia
Adapted from Library of Congress

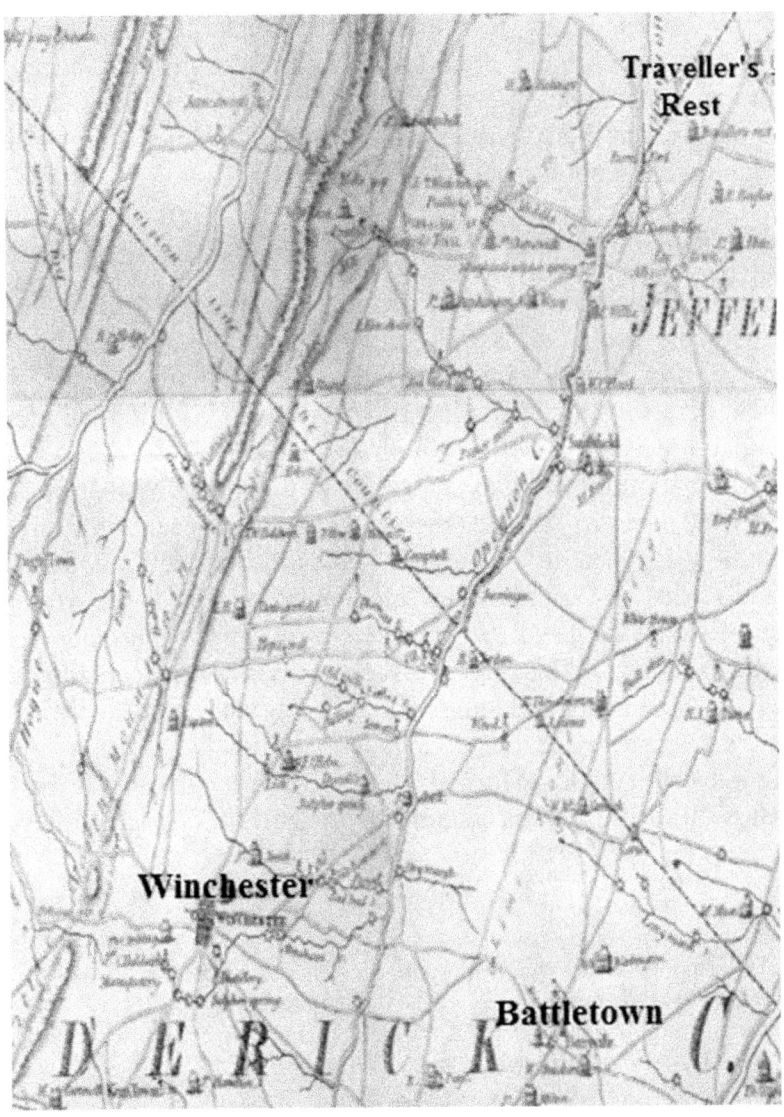

Yet, despite such praise and esteem, Morgan's service to the United States and his many accomplishments on the battlefield are unknown to most Americans today. When Americans think of the heroes of the Revolution, they think of Washington, Jefferson, Adams and Franklin, all important players indeed. But many others deserve to be recognized and remembered for their service in the American Revolution and Daniel Morgan of Virginia ranks among the first of these.

Morgan Arrives in Virginia

Very little is known about Daniel Morgan's early life; it was a topic he rarely discussed. Some accounts claim he was born in 1736 in Pennsylvania, but most identify his birthplace as New Jersey. Wherever Morgan was raised, his childhood was apparently spent under very humble conditions.

It is not until Morgan arrived in Virginia in 1753 that more specific details of his life emerge. He reportedly left his family in New Jersey at age 17 after a heated dispute with his father and settled in Virginia a few months later.[2] Burdened with a limited education and, "*so poor that he hardly had any cloaths,*" Morgan relied on his physical strength (he was six feet tall and broad shouldered) and found work as a day laborer or "*grubber*" on a farm near Charlestown (West Virginia).[3] After a few months in the fields, Morgan took a job as a wagoner for Robert Burwell, a prosperous landowner in the Shenandoah Valley,

---

[2] Don Higginbotham, *Daniel Morgan: Revolutionary Rifleman*, (Chapel Hill: University of North Carolina Press, 1961), 2

[3] "Notes from Benjamin Berry on Daniel Morgan," Virginia Historical Society (Henceforth referred to as Benjamin Berry Notes) and
"A Return of the 2nd Company of Rangers Commanded by Capt. John Ashby, 21 October, 1755," *George Washington Papers at the Library of Congress, 1741-1799*: Series 4, General Correspondence, 1697-1799. (Accessed through the Library of Congress website)

and hauled freight from Frederick County to the eastern towns of Leesburg, Alexandria, Dumfries, and Fredericksburg.[4]

Involvement in the French and Indian War

By the outbreak of the French and Indian War, just a year after Morgan's arrival in Virginia, the ambitious youth of eighteen had purchased his own team of horses and a wagon. Morgan hauled supplies to Fort Cumberland (Maryland) for General Edward Braddock's ill-fated expedition in 1755 and witnessed the disaster that ensued at the British defeat.[5]

At some point in his service as a wagoner for the army, Morgan was severely punished (whipped) by the British for misconduct. The specific details are a bit unclear. One account, attributed to Morgan, claimed that he *"knocked down a sentinel"* for which he was sentenced to 400 lashes, while another account, also attributed to Morgan, claimed that insubordination towards an officer earned him 500 lashes.[6] Whatever the details (perhaps both actions occurred), Daniel Morgan found great delight in frequently recounting in a, *"jocular way, that King George was indebted one lash yet, for the drummer miscounted one…so that he only received 499 when he had promised him 500."*[7]

---

[4] William Hill Notes and Benjamin Berry Notes
and
James Graham, *Life of General Daniel Morgan,* (Bloomingburg, NY: Zebrowski: Historical Services Publishing Co., 1993), 21
(Originally published in 1856)
[5] Graham, 23-25
[6] William Maxwell, ed., "A Recollection of the American Revolutionary War," *Virginia Historical Register and Literary Companion,* Vol. 6, (Richmond: MacFarland & Fergusson, 1853), 210
and
William Hill Notes
[7] William Hill Notes

Despite such harsh treatment by the British, Morgan recovered and joined Captain John Ashby's ranger company in late August 1755.[8] Morgan knew Ashby well; both men had worked for Robert Burwell before the war, Morgan as a wagoner and Ashby as an overseer who, in part, supervised Morgan.

After a rather uneventful fall campaign with Ashby's rangers on the frontier, Morgan was granted a furlough to return to Frederick County for the winter. On his way back to Captain Ashby's company in mid-April, Morgan and another soldier were ambushed by several Indians.[9] Morgan's companion was shot off his horse and killed. Morgan barely avoided a similar fate, suffering a serious neck wound from a musket ball that entered the back of his neck, grazed his jaw bone and passed through his left cheek, taking some of his lower left teeth with it.[10] Despite the grievous wound, (which left him with a permanent scar on his cheek) Morgan somehow managed to remain on his horse and escape, riding fourteen miles to Fort Edward where he eventually recovered.[11]

It appears that when Morgan's service in Captain Ashby's company ended in the fall of 1756 he returned to Frederick County and resumed his work as a wagoner, delivering supplies to several military outposts on the Virginia frontier, but also making non-military hauls to the east. It is unclear how long Morgan continued to deliver military supplies; the need to maintain Virginia's frontier outposts diminished as the fighting on the frontier subsided. Morgan's participation in the French

---

[8] "A Return of the 2nd Company of Rangers Commanded by Capt. John Ashby, 21 October, 1755," *George Washington Papers at the Library of Congress, 1741-1799*: Series 4, General Correspondence, 1697-1799.

[9] W.W. Abbot, ed., "John Fenton Mercer to Colonel Washington, 17 April, 1756," *The Papers of George Washington, Colonial Series,* Vol. 3, (Charlottesville: University Press of Virginia, 1984), 11

[10] Ibid., and William Hill notes

[11] Abbot, ed., "John Fenton Mercer to Colonel Washington, 17 April, 1756," *The Papers of George Washington, Colonial Series,* Vol. 3, 11

and Indian War likely ceased well before the end of the decade. He returned to Frederick County where he quickly earned a rather dubious reputation.

Morgan the Notorious Brawler

Daniel Morgan eagerly embraced his return to civilian life in Frederick County and embarked on a path of riotous behavior, drinking, gaming, and fighting at an alarming rate.[12] Much of his disorderly behavior occurred in a small settlement a few miles east of Winchester called Battletown (no doubt due to the numerous fights that occurred at the tavern located there).[13]

By the early 1760's, however, a new influence emerged on Daniel Morgan's life, one that gradually tamed his riotous behavior. Abigail Curry was the daughter of a Frederick County farmer and it appears she captured Morgan's eye as early as 1761.[14] A series of purchases, some made by Morgan and others charged by Abigail to his account, appear in the ledger of a local merchant at this time.[15]

By 1763 the young couple shared a home together out of wedlock, a not uncommon arrangement on the frontier.[16] Two daughters were born from this union in the 1760's, Nancy and Betsy, and by the start of the next decade Morgan had purchased land near Battletown on which he grew wheat and hemp.[17]

---

[12] William Hill Notes and Benjamin Berry Notes
[13] Ibid.
[14] Higginbotham, 11
[15] Peggy Shomo Joyner, ed., "Allason Papers: Store Day Book, 1761-63," *Magazine of Virginia Genealogy*, Vol. 34, No. 4, (Fall 1996), 294, 296, 302, 305 and Higginbothan, 11, Note 19
[16] Higginbotham. Note: Higginbotham asserts that Daniel and Abigail were formally married in 1773.
[17] Curtis Chappelear, "The George Carter Tract," *Proceedings of the Clarke County Historical Association*, Vol. 3, (1943), 18-19

Debt was a constant concern for Morgan, as it was for many Virginia farmers, but Morgan managed his affairs deftly enough that by the 1770's he was a respected member of the community. This was evident in 1771 when county leaders appointed Morgan to command a company of county militia.[18] Morgan's ownership of slaves, which numbered ten in 1774, likely further enhanced his successful status in Frederick County.[19]

The poor, uneducated lad from New Jersey with no family connections in Virginia had seemingly done quite well for himself in the two decades since his arrival in the Shenandoah Valley. Morgan's high stature and regard among his neighbors in Frederick County was confirmed in 1774 when scores of volunteers stepped forward to serve under Captain Morgan in yet another frontier conflict with the Indians.

Dunmore's War 1774

A series of clashes in the early 1770's along Virginia's frontier between colonial settlers moving west for land and the Indians who already lived there, erupted into a full-fledged frontier war in 1774. While Virginia's royal governor, John Murray, the Earl of Dunmore, acknowledged that both sides were responsible for the conflict, he heeded the appeals of the settlers to, "*put* [the frontier] *in a State of defence,*" and, "*bring the Indians to terms.*"[20] Dunmore proposed a plan to mobilize the militia to the House of Burgesses in May, but the burgesses, who were focused on supporting Boston in its struggle with the British Parliament, declined to support Dunmore.

---

[18] *Frederick County Order Book Abstracts, Order Book 15,* "10 May, 1771," 211

[19] Higginbotham, 14

[20] Reuben Gold Thwaites and Louise Phelps Kellog, eds., "Dunmore to Dartmouth, 24 December, 1774," *Documentary History of Dunmore's War : 1774,* (Madison, WI: Wisconsin Historical Society, 1905), 379

Citing an act that allowed Virginia's governors to employ the militia against invasions and insurrections, Lord Dunmore responded with an order for the militia of the frontier counties to muster in preparation for an expedition against the Shawnee Indians and their allies.[21]

Captain Daniel Morgan answered Dunmore's call and raised a company of militia volunteers. They joined several other companies and fell under the command of Major Angus McDonald, a veteran of the French and Indian war and fellow resident of Frederick County. McDonald's force, numbering over 400 men, rendezvoused at Wheeling Creek on the Ohio River (present day Wheeling, WV) in July and constructed a fort.[22]

With few signs of hostile Indian activity in the immediate area, Major McDonald lead the bulk of his force, including Captain Morgan's company, westward across the Ohio River into Shawnee territory. They marched in late July with only a week's worth of provisions and travelled nearly 90 miles before they stumbled upon an Indian ambush near the Muskingum River.[23] Captain James Wood (of Winchester) commanded Major McDonald's lead company and bore the brunt of the ambush, but Captain Wood and his men were quickly reinforced by Captain Morgan and his company, who rushed forward in support.[24] The ensuing skirmish was brief but intense, and both sides suffered a handful of casualties.[25] The Indians withdrew across the Muskingum River, pursued by the Virginians, who paused for the night on the riverbank and crossed the following day against minimal resistance. Several abandoned Shawnee towns were burned and approximately 70 acres of corn destroyed. Another three to four hundred bushels

---

[21] Ibid.
[22] Thwaites and Kellog, 155
[23] Ibid.
[24] Higginbotham, 17
[25] Thwaites and Kellog, 155

of old (harvested) corn were also burned before Major McDonald led his force back to Wheeling.[26]

Governor Dunmore, with a large body of militia from the northern counties of the Shenandoah Valley, joined Major McDonald at Wheeling and this combined force proceeded down the Ohio River in late September to rendezvous with Colonel Andrew Lewis and approximately 1,100 militia from southwestern Virginia.[27] Dunmore halted at the mouth of the Hockhocking River where he waited at newly built Fort Gower for the arrival of Indian representatives whom he expected to negotiate a peace treaty with.

The governor soon learned, however, that the Shawnee refused to meet with him and, *"were resolved to prosecute their designs against the People of Virginia."*[28] In response, Dunmore marched his force westward, into Shawnee territory, *"to defeat* [the Shawnee] *and destroy their Towns, in case they should refuse* [further] *offers of Peace."*[29] After a few days on the march (against little opposition) a report reached Dunmore of a significant battle at the confluence of the Ohio and Kanawha Rivers. Colonel Lewis's force of 1,100 men, (encamped at Point Pleasant on the Virginia side of the Ohio River) engaged a slightly smaller force of Indians on October 10th, and after, *"a very warm engagement,"* the Indians broke off contact, withdrew back across the Ohio River, and asked for peace terms from Dunmore.[30]

The governor, who was encamped deep in Shawnee territory on the Scioto River, credited the new found desire of the Shawnee for peace to their disappointment with the outcome of the battle at Point Pleasant (which actually resulted in twice as many militia casualties as Indian losses) and their concern for

---

[26] Thwaites and Kellog, 156, 154
[27] Ibid., Note 15, 302
[28] Thwaites and Kellog, eds., "Dunmore to Dartmouth, 24 December, 1774," *Documentary History of Dunmore's War : 1774*, 384
[29] Ibid.
[30] Ibid., 384-385

their families and towns threatened by the presence of Dunmore's large detachment. Lord Dunmore reported to his superiors in England that after a few days of negotiation the Shawnee resolved to

> Make no further efforts against a Power they saw so far superior to theirs, [and] determined to throw themselves upon our Mercy.[31]

Although most of the Indian leaders accepted the peace terms offered by Dunmore -- which included the return of all white captives held by the Indians as well as any horses captured during the years of frontier conflict in exchange for Dunmore's recognition of the Ohio River as a boundary and barrier to white encroachment -- several Mingo leaders balked at the treaty and attempted to escape west towards the Great Lakes with their people and captives. When Lord Dunmore learned of this, he ordered Major William Crawford, a veteran of the French and Indian War, to march westward with 240 men (including Captain Morgan and his company) to prevent the Mingoes from escaping.[32]

After a forced march of approximately 40 miles, Crawford's detachment reached the fugitive Mingoes. Crawford allowed his troops to rest for a few hours in the early morning darkness, then ordered them into position to attack at dawn. One of Crawford's men was discovered by an Indian, however, and the confrontation that ensued alarmed the Indian encampment. Major Crawford, whose grasp of spelling was rudimentary, confided to Colonel George Washington (his former commander in the French and Indian War) after the encounter that the, "*Chief part* [of the Indians] *maid there Eascap in the*

---

[31] Ibid., 385
[32] Beverly H. Runge, ed., "Colonel William Crawford to Colonel George Washington, 14 November, 1774," *The Papers of George Washington, Colonial Series,* Vol. 10, (Charlottesville, VA: University Press of Virginia, 1995), 182

dark but we got 14 Prisoners and killd 6 and wounded Saveral more, got all there bagege and horses 10 of there Guns and [two] *white Prisoners*...."[33] Crawford apparently did not suffer any casualties in the brief fight and declined to pursue the fugitives any further.

Fort Gower Resolves

By early November, Captain Morgan was back at Fort Gower on the Ohio River where he participated in the adoption of an extraordinary set of resolves by the militia officers assembled there.[34] Morgan and his fellow soldiers were well aware of the intensifying dispute between the colonies and British Parliament over the latter's colonial policies and recent crackdown on Boston. A series of oppressive parliamentary acts against Massachusetts (dubbed the Intolerable Acts by those allied with Boston) had led to a gathering of colonial delegates in Philadelphia at the same time that Dunmore's expedition against the Shawnee took place.

Although Captain Morgan and his comrades at Fort Gower were unaware of the outcome of the meeting in Philadelphia, they wanted it known that they were willing to do their part to defend American liberty:

> *Having now concluded the Campaign...it only remains that we give our Country the strongest Assurance that we are ready, at all Times, to the utmost of our Power to maintain and defend her just Rights and Privileges.*[35]

The confident veterans of Dunmore's campaign announced that they were, "*a respectable body,*" whose recent experience in the field (and wilderness) meant that, "*our Men can march and*

---

[33] Ibid.
[34] Graham, 52
[35] Purdie & Dixon, "A Meeting of Officers...," *Virginia Gazette*, 22 December, 1774, 1

shoot with any in the known World."³⁶ They went on to declare that although they bore the most faithful allegiance to the King, their, "*Love of Liberty, and Attachment to the real Interests and just Rights of America outweigh every other consideration.*"³⁷ They therefore resolved to

> *Exert every Power within us for the Defense of American liberty, and for the support of her just Rights and Privileges, not in any precipitate, riotous, or tumultuous Manner, but when regularly called forth by the unanimous Voice of our Countrymen.*³⁸

And with that bold statement, Captain Morgan and the rest of Dunmore's force returned to their homes.

---

[36] Ibid., 2
[37] Ibid.
[38] Ibid.

Chapter Two

"Remarkably Stout and Hardy Men"

1775

Upon Daniel Morgan's return to Frederick County, he discovered that the Continental Congress in Philadelphia had also declared its determination to defend the rights of the colonists, but the delegates declined to encourage militant measures and opted instead to employ economic measures to oppose Parliament's Intolerable Acts against Boston. A handful of Virginia counties acted on their own to form independent militia companies, but most, including Frederick County, initially chose only to create committees to implement the continental boycott.

Reports over the winter of a steady British military build-up in Boston and a British ban on shipments of gunpowder and arms to the American colonies, coupled with growing disillusionment among many colonists at the lack of support from either the British people or King, convinced many Virginians to support a more militant stance against Parliament in the spring of 1775. This was demonstrated at the 2nd Virginia Convention in March when county representatives assembled in Richmond and debated a resolution proposed by Patrick Henry to place Virginia in a "posture of defense." Henry's argument that armed conflict with Great Britain was inevitable and his stirring declaration of, "Give Me Liberty or Give Me Death" helped convince a narrow majority of the Convention delegates to adopt his resolution to better organize the militia.

All of these events in the winter and spring of 1775 increased tension and widened the rift between Great Britain and her American colonies, but not irreparably. In late April, however, two incidents just days apart, one in Massachusetts at Lexington and Concord (the opening battle of the Revolutionary War) and the other in Williamsburg (Governor Dunmore's seizure of gunpowder from the capital) outraged Virginians to such a degree that war fever spread throughout the Old Dominion.

This sentiment was very evident in Daniel Morgan's adoptive hometown of Winchester in early June of 1775 when the Reverend Philip Fithian passed through on his travels in the Shenandoah Valley. On June 6th, Fithian recorded in his journal that

> *Mars, the great God of Battle, is now honoured in every Part of this spacious Colony but here* [Winchester] *every Presence is warlike, every Sound is martial! Drums beating, Fifes & Bag-Pipes playing, & only sonorous & heroic Tunes—Every Man has a hunting-shirt, which is the Uniform of each Company—Almost all have a Cockade, & bucktale in their Hatts, to represent that they are hardy, resolute, & invincible Natives of the Woods of America.*[1]

Fithian observed this same martial spirit ten days later on another visit to Winchester:

> *This Town in Arms. All in a Hunting-Shirt uniform & Bucks Tale in their Hats. Indeed they make a grand Figure.*[2]

Similar scenes occurred throughout Virginia, but the men of Frederick County were offered an opportunity in June not given to most of their fellow Virginians; a chance to enlist in one of two continental rifle companies raised in Virginia and authorized by the Continental Congress in Philadelphia.

---

[1] Robert Albion and Leonidas Dodson Philip, eds., "Diary Entry, 6 June, 1775," *Philip Vickers Fithian: Journal, 1775-1776, Written on the Virginia-Pennsylvania Frontier and in the Army Around New York*, (Princeton: Princeton University Press, 1934), 24

[2] Ibid. , "Fithian Diary Entry, 17 June, 1775", 31

Congress had authorized the formation of ten continental rifle companies on June 14, 1775 to reinforce the American army that sat outside of Boston after the fighting at Lexington and Concord. Six of the rifle companies were to be raised in Pennsylvania, two in Maryland, and two in Virginia. All of these companies were ordered to march to Boston as soon as possible to serve as light infantry under the newly appointed commander in chief of the continental army, General George Washington.[3]

It appears that the congressional delegations from Pennsylvania, Maryland and Virginia took the authority upon themselves to select the counties in their respective colonies from which to raise the rifle companies.[4] In Virginia, Berkeley County (present day Jefferson County, West Virginia) and Frederick County were selected by Virginia's congressional delegation to each raise a company of Virginia riflemen. On June 22nd, 1775 Frederick County's leaders agreed to do so and unanimously appointed Captain Daniel Morgan to command the rifle company. Morgan's commission read in part,

In obedience to a resolve of the Continental Congress...this committee, reposing a special trust in the courage, conduct, and reverence for liberty under the spirit of the British constitution, of Daniel Morgan, Esq., do hereby certify that we have unanimously appointed him to command a Virginia company of riflemen to march from this county. He is hereby directed to act, by exercising the officers and soldiers under his command, taking particular

---

[3] Worthington C. Ford, "14 June, 1775," *Journals of the Continental Congress: 1774-1789,* Vol. 2, (Washington: Government Printing Office, 1905), 89

[4] Paul H. Smith, ed., "Pennsylvania Delegation to the Cumberland County Committee of Correspondence, (Circular Letter) 15 June, 1775," *Letters of Delegates to Congress*, Vol. 1, (Washington, D.C.: Library of Congress, 1976), 492

care to provide them with the necessaries, as the 1st Resolves of Congress directs...[5]

Daniel Morgan was just shy of 40 years old when he was selected to command one of Virginia's two rifle companies.[6] Respected throughout Frederick County for his leadership, character, and strength, Morgan was an excellent choice to lead the young men of Frederick County off to war.

Raising the Rifle Company

Captain Morgan started recruiting his company of riflemen immediately upon word of his appointment. He wanted to get a jump on Hugh Stephenson, captain of the other Virginian rifle company in neighboring Berkeley County. Henry Bedinger, a member of Captain Stephenson's company, recalled that,

> *Great exertions were made by each Captain to complete his company first, that merit might be claimed on that account. Volunteers presented themselves from every direction, in the vicinity of these Towns; [Winchester and Shepherdstown] none were received but young men of Character, and of sufficient property to Clothe themselves completely, find their own arms, and accoutrements, that is, an approved Rifle, handsome shot pouch, and powder-horn, blanket, knapsack, with such decent clothing as should be prescribed, but which was at first ordered to be only a Hunting shirt and pantaloons, fringed on every edge, and in Various ways. Our Company was raised in less than a week. Morgan had equal success.*[7]

---

[5] Graham, 53
[6] Higginbotham, 2
[7] Danske Dandridge, "Henry Bedinger to --- Findley," *Historic Shepherdstown*, (Charlottesville, VA: Michie Co., 1910), 79

Daniel Morgan 1775
Source: Library of Congress

"I recruited 96 men in a few days," Daniel Morgan proudly recalled years later.[8] Men flocked to Winchester, willing to serve for a year in far off Boston to defend their threatened liberties.

> *"So great was the enthusiasm of the moment,"* recalled Peter Bruin, a 21 year old ensign in Captain Morgan's company, *"that the difficulty did not depend on raising the number of men required but in selecting from those who crowded to the standard for admission, so that but a short time was employed in mustering and equiping the company."*[9]

Along with Ensign Bruin, who was the most junior officer in the company, Captain Morgan had two able lieutenants to assist him.

Lieutenant John Humphreys was Morgan's first lieutenant. Although he was Morgan's senior by seventeen years (56 years old) and far older than most lieutenants, Humphreys had served with Morgan during Lord Dunmore's War and had apparently earned Morgan's respect.[10] Second Lieutenant William Heth had also served under Captain Morgan in 1774. Destined to rise to the rank of colonel during the Revolutionary War, the twenty-five year old 2nd lieutenant possessed a degree of

---

[8] Henry B. Dawson, "General Daniel Morgan, An Autobiography", *The Historical Magazine and Notes and Queries Concerning the Antiquities, History and Biography of America, 2nd Series* Vol. 9 (1871), 379

[9] John Dorman, ed., "Peter Bruin Pension Application," *Virginia Revolutionary Pension Applications,* Vol. 12, (Washington, D.C.: 1965), 3

[10] Lloyd D. Bockstruck, *Virginia's Colonial Soldiers*, (Baltimore, MD: 1990), 138
and
DAR Patriot Index, Vol. 2 (Baltimore, MD: Gateway Press, Inc., 2003), 1406

confidence, (viewed as arrogance by many) that earned the ire of some in the army.[11]

The men of Morgan's rifle company, like most of the riflemen raised in 1775, were all excellent shots, the "marksmen" of their day. In an age when most soldiers used smoothbore muskets with an effective range of 50 to 100 yards, experienced riflemen could consistently hit their mark at more than 200 yards. The advantage that rifles had in accuracy, however, was somewhat negated by their lower rate of fire. Musket-men, using pre-rolled cartridges containing powder and ball, could fire up to four rounds a minute. Riflemen, on the other hand, typically measured each charge from a powder horn. Furthermore, achieving the greater accuracy of a spinning projectile, as created by the rifle's grooved barrel, meant that a tight fitting lead ball, wrapped in a greased cloth patch, had to be forced down the barrel. As a result, it typically took riflemen two to three times longer to load their rifle as compared to a musketman. Another disadvantage of rifles was that, in most cases, bayonets could not be attached to them. Thus, in close combat situations, riflemen found themselves at a distinct disadvantage to their bayonet wielding enemy.

This disadvantage was not very obvious to the confident colonists in 1775. In fact, many believed that riflemen would be decisive in a conflict. Richard Henry Lee, writing about his fellow Virginia riflemen, stated that

---

[11] *Orderly Book of Major William Heth of the Third Virginia Regiment, May 15 – July 1, 1777*, (Richmond, 1892). 321-22
and
   Kenneth Roberts, ed., "John Joseph Henry Journal," *March to Quebec: Journals of the Members of Arnold's Expedition*, (Garden City, NY: Doubleday & Co., 1940), 335
and
   Michael Cecere, *They Behaved Like Soldiers: Captain John Chilton and the Third Virginia Regiment*, (Heritage Books, 2004), 52-53

Rifleman Image
Source: Library of Congress

The six frontier Counties can produce 6000 of these Men who from their amazing hardihood, their method of living so long in the woods without carrying provisions with them, the exceeding quickness with which they can march to distant parts, and above all, the dexterity to which they have arrived in the use of the Rifle Gun. There is not one of these Men who wish a distance less than 200 yards or a larger object than an Orange. – Every shot is fatal.[12]

Informed of the deadly accuracy of the frontier riflemen, John Adams of Massachusetts confidently reported to his friend, Elbridge Gerry that

These riflemen are said to be all exquisite marksmen, and by means of the excellence of their firelocks, as well as their skill in the use of them, to send sure destruction to great distances.[13]

Come Boys, Who's For Cambridge

Although Morgan's company was raised in a week, it took two more weeks for Morgan's men to secure enough rifles, gear, and provisions for the long march to Boston.[14] By mid-July they were ready to go, as were Captain Stephenson and his company of Virginians in Shepherdstown. One of Stephenson's men, Henry Bedinger, claimed that the two Virginia rifle commanders had agreed to rendezvous in Frederick, Maryland and then proceed to Massachusetts together, but Morgan began his march early and never looked

---

[12] James C. Ballagh, ed., "Richard Henry Lee to Arthur Lee, 24 February, 1775," *Letters of Richard Henry Lee,* Vol. 1 (New York: Macmillan Co., 1911), 130-131

[13] Smith, ed., "John Adams to Elbridge Gerry, 18 June, 1775," *Letters of Delegates to Congress*, Vol. 1, 503

[14] Higginbotham, 23

back.[15] Historian Lyman C. Draper, who collected accounts of the Revolutionary War from numerous veterans and their descendants, claimed that Morgan purposefully deceived Stephenson into delaying his departure from Shepherdstown so that he could, "*steal a march on Stephenson and have the honor of being the first to reach the army in Boston.*"[16]

Whatever his motivation, Captain Morgan and his company left Winchester on July 15th, and crossed the Potomac River at Harper's Ferry.[17] When they reached the outskirts of Frederick, Maryland two days later, they were greeted by the local militia and escorted into town, "*amidst the acclamation of all the inhabitants that attended them.*"[18] One resident described their appearance:

> *Capt. Morgan, from Virginia, with his company of riflemen (all chosen), marched through this place on their way to Boston. Their appearance was truly martial; their spirits amazingly elated; breathing nothing but a desire to join the American army and to engage the enemies of American liberties....*[19]

The reception that Captain Morgan and his company received in Frederick was typical of nearly every community they marched through. All along the route the riflemen were greeted as heroes. Henry Bedinger, of Captain Stephenson's company (who trailed behind Morgan) recalled that throughout the march

---

[15] Dandridge, "Henry Bedinger to --- Findley," *Historic Shepherdstown*, 81
[16] Dandridge, *Historic Shepherdstown*, 81
[17] Dandridge, "Henry Bedinger to --- Findley," *Historic Shepherdstown*, 81
[18] Dandridge, "Extract of a Letter from a Gentleman in Frederick Town to His Friend, in Baltimore Town, Dated July 19, 1775," *Historic Shepherdstown*, 95
[19] Ibid.

Morgan's March to Boston
Adapted from Library of Congress

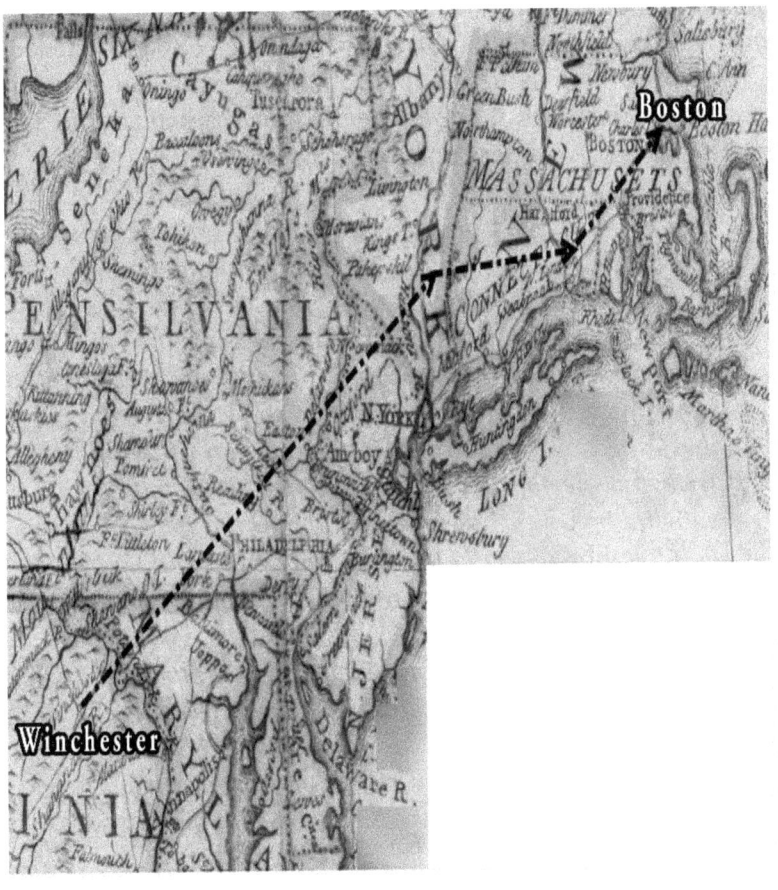

> *We were Met by a Number of Men and Women out of the Country who Brought us churns of Beer, Cyder, and Buttermilk, apples, cheries, etc., etc. We honoured them by firing at our parting.*[20]

Sometimes the firing demonstrations produced quite the spectacle. A Maryland rifle company under Captain Michael Cresep (marching in the wake of Captain Morgan and his men) dazzled the residents of one town with their marksmanship (and recklessness). A witness reported that

> *A clap-board with a mark the size of a dollar was put up; they began to fire off-hand, and the by standers were surprised, few shots being made that were not close or into the paper. When they had shot for some time in this way, some lay on their backs, some on their breasts or sides; others ran twenty or thirty steps and, firing as they ran, appeared to be equally certain of the mark. With this performance the company were more than satisfied, when a young man took up the board in his hand, not by the end but by the side, and holding it up, his brother walked to the distance and coolly shot into the white; laying down his rifle, he took the board, and holding it as it was before, the second brother shot as the former had done. By this exhibition I was more than astonished than pleased. But will you believe me when I tell you that one of the men took the board, and placing it between his legs, stood with his back to the tree while another drove the center?*[21]

Although it is very likely that Captain Morgan's company participated in similar activities on their march, such stops were brief, for they had nearly 600 miles to march to reach Boston.

---

[20] Dandridge, "Henry Bedinger Journal," *Historic Shepherdstown*, 100
[21] Dandridge, "Extract of a Letter from Frederick Town dated August 1, 1775," *Historic Shepherdstown*, 94-95

On July 24th, Morgan and his men passed through Bethlehem, Pennsylvania, approximately 205 miles from Winchester.[22] Three days later, at Sussex Court House, New Jersey, (a little more than halfway to Boston) they fell in with a company of Pennsylvania riflemen. The Virginians soon outpaced the Pennsylvanians however, and crossed the Hudson River at Fishkill, New York.[23] Captain Morgan and his men raced on, through Litchfield and Hartford, Connecticut and arrived in Cambridge, Massachusetts on August 6th, five days ahead of Captain Stephenson but ten days after the first Pennsylvania rifle company reached Boston.[24]

Siege of Boston

The arrival of the rifle companies in late July and early August sparked a wave of excitement among the New England troops outside Boston. Riflemen were largely unknown in New England and their appearance and reputation made quite an impression. A Pennsylvania rifle officer described the reception that he and his fellow riflemen received:

> *You will think me vain should I tell you how much the Riflemen are esteemed. Their dress, their arms, their size, strength and activity, but above all their eagerness to attack the enemy, entitle them to the first rank. The hunting shirt is like a full suit at St. James's.*

---

[22] John W. Jordan, ed., "Bethleham During the Revolution," *Pennsylvania Magazine of History and Biography,* Vol. 12 (1888), 387

[23] Dandridge, "Henry Bedinger Journal," *Historic Shepherdstown,* 101
  Note: It is very likely that Captain Stephenson marched along the same route that Captain Morgan marched in his effort to catch up to him.

[24] B. Floyd Flickinger, "Captain Morgan and His Riflemen," *Winchester-Frederick County Historical Society Journal,* Vol. 14, (2002), 56-57
and
  Robert J. Taylor, ed., "James Warren to John Adams, 9 August, 1775," T*he Papers of John Adams,* Vol. 3, (Cambridge, MA: Harvard University Press, 1979), 115

> *A Rifleman in his dress may pass sentinels and go almost where he pleases, while officers of other Regiments are stopped.*[25]

Surgeon's Mate James Thacher, of Massachusetts, was equally impressed and described the riflemen as

> *Remarkably stout and hardy men; many of them exceeding six feet in height. They are dressed in white frocks, or rifle-shirts, and round hats. These men are remarkable for the accuracy of their aim; striking a mark with great certainty at two hundred yards distance. At a review, a company of them, while on a quick advance, fired their balls into objects of seven inches diameter, at a distance of two hundred and fifty yards. They are now stationed on our lines, and their shot have frequently proved fatal to British officers and soldiers who expose themselves to view, even at more than double the distance of common musket-shot.*[26]

The deadly aim of the riflemen was also noticed by the enemy. The *London Chronicle* reported that American riflemen have, *"rifles particularly adapted to take off the officers of a whole line..."*[27] Another London newspaper wrote that, *"...with their cursed twisted gun, [riflemen are] the most fatal widow and orphan makers in the world."*[28]

An observer in the American camp noted that, *"since the riflemen arrived, they have killed six or eight officers of*

---

[25] William W. Williams, ed., "Robert Magaw to the Carlisle Committee of Correspondence, 13 August, 1775," *Magazine of Western History*, Vol. 4, (May-October, 1886), 674

[26] James Thacher, M.D., *Military Journal of the American Revolution*, (Gansevoort, New York: Corner House Historical Publications, 1998), 31

[27] Richard B. LaCrosse Jr., *The Frontier Rifleman*, (Union City, TN: Pioneer Press, 1989), 83

[28] Ibid. 81

distinction."[29] Even General Washington, in a letter to Congress, noted the impact of the riflemen:

> *I last Saturday Evening ordered some of the Riflemen down to make a Discovery, or bring off a Prisoner…Since that Time we have on each side drawn in our sentries and there have been scattering Fires along the Lines. This Evening we have heard of three Captains who have been taken off by the Rifle Men…*[30]

Although the riflemen initially lived up to their reputation as deadly marksmen, the shortage of gunpowder in the American army soon compelled General Washington to curtail their frequent firing.[31] It seemed that whenever the riflemen engaged the enemy, scores of American musket men joined in, ineffectively firing their smoothbore weapons. General Washington complained in the general orders of August 4th, that

> *Contrary to all Orders, straggling Soldiers do still pass the Guards, and fire at a Distance, where there is not the least probability of hurting the enemy, and where no other end is answer'd, but to waste Ammunition, expose themselves to the ridicule of the enemy, and keep their own Camps harrassed by frequent and continual alarms….*[32]

It is unclear whether Washington included the riflemen in his charge of wasting ammunition. James Warren, President of the

---

[29] Margaret Willard, ed., *Letters on the American Revolution: 1774-1776,* (Boston & New York: Houghton Mifflin Co., 1925), 185
[30] Philander D. Chase, ed., "General Washington to John Hancock, 4 August, 1775," *The Papers of George Washington: Revolutionary War Series,* Vol. 1, June – September 1775, (Charlottesville: University Press of Virginia, 1985), 226
[31] Chase, ed., "General Orders, 4 August, 1775," *The Papers of George Washington:* Vol. 1, June – September 1775, 218-19
[32] Ibid.

Massachusetts Provincial Congress, informed John Adams on August 9th, that

> *The General [Washington] has been obliged from Principles of frugality to restrain his rifle men. While they were permitted Liberty to fire on the Enemy, a great number of the Army would go and fire away great quantitys of Ammunition to no Purpose.*[33]

In other words, to save gunpowder and shot, Washington reigned in the rifle companies, much to their chagrin.

Captain Morgan and his company were posted in the lines at Roxbury, directly across from the British fortifications on Boston Neck.[34] They, along with Captain Stephenson's rifle company and the two Maryland rifle companies, were part of the right wing of the American army outside of Boston.[35] As such, they fell under the command of General Artemas Ward. It was General Ward who relinquished command of the army to General Washington upon Washington's arrival in Cambridge in early July.

Restrained by General Washington's August 4th orders to limit small arms fire in the lines, the riflemen chafed at the monotony of camp life and guard duty. Many grew restless and what little discipline existed among the riflemen deteriorated with the inactivity.

Captain Morgan and his men did not remain inactive for long, however. In early September, Morgan and two rifle company commanders from Pennsylvania were selected to participate in an expedition through the Maine wilderness to

---

[33] Taylor, ed., "James Warren to John Adams, 9 August, 1775," *The Papers of John Adams*, Vol. 3, 114-115

[34] Williams, ed., "Robert Magaw to the Carlisle Committee of Correspondence, 13 August, 1775," *Magazine of Western History*, Vol. 4, (May-October, 1886), 675

[35] Ibid.

capture the fortress city of Quebec.[36] The three rifle companies joined ten musket companies from the New England regiments, all under the command of Colonel Benedict Arnold of Connecticut, and together this 1,100 man force prepared to march.

---

[36] Wm. H. Egle, ed., "The Journal of Captain William Hendricks and Captain John Chambers," *Pennsylvania Archives, 2nd Series*, Vol. 15 (1890), 31

Map of the Siege of Boston
Adapted from Library of Congress

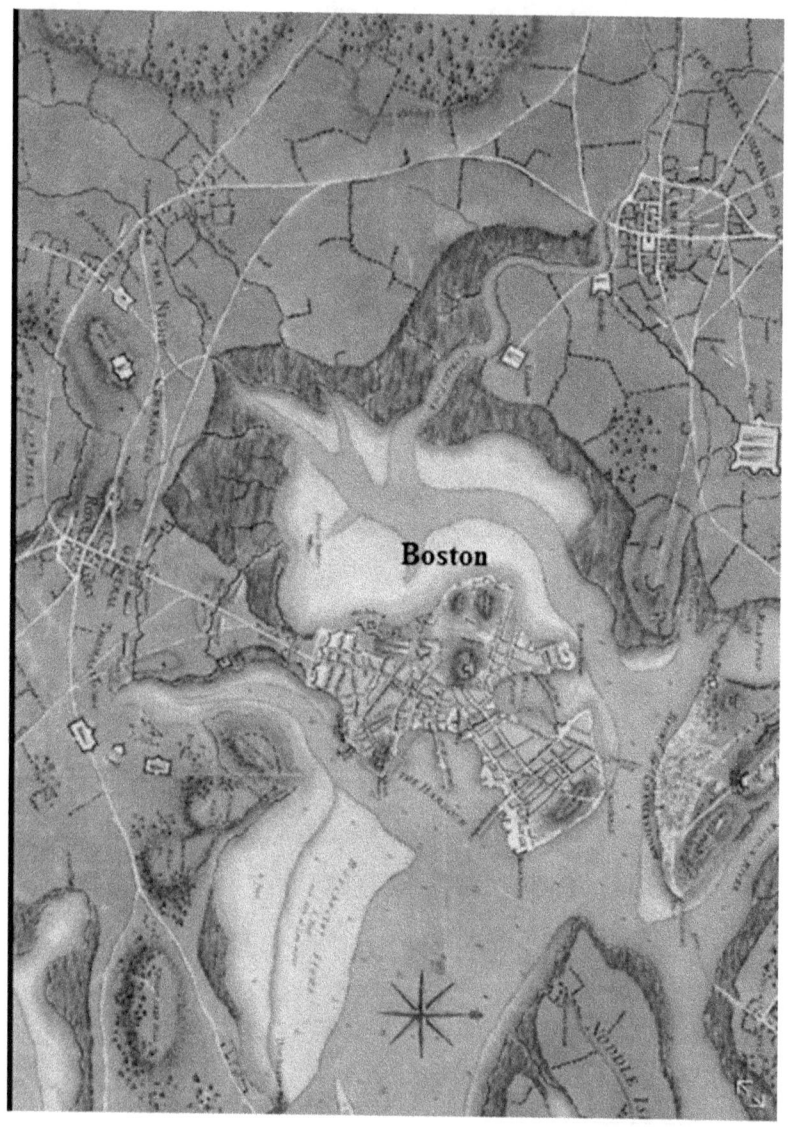

Chapter Three

"A Scene of Trouble to Go Through"

Arnold's Expedition to Quebec : 1775

General Washington first conceived of a coordinated two pronged attack on Quebec in mid-August and proposed the idea to General Philip Schuyler, the commander of American troops at Fort Ticonderoga in New York. Washington informed Schuyler on August 20th, that he could spare 1,200 men from the main army for a joint expedition against Canada.[1] Washington proposed to send this detachment up the Kennebec River and through the Maine and Canadian wilderness to approach Quebec from the south while General Schuyler led a second detachment into Canada from Lake Champlain to distract and occupy the British forces posted in Montreal and Quebec.[2] General Washington explained to Schuyler that such a coordinated movement would force the British commander in Canada, Governor Guy Carleton, to

> Either break up and follow [Arnold's] *Party to Quebeck, by which he will leave you a free Passage, or he must suffer that important place to fall into our Hands, an Event, which would have a decisive Effect and influence on the publick Interest.*[3]

The decision to proceed with the two pronged attack rested with General Schuyler, who informed Washington in late August that he would indeed march north into Canada, but not with the numbers either general desired:

---

[1] Chase, ed., "General Washington to Major General Philip Schuyler, 20 August, 1775," *The Papers of George Washington*, Vol. 1, 332
[2] Ibid.
[3] Ibid.

The force I shall carry is far short of what I would wish. I believe It will not Exceed Seventeen Hundred men, and this will be a body Insufficient to Attempt Quebec [alone]...*Should the detachment of Your body penetrate Into Canada and we meet with Success, Quebec must Inevitably fall into our hands...*[4]

Schuyler's reply prompted General Washington to set his plan in motion. First, he made arrangements for transport ships to assemble in the coastal town of Newburyport, near the border of Massachusetts and New Hampshire.[5] Next, Washington employed Reuben Colburn, the owner of a small shipyard and sawmill on the Kennebec River in Maine to proceed, *"with all Expedition and without delay...* [with] *the Construction of Two Hundred Batteaus."*[6] These craft, designed to haul cargo on shallow rivers and lakes, were needed to transport Arnold's expedition further up the Kennebec River, beyond where the sailing vessels could go. Colburn was also instructed to procure as much pork and flour from the local inhabitants as was available for the expedition.[7]

After the transport and provision issues were addressed, General Washington issued orders to form Colonel Arnold's detachment:

"A Detachment consisting of two Lieut. Colonels, two Majors, ten Captains, thirty Subalterns, thirty Serjeants, thirty Corporals, four Drummers, two Fifers, and six hundred and seventy six privates; to parade tomorrow morning at eleven O' Clock, upon

---

[4] Chase, ed., "General Schuyler to General Washington, 27 August, 1775," *The Papers of George Washington,* Vol. 1, 368
[5] Chase, ed., "General Washington to Nathaniel Tracy, 2 September, 1775," *The Papers of George Washington,* Vol. 1, 404-405
[6] Chase, ed., "General Washington to Reuben Colburn, 3 September, 1775," *The Papers of George Washington,* Vol. 1, 471
[7] Ibid.

the Common, in Cambridge, to go upon Command with Col. Arnold of Connecticut; one Company of Virginia Rifle-men and two Companies from Col. Thompson's Pennsylvania Regiment of Rifle-men, to parade at the same time and place, to join the above Detachment. Tents and Necessaries proper and convenient for the whole, will be supplied by the Quarter Master Genl. immediately upon the Detachment being collected.[8]

Washington's orders specified that only men who, *"are active Woodsmen, and well acquainted with bateaus,"* should volunteer for this service.[9]

Nearly a week passed before any of Arnold's detachment was ready to march. Captain Morgan and the three rifle companies (about 250 strong) set out first on September 11th. The 40 mile march from Cambridge took two days. Upon their arrival at Newburyport they boarded transport ships that were described by one soldier as little more than, *"dirty coasters and fish boats"*.[10] The rest of Colonel Arnold's detachment followed the riflemen two days later.

---

[8] Chase, ed., "General Orders, 5 September, 1775," *The Papers of George Washington,* Vol. 1, 415

[9] Ibid.

[10] Stephen Clark, *Following Their Footsteps: A Travel Guide & History of the 1775 Secret Expedition to Capture Quebec,* (2003), 10-11
and
Thomas A. Desjardin, *Through A Howling Wilderness: Benedict Arnold's March to Quebec, 1775,* (New York: St. Martin's Griffin, 2007), 20

Newburyport to Fort Western
Adapted from Library of Congress

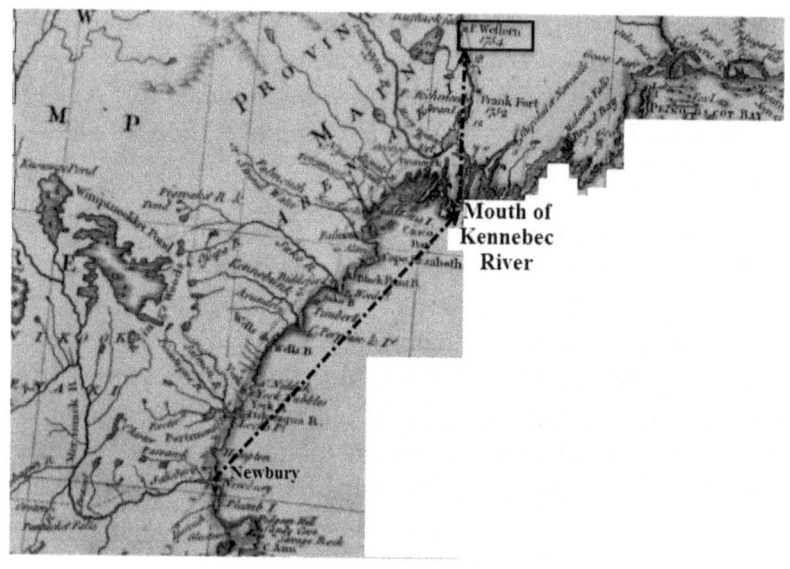

Delayed at Newburyport by poor weather, Arnold's expedition finally set sail on September 19th. Eleven transport ships loaded with nearly 1,100 troops, ammunition, and provisions set sail for the Kennebec River with the ebb tide.[11] Abner Stocking, a private in one of Arnold's musket companies, recalled that the expedition left Newburyport with much fanfare. *"Many pretty Girls stood upon the shore, I suppose weeping for the departure of their sweethearts."*[12]

Up the Kennebec

The voyage to the Kennebec River, some 90 miles from Newburyport, was completed in a day without incident (excluding some stormy weather and widespread seasickness among the troops).[13] Most of the ships reached the mouth of the river by midnight and anchored until sunrise.

Navigating up the Kennebec River was a challenge, but strong tides and favorable winds propelled the ships upriver, albeit in a rather scattered state. By September 22nd, the first of Arnold's ships arrived at Reuben Colburn's shipyard [in present day Pittston, Maine]. Most of the transport ships, laden with men and supplies, were unable to sail any further upriver, the river's depth was too shallow to continue. Luckily, two hundred newly built bateaux were waiting on the east bank of the river to ferry Arnold's troops and their supplies twelve miles further upriver to Fort Western.[14] This fort, built during the French and Indian War and converted into a residence and trading post after the war, was the base

---

[11] Kenneth Roberts, ed., "Benedict Arnold's Journal, 19 September, 1775,"*March to Quebec: Journals of the Members of Arnold's Expedition*, (New York: Country Life Press, 1938), 44b
[12] Roberts, ed., "Abner Stocking's Journal,19 September, 1775," 546
[13] Clark, 15-17
[14] Ibid., 19

Fort Western

camp for the expedition, the place where Colonel Arnold made his final preparations for the long journey upriver.

Dispute Over Command

Arnold initially intended to send Lieutenant-Colonel Christopher Greene of Rhode Island ahead of the rest of the expedition with an advance party of two musket companies and a rifle company, but Captain Morgan and the other rifle captains objected. They claimed that the rifle companies were an independent command and as such answered only to Colonel Arnold, not the other staff and company officers of the expedition. Colonel Arnold informed General Washington of Morgan's objection and sought his guidance on the matter:

> *I intended Col. Green should have gone on with the first Division of one Company of Riffle-Men, & two Companies of Musketeers – This was objected to by the Captains of the Riffle Companies, who insist on being commanded by no other Person than Captain Morgan & my self – This, Capt. Morgan tells me, was your Excellency's Intention, but as I was not acquainted with it before I came away, I should be very glad of particular Instructions on that Head....*[15]

General Washington received the news of Morgan's objection and conduct and wrote directly to the rifle commander with a gentle reprimand:

> *I write you in Consequence of Information I have received that you & the Captains of the Rifle Companies on the Detachment agt Quebec claim an*

---

[15] Philander D. Chase, ed., "Colonel Benedict Arnold to General George Washington, 25-27 September, 1775," *The Papers of George Washington, Revolutionary War Series*, Vol. 2, (Charlottesville: University Press of Virginia, 1987), 41

Exemption from the Command of all the Field Officers except Col. Arnold. I understand this Claim is founded upon some Expression of mine, but if you understood me in this Way, you are much mistaken in my meaning. My intention is and ever was that every Officer should Command according to his Rank – to do otherwise would Subvert all military Order & Authority which I am Sure you could not wish or expect – Now that the Mistake is rectified I trust you will exert yourself to Support my Intentions, ever remembering that by the Same Rule that You claim an independent Command & break in upon military Authority others will do the same by you: And of Consequence the Expedition must terminate in Shame & Disgrace to yourselves and the Reproach and Detriment of your Country – To a Man of true Spirit & military Character farther Argument is unnecessary I shall therefore recommend you to preserve the utmost Harmony among yourselves to which a due Subordination will much Contribute & wishing you all Health & Success I remain
Your very Hbble Sevt.[16]

It is uncertain when Captain Morgan received General Washington's letter, but assuming he did receive it Washington's words must have stung Morgan.

At the time the commander-in-chief penned the letter, Morgan and his riflemen were ten days into their journey up the Kennebec River. Colonel Arnold had acquiesced to Captain Morgan and altered his plan, sending all three rifle companies under Morgan's command up the river on September 25th, They trailed two small scouting parties that started upriver two days earlier.

---

[16] Chase, ed., "General Washington to Captain Daniel Morgan, 4 October, 1775," *The Papers of George Washington*, Vol. 2, 93

Colonel Arnold designated Morgan's detachment the 1st division of the expedition and the riflemen carried with them 45 days of provisions. They were instructed to proceed to the Great Carrying Place (a 12 mile portage between the Kennebec and Dead Rivers) to cut a road for the rest of the expedition.[17] Three divisions of musket men, under Lieutenant Colonel Christopher Greene, Major Return Meigs, and Lieutenant Colonel Roger Enos, followed in Morgan's wake with the rest of the supplies.

The Real Struggle Begins

Unlike the scouting parties, which used lightweight, birch bark canoes that were well suited for the shallow waters of the Kennebec River, the rest of Arnold's force, including Captain Morgan's division, struggled to move their heavy bateaux upriver against the swift current and numerous shoals (rapids).[18]

Colonel Arnold staggered the departure of the divisions from Fort Western over four days in the hopes of avoiding bottlenecks and delays at the numerous portages on the river. As each division started up the Kennebec (some men marching along the river through the brush and the rest paddling and poling the bateaux loaded with supplies upriver) the men in the boats discovered they had the harder task. Private Caleb Haskell with Major Meigs's third division noted in his journal just a day into the movement upriver that

> *We begin to see that we have a scene of trouble to go through in this river, the water is swift and the shoal full of rocks, ripples, and falls, which oblige us to wade a great part of the way.*[19]

---

[17] Roberts, ed., "Benedict Arnold's Journal, 25 September, 1775," 44b
[18] Roberts, ed., "John Joseph Henry's Journal," 303
[19] Roberts, ed., "Caleb Haskell's Journal, 28 September, 1775," 474

The Expedition Struggles Upriver
Source: Library of Congress

Private George Morison, a Pennsylvania rifleman marching in Morgan's division, also commented on the difficult passage upriver:

> *Poled up the river all day. The water in many places being so shallow, that we were often obliged to haul the boats after us through rock and shoals, frequently up to our middle and over our heads in the water; and some of us with difficulty escaped being drowned.*[20]

The men marching onshore did not escape work; they were frequently called upon to assist with the boats, especially when difficult rapids or waterfalls were encountered. Abner Stocking, with the third division, noted that

> *We arrived to the second carrying place...* [present day Skowhegan, Maine] *it occasioned much delay and great fatigue. We had to ascend a ragged rock, near on 100 feet in height and almost perpendicular. Though it seemed as though we could hardly ascend it without any burden, we succeeded in dragging our bateaus and baggage up it.*[21]

The weather also proved a challenge, turning cold and raw. Captain Simeon Thayer, with the Lieutenant Colonel Greene's second division, noted on September 30th that, *"Last night, our clothes being wet, were frozen a pane of glass thick, which proved very disagreeable, being obliged to lie in them."*[22]

A week into the journey, Captain Morgan's division encountered Norridgewock Falls, a rock strewn section of river that required a steep, mile and a quarter long portage. Colonel Arnold, who started near the rear of the expedition in

---

[20] Roberts, ed., "George Morison's Journal, 28 September, 1775," 511
[21] Roberts, ed., "Abner Stocking's Journal, 29 September, 1775," 548
[22] Roberts, ed., "Simon Thayer's Journal, 30 September, 1775," 250

Portage Over Skowhegan Falls
Source: Library of Congress

a birch bark canoe, caught up to Morgan and the 1st Division at Norridgewock Falls on October 2nd, as the riflemen hauled the last of their provisions up the portage.[23] Morgan and his riflemen pressed on upriver while Colonel Arnold briefly halted the other divisions at Norridgewock to repair their leaking bateaux and salvage whatever provisions could be saved. Dr. Isaac Senter, travelling with the 2nd division, explained in his journal how water had seeped into the casks of food and spoiled much of it:

> *The bread casks not being water-proof, admitted the water in plenty, swelled the bread, burst the casks, as well as soured the whole bread. The same fate attended a number of fine casks of peas. These with the others were condemned. We were now curtailed of a very valuable and large part of our provisions…Our fare was now reduced to salt pork and flour. Beef we had now and then, when we could purchase a fat creature, but that was seldom. A few barrels of salt beef remained on hand, but of so indifferent quality, as scarce to be eaten, being killed in the heat of summer, took much damage after salting, that rendered it not only very unwholesome, but very unpalatable."*[24]

While Colonel Arnold and his musket companies repaired the bateaux and repacked the provisions, Captain Morgan and the riflemen pushed upriver. They reached the entrance to the Great Carrying Place on October 7th, and after a day of rest in their tents due to heavy rain, proceeded to clear the trail for the detachments to come and haul their bateaux and gear to the Dead River, 12 miles away.[25]

Captain Morgan, described by a Pennsylvanian rifleman as, *"large,* [with] *a commanding aspect and stentorian voice,"*

---

[23] Roberts, ed., "Benedict Arnold's Journal, 2 October, 1775," 46-47
[24] Roberts, ed., "Isaac Senter's Journal, 5 October, 1775," 203
[25] Roberts, ed., "George Morison's Journal, 7-9 October, 1775," 513

worked alongside his men on the trail.[26] Dressed like his men *"in the Indian style,"* (which included a fringed hunting shirt, breach cloth and leather leggings) Pennsylvanian rifleman Joseph Henry recalled that Morgan's thighs were cut up by the brush and thorns that the riflemen cleared away.[27]

The Great Carrying Place

Three ponds linked the long portage between the Kennebec and Dead Rivers, making the overland trek a bit easier. Nevertheless, hauling the heavy boats and supplies over the rough, steep, terrain was a daunting task. Rifleman George Morison described the difficulties they endured.

> *This morning we hauled out our Batteaux from the river and carried thro' brush and mire, over hills and swamps (for we had not even the shape of a road but as we forced it) to a pond which we crossed, and encamped for the night. This transportation occupied us three whole days, during which time we advanced but five miles. This was by far the most fatiguing movement that had yet befell us. The rains had rendered the earth a complete bog; insomuch that we were often half leg deep in the mud, stumbling over old fallen logs, one leg sinking deeper in the mire than the other, then down goes a boat and the carriers with it, a hearty laugh prevails. The irritated carriers at length get to their feet with their boat, plastered with mud from neck to heel, their comrades tauntingly asking them how they liked their washing and lodging....* [28]

---

[26] Roberts, ed., "John Joseph Henry's Journal, 17 October, 1775," 327 and Higginbotham, 30

[27] Roberts, ed., "John Joseph Henry's Journal, 17 October, 1775," 327

[28] Roberts, ed., "George Morison's Journal, 9 October, 1775," 513-514

The Great Carrying Place Portage
Source: Library of Congress

Morison continued:

> *Our encampments these two last nights were almost insupportable; for the ground was so soaked with rain that the driest situation we could find was too wet to lay upon any length of time; so that we got but little rest. Leaves to bed us could not be obtained and we amused ourselves around our fires most all the night...The incessant toil we experienced in ascending the river, as well as the still more fatiguing method of carrying our boats, laden with the provisions, camp equipage etc., from place to place, might have subdued the resolution of men less patient and less persevering than we were.*[29]

It was not possible to move the bateaux and supplies across the portage in one haul, so the men trudged back and forth numerous times over the trail. The ponds offered brief respites (and some nourishment from the bountiful fish that were caught) but the, *"incessant toil...of carrying* [the] *boats laden with provisions, camp equipage, etc.,"* greatly fatigued Captain Morgan and his men.[30] The divisions that followed were equally exhausted (despite Morgan's efforts to improve the trail). Dr. Isacc Senter described the challenge of the portage from the perspective of one of the musket divisions:

> *The army was now much fatigued, being obliged to carry all the batteaus, barrels of provisions, warlike stores, etc. over on their backs through a most terrible piece of woods conceivable. Sometimes in the mud knee deep, then over ledgy hills, etc.*[31]

---

[29] Ibid., 514
[30] Roberts, ed., "George Morison's Journal, 12 October, 1775," 514-515
[31] Roberts, ed., "Isaac Senter's Journal, 13 October, 1775," 204-205

The Dead River Floods

The backbreaking work of crossing the portage continued for a week. When Lieutenant Colonel Greene's 2nd division caught and passed Morgan and his men, the rifle commander ordered his riflemen to remove just the large obstacles (fallen trees and heavy brush) from the trail.[32] Morgan was determined to regain the head of the expedition and did so on October 17th, when Greene's division halted on the Dead River to re-distribute their scant food stores and make cartridges.[33] Once he regained the head of the expedition, Morgan pushed his riflemen up the deeper Dead River, covering 36 miles in two days.[34] Poor weather finally halted their progress and the riflemen encamped along the river to wait for both the weather to improve and the rest of the expedition to catch up.

During this delay, rifleman John Henry witnessed an incident involving Captain Morgan that left a lasting impression on him. Morgan, whom Henry described as a, *"strict disciplinarian,"* had ordered the riflemen to cease firing their rifles to clear them (as opposed to drawing unspent rifle balls and powder out of the barrels with their ramrods to be re-used). Henry recalled that

> *One Chamberlaine, a worthless fellow, who did not think it worth while to draw his bullet, had gone some hundreds of yards into the woods, and discharged his gun. Lieut. Steele happened to be in that quarter at the time; Steele had but arrived at the fire, where we sat, when Morgan, who had seen him coming, approached our camp, and seated himself within our circle. Presently Chamberlaine came, gun in hand, and was passing our fire, towards that of his mess. Morgan called to the soldier, accused him as the defaulter; this the man (an arrant liar) denied. Morgan*

---

[32] Higginbotham, 30
[33] Roberts, ed., "Benedict Arnold's Journal, 17 October, 1775," 53
[34] Roberts, ed., "George Morison's Journal, 18 October, 1775," 515

> appealed to Steele. Steele admitted he heard the report, but knew not the party who discharged the gun. Morgan suddenly springing to a pile of billets, took one, and swore he would knock the accused down unless he confessed the fact. Instantly, [Captain] Smith [Chamberlaine's company commander] seized another billet, and swore he would strike Morgan if he struck the man. Morgan knowing the tenure of his rank, receded.[35]

It was rare for Daniel Morgan to back down from a fight, but to push the dispute further risked fracturing his command and undermining his authority with the Pennsylvanians, so Morgan dropped the matter.

Morgan's attention shifted to the deteriorating weather conditions that befell the expedition, the remnants of an apparent hurricane. For four miserable days Morgan's division waited along the flooded Dead River for the heavy rain to abate.[36] Rifleman John Henry described the storm's impact:

> A most heavy torrent of rain fell upon us, which continued all night...towards morning we were awakened by the water that flowed in upon us from the river. We fled to high ground. When morning came, the river presented a most frightful aspect: it had risen at least eight feet, and flowed with terrifying rapidity.[37]

The weather finally cleared on October 22nd, and Captain Morgan's division pushed on. Rifleman Henry recalled that

---

[35] John Joseph Henry, *Account of Arnold's Campaign Against Quebec*, (New York Times & Arno Press, 1968, 50
   Originally published in 1877
[36] Roberts, ed., "George Morison's Journal, 18-22 October, 1775," 515
[37] Roberts, ed., "John Joseph Henry's Journal, 23 October, 1775," 330

None but the most strong and active boatmen entered the boats. The army marched on the south side of the river, making large circuits to avoid the overflowing (river)...This was one of the most fatiguing marches we had as yet performed, though the distance was not great in a direct line. But having no path, and being necessitated to climb the steepest hills and without food, for we took none with us, thinking the boats would be near us all day.[38]

In the evening, Colonel Arnold, who had once again caught up to Morgan's division, held a war council with the officers of Captain Morgan's 1st division and Major Meigs's 3rd division. Supply problems had caused Lieutenant Colonel Greene's 2nd division to drop back in the order of march.

Arnold's war council decided to send the sick men, which numbered 26 men between the two divisions, back to Fort Western.[39] Orders were sent to Lieutenant Colonel Greene and Lieutenant Colonel Enos (who brought up the rear of the expedition with the 4th division) to send their sick back as well and to take the extra step of sending back as many men in poor condition as necessary so that 15 days of provisions could be distributed among those who remained.[40]

In an effort to obtain more provisions as quickly as possible, the war council also endorsed Arnold's decision to send Captain Oliver Hanchet's company of musket-men ahead of the expedition with orders to seek supplies from the inhabitants of Sartigan, the southernmost French settlement on the Chaudiere River, and forward them back to the rest of the expedition.[41] Colonel Arnold followed Hanchet's company the next day in a birch bark canoe with a similar mission and eventually passed

---

[38] Ibid.
[39] Roberts, ed., "Benedict Arnold's Journal, 24 October, 1775," 55
[40] Ibid.
[41] Ibid.

them.[42] In doing so, Arnold was temporarily out of touch with the rest of the expedition; his absence proved crucial, for a crisis erupted in the rear of the column.

The Expedition Nearly Collapses

Lieutenant Colonel Roger Enos and the officers of the 4th division, claiming excessive fatigue and the lack of provisions, announced on October 25th, at their own officer's council with Lieutenant Colonel Greene and his officers, that they were abandoning the expedition and returning to Fort Western.[43] Had Colonel Arnold been aware of this he would have undoubtedly prevented it, but without his commanding presence, more than a quarter of the expedition's troop strength, as well as several barrels of provisions desperately needed by all of the men, vanished. Enos left just two barrels of flour behind for Lieutenant Colonel Greene's starving division.[44] When word of the 4th division's return spread among the rest of the expedition, contempt, anger, and disgust were the most common sentiments expressed.[45]

The situation for Captain Morgan and the rest of Arnold's expedition only grew worse in the last week of October. Soon after Colonel Arnold's departure, several of the rifle division's bateaux were overset while passing through rapids, dumping flour, ammunition, and a number of rifles into the Dead River.[46] The next night, October 25th, a snowstorm blew in and the frigid temperatures only added to the distress of the men.[47]

Captain Morgan and his division reached a segment of the route called the Height of Land the following day. This was the highest point of elevation on the journey, the point in which the

---

[42] Ibid., 56
[43] Roberts, ed., "Simeon Thayer's Journal, 25 October, 1775," 256
[44] Ibid.
[45] Roberts, ed., "Henry Dearborn's Journal, 27 October, 1775," 137
[46] Roberts, ed., "George Morison's Journal, 24 October, 1775," 517
[47] Ibid., 517-518

rivers and creeks began to flow northward, towards the St. Lawrence River and Quebec. Crossing this point involved a brutal portage which was described by Pennsylvania rifleman George Morison:

> *The Terrible Carrying Place; a dismal portage indeed of two miles and fifty perches* [825 feet]; *intersected with a considerable ridge covered with fallen trees, stones and brush. The ground adjacent to this ridge is swampy, plentifully strewed with old dead logs, and with everything that could render it impossible. Over this we forced a passage, the most distressing of any we had yet performed. The ascent and descent of the hill was inconceivably difficult. The boats and carriers often fell down into the snow, some of them were much hurt by reason of their feet sticking fast among the stones.... We were very feeble from former fatigues and short allowance of but a pint of flour each man per day for nearly two weeks past, so that this day's movement was by far the most oppressive of any we had experienced.*[48]

Morgan's Virginians were the first of the riflemen to cross the Height of Land, hauling their seven remaining bateaux into Canada.[49] It is not clear whether Captain Morgan received Colonel Arnold's instructions to abandon the bateaux at the Height of Land, but the Pennsylvania rifle captains, who had fallen behind Morgan's Virginians, apparently did for each company hauled just one bateaux across for the use of their sick.[50] The extra burden endured by the Virginians was described by Pennsylvania riflemen John Henry:

---

[48] Roberts, ed., "George Morison's Journal, 27 October, 1775," 522-523
[49] Clark, 72-73
[50] Roberts, ed., "John Joseph Henry's Journal, 28 October, 1775," 335

> *It would have made your heart ache to view the intolerable labors of these fine fellows. Some of them, it was said, had the flesh worn from their shoulders, even to the bone. By this time an antipathy had arisen against Morgan, as too strict a disciplinarian.*[51]

The Virginians were not alone in their suffering, however. The great physical exertions of the last month and lack of provisions took its toll on all the men. George Morison reported that

> *Never perhaps was there a more forlorn set of human beings...Every one of us shivering from head to foot, as hungry as wolves, and nothing to eat save a little flour we had left, which we made dough of and baked in the fires...*[52]

Private Henry noted that the situation was so desperate that,

> *The men were told by the officers that order would not be required in the march – each one must put their best foot foremost.*[53]

In other words, it was now every man for himself. Dr. Senter confirmed the desperate situation, writing on November 1st that,

> *We had now arrived...to almost the zenith of distress. Several had been entirely destitute of either meat or bread for many days...The voracious disposition many of us had now arrived at, rendered almost anything admissible...In company was a poor dog, [who had] hitherto lived through all the tribulations...This poor animal was instantly devoured, without leaving any vestige of the sacrifice. Nor did the shaving soap,*

---

[51] Ibid., 335-336
[52] Roberts, ed., "George Morison's Journal, 30 October, 1775," 524
[53] Roberts, ed., "John Joseph Henry's Journal, 30 October, 1775," 336

> *pomatum, and even the lip salve, leather of their shoes, cartridge boxes, &c., share any better fate...*[54]

Private Morison and many of his comrades resorted to roasting and eating their leather shot pouches:

> *This day [November 2nd] I roasted my shot-pouch and eat it. It was now four days since I had eat anything save the skin of a squirrel I had picked up in a tent some time before, and had accidently put it into my pocket. A number resorted to the same expedient; and in a short time there was not a shot-pouch to be seen among all those within my view.* [55]

After struggling through a swamp and across a large lake [Lake Megantic] Captain Morgan and his company of Virginians started down the Chaudiere River in their seven bateaux, ahead of the other rifle companies. They initially made good progress, but disaster struck when they suddenly came upon a heavy set of rapids that dashed their bateaux to pieces and drowned one of the Virginians.[56] Private Abner Stocking encountered Morgan's men a day after their mishap and recorded in his journal that

> *We learnt to our great sorrow, that in attempting to go down the river in their bateaus, which they brought to this place, they were carried down by the rapidity of the stream and dashed on rocks; that they had lost most of their provisions and that a waiter of Captain Morgan was drowned. Their condition was truly deplorable – they had not...a mouthful of provisions of any kind, and we were not able to relieve them, as hunger stared us in the face. Some of us were entirely*

---

[54] Roberts, ed., "Isaac Senter Journal, 1 November, 1775," 218-219
[55] Roberts, ed., "George Morison's Journal, 2 November, 1775," 528
[56] Roberts, ed., "Abner Stocking's Journal, 30 October, 1775," 554-555

> destitute and others had but a morsel of bread, and we now supposed ourselves 70 miles from the nearest inhabitants. Some of Captain Morgan's company we were told had perished with the cold.[57]

Captain Morgan and his famished men re-joined the march northward. The column of emaciated men were scattered along twenty miles. Some could go no further and collapsed, resigned to their fate in the wilderness.[58] The rest pressed on.

Then, on November 2nd, the front of the column sighted a small party of men driving livestock towards them. It was the American advance party with desperately needed provisions from the local inhabitants. Arnold's expedition had made it out of the wilderness! They had survived six weeks of hardship and misery and in doing so, completed one of the most difficult marches in American military history.

Some of the livestock were immediately butchered and the famished men gorged themselves on fresh beef and other provisions. Rejuvenated by this new found nourishment, some returned to the wilderness to retrieve their exhausted comrades. Arnold's march through the wilderness was over, but more challenges lay ahead.

---

[57] Ibid.
[58] Roberts, ed., "Abner Stocking's Journal, 2 November, 1775," 556

Chapter Four

"Betwixt Every Peal [of Gunfire], the Awful Voice of Morgan is Heard"

Quebec: 1775

Although Arnold's expedition had made it through the wilderness, they were still approximately 75 miles from Quebec and in pitiful condition. Several days of hard marching lay ahead but the men, revived by the fresh provisions, pushed on. Advance troops of the expedition reached the St. Lawrence River, opposite Quebec, on November 7th, and over the next few days the rest of the expedition caught up.[1]

While Arnold's force encamped at Point Levi and prepared to cross the river, a small landing party from a British warship in the river approached the Americans, unaware of the American presence. Rifleman John Joseph Henry recalled that, *"a hurried and boisterous report came from head-quarters, that the British were landing on our left at a mill, about a mile off."*[2]

Captain Morgan and some of his men, accompanied by several Indians who had recently arrived in camp, raced towards the mill to confront the British. Henry noted that, *"the running was severe"* and when they reached the brow of a hill overlooking the shore they observed a single longboat unload a midshipman in the water near the mill and then row towards a better spot to load spars and oars from the mill.[3]

Concerned that they had been discovered, Captain Morgan fired a shot at the boat which was immediately followed by a volley from the men with Morgan. The startled British midshipman desperately tried to return to the boat; its crew,

---

[1] Roberts, ed., "George Morison's Journal, 8-13 November, 1775," 531
[2] Roberts, ed., "John Joseph Henry's Journal, 11 November, 1775," 349
[3] Ibid.

however, was more concerned for their own safety and abandoned him, rowing furiously away from shore to get out of range of the Americans.[4] Rifle balls whizzed past the midshipman's head as he swam after the boat, but he soon realized the futility of his efforts and headed back to shore, resigned to his capture.[5]

Henry participated in this affair and noted that the young midshipman had another close brush with death on shore when an Indian raced forward, scalping knife at the ready, intent on claiming a prize. Henry recalled that

> The humanity of Morgan and [Lieutenant] Humphreys, towards a succumbent foe, was excited. One or the other of them, it is not now recollected which in particular, by his agility and amazing powers of body, was enabled to precede the Indian by several yards. This contest of athleticism was observed from the shore, where we were, with great interest. Morgan brought the boy, (for he was really such,) to land, and afterwards esteemed him, for he merited the good-will of a hero.[6]

On the Outskirts of Quebec

A few days after this incident the bulk of Arnold's force (approximately 550 men) crossed the St. Lawrence River under cover of night, avoiding detection by the British warships and tenders that patrolled the river.[7] In a brief, incomplete autobiography, Captain Morgan recounted the crossing:

---

[4] Ibid
[5] Ibid.
[6] Ibid., 350
[7] Roberts, ed., "Colonel Arnold to General Montgomery, 14 November, 1775," 87

Quebec

Source: Library of Congress

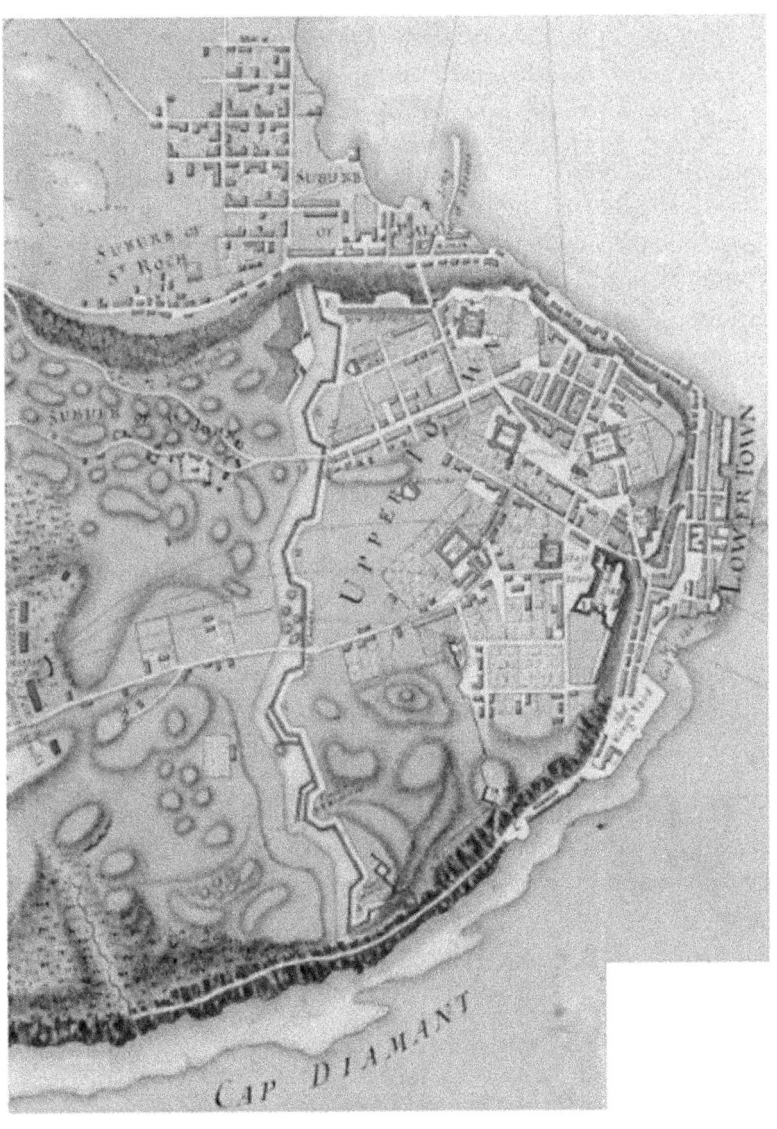

> *We crossed the river in some small craft which we found drawn up in the guts, and some bark canoes, (which we purchased from the Indians,) we passed between two men of war, in point blank shot; but we slipped through, undiscovered.*[8]

Morgan's recollection was not entirely accurate; a British barge discovered the crossing early in the morning but was chased away when the Americans fired upon it. Colonel Arnold described the incident to General Washington and cited it as one of the reasons he chose not to attack the city upon landing ashore.

> *I passed the St. Lawrence without obstruction, except from a barge, into which we fired, and killed three men; but as the enemy were apprised of our coming and the garrison augmented to near seven hundred men, besides the inhabitants, it was not thought proper to storm the place, but cut off their communication with the country, until the arrival of Gen. Montgomery. We accordingly invested the town with about 550 men...We marched up several times near the walls, in hopes of drawing them out but to no effect, though they kept a constant cannonading and killed us one man.*[9]

In hindsight, the Americans may have squandered an opportunity to capture Quebec as the garrison within the walls was unaware of Arnold's presence for several hours after their landing and the gates to the city were open and lightly guarded.[10] Of course, Arnold was unaware of this at the time

---

[8] Dawson, "General Daniel Morgan: An Autobiography," *The Historical Magazine and Notes and Queries Concerning the Antiquities, History and Biography of America,* 2nd Series, Vol. 9 379

[9] Chase, ed., "Colonel Benedict Arnold to General George Washington, 20 November, 1775," *The Papers of George Washington,* Vol. 2, 403

[10] Roberts, ed., "John Joseph Henry's Journal, 15 November, 1775," 352

he made his decision, which was based in large part on the assumption that the gunfire on the river had alarmed the city. Thus, Arnold uncharacteristically opted for caution at a council of war with his officers and in doing so, lost his best chance to capture Quebec.

Biographers of Daniel Morgan contend that he was one of the officers at the war council that advocated an immediate attack upon the city, but Morgan said nothing of this in a letter written many years later that is considered an unfinished autobiography of the rifle commander. In the letter, Morgan recalled that upon landing undetected in Wolfe's Cove,

> *I led the forlorn hope...marched up General Wolfe's Cove, and formed on the Plains of Abraham, where I expected to be attacked. We however, remained undiscovered.*[11]

With daylight approaching, Colonel Arnold ordered most of his troops onto the Plains of Abraham. They headed towards the residence of Major Henry Caldwell, commander of the British militia in Quebec. Caldwell was the tenant of a fine manor house with numerous outbuildings outside the walls of Quebec, but he had recently moved into town. Many of his servants, however, as well as a detachment of British troops, remained at the residence. The Americans desired both the manor house and its outbuildings for shelter, and Captain Morgan once again led the forlorn hope (advance guard) forward to seize them. He proudly recalled

> *We...marched to Caldwell's house, in which strong building the enemy had posted a considerable force. We carried it, sword in hand.*[12]

---

[11] Dawson, "General Daniel Morgan: An Autobiography," *The Historical Magazine and Notes and Queries Concerning the Antiquities, History and Biography of America,* 2nd *Series,* Vol. 9, 379

[12] Ibid.

Many of Arnold's men took advantage of their fine accommodations and had their first comfortable rest in weeks. A few unlucky men, however, had to remain on guard duty, and one such sentinel, George Merchant, a popular rifleman in Captain Morgan's company, was boldly seized in broad daylight by a detachment from Quebec that managed to sneak up on the unfortunate (and perhaps inattentive) sentinel while he stood guard.

Merchant's capture sparked a flurry of activity among the Americans; many initially thought they were under attack.[13] Colonel Arnold formed his men and marched them to within a few hundred yards of the town, hoping to draw the enemy out from behind their walled town to fight. A rather comical encounter occurred of Arnold's men and Quebec's defenders taunting, cheering, and ineffectually firing at each other. The defenders wisely refused to accommodate the Americans and remained safely behind their massive fortifications and Arnold eventually withdrew.

Not everyone saw humor in this incident. Private John Joseph Henry admitted that

> *It must be confessed that this ridiculous affair gave me a contemptible opinion of Arnold. This notion was by no means singular. Morgan, Febiger, and other officers, who had seen service, did not hesitate to speak of it in that point of view.*[14]

Apparently none of these men appreciated the reckless way Arnold risked the lives of his men.

This incident was likely still on Captain Morgan's mind when he met with Arnold the next day to discuss what he and his riflemen believed were inadequate rations for the troops. All three rifle captains approached Colonel Arnold to request

---

[13] Roberts, ed., "John Joseph Henry's Journal, 15 November, 1775," 353-354

[14] Ibid., 354

that the rations be increased. A heated confrontation developed between Morgan and Arnold. Captain Matthew Smith described the tense exchange afterwards to some of his men, one of whom was Joseph Henry who recorded that

> *Altercation and warm language took place* [between Morgan and Arnold]. *Smith, with his usual loquacity, told us that Morgan seemed at one time on the point of striking Arnold.*[15]

Although Colonel Arnold was apparently just as defiant and combative as Morgan and refused to accommodate the rifle commanders at the meeting, the rations of the riflemen were increased the next day and the matter was closed.[16]

Retreat and Reinforcement

Colonel Arnold had much more serious matters to contend with than the dissatisfaction of his men over their rations. His force of only 550 men was not only far too weak to attack Quebec, but also too weak to effectively besiege the city, especially given the absence of cannon. Additionally, when it appeared that Arnold might get his wish and draw the enemy out of Quebec to fight, an examination of the arms and ammunition of his troops revealed that there was no more than five rounds per man available.[17] As a result, on November 20th, Colonel Arnold withdrew his force twenty miles up the St. Lawrence River to Point Aux Trembles where he waited to rendezvous with General Richmond Montgomery's force from New York.

General Montgomery had assumed command of the second prong of the American invasion force of Canada from General Schuyler, who had become too ill to proceed, and was marching

---

[15] Ibid., 356
[16] Higginbotham, 40
[17] Chase, ed., "Colonel Benedict Arnold to General George Washington, 20 November, 1775," *The Papers of George Washington*, Vol. 2, 403

towards Quebec from Montreal. Several successful engagements on the march into Canada had actually reduced Montgomery's numbers because detachments were left behind to secure the route back to Fort Ticonderoga. Sickness also took a high toll, so high that by the time General Montgomery joined Arnold at Point Aux Trembles on December 2nd, he only had 300 men with him. Fortunately, Montgomery also brought several cannon and much needed clothing and ammunition for Arnold's men.[18] He assumed command of the combined American force, which numbered just under 900 men, and led them back to Quebec.

Waiting for Montgomery on the outskirts of the city was Captain Morgan and his riflemen; they had returned to Quebec a few days earlier to reconnoiter and prevent British parties from punishing French inhabitants outside of Quebec who had cooperated with the Americans.[19] While posted outside the town, Morgan's men captured several prisoners.[20] Information obtained from the captives did not present a promising picture for the Americans. Outnumbered nearly two to one by an enemy protected behind strong walls, it appeared that there was little the Americans could do to convince Governor Guy Carleton and the inhabitants of Quebec to surrender.

General Montgomery's demands in early December for such a surrender were scornfully rejected by Governor Carleton so Montgomery resorted to an ineffective "siege" and bombardment of the town. It soon became apparent that the Americans lacked the firepower, men, or time to conduct a successful siege and that the only option left to dislodge the

---

[18] Chase, ed., "Colonel Benedict Arnold to General George Washington, 5 December, 1775," *The Papers of George Washington,* Vol. 2, 495
[19] Desjardin, 156
[20] Dawson, "General Daniel Morgan: An Autobiography," *The Historical Magazine and Notes and Queries Concerning the Antiquities, History and Biography of America, 2nd Series,* Vol. 9, 379

Attack on Quebec
Adapted from the Library of Congress

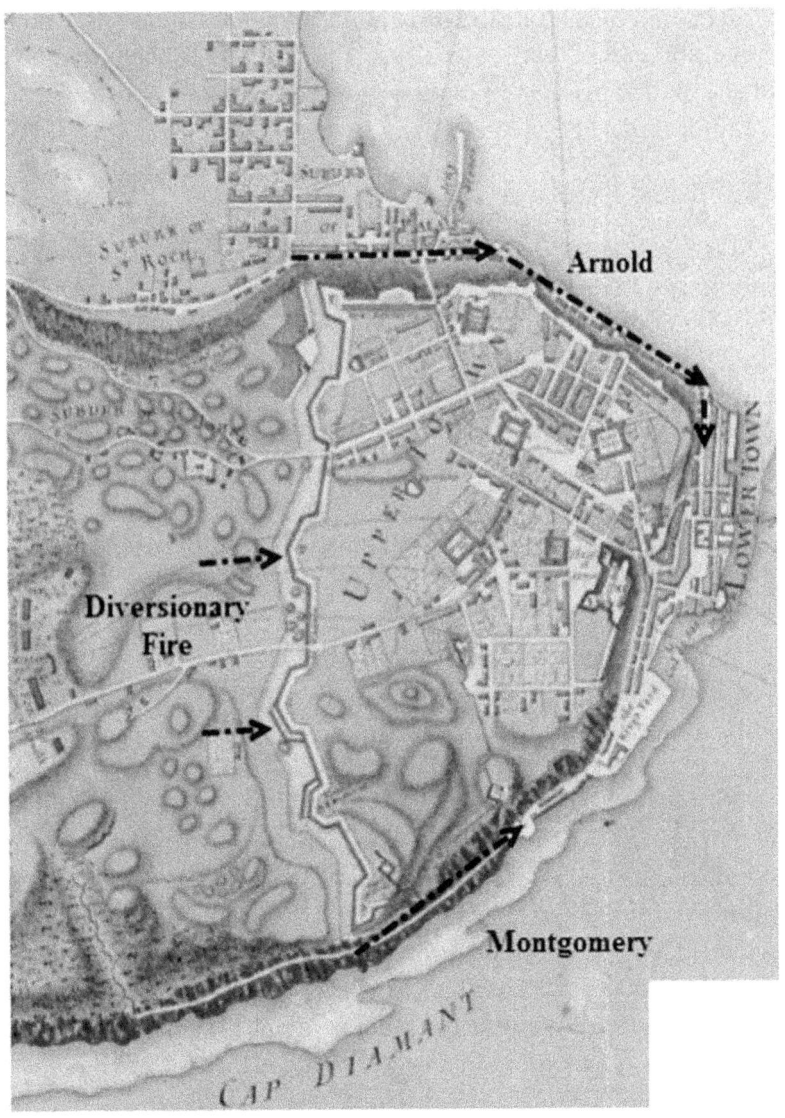

British from Quebec was a direct assault on the walled city. General Montgomery waited impatiently for the right weather conditions, preferably a storm, to launch his attack. With the enlistments of many of his men due to expire at the end of the December, the weather finally cooperated on December 30th, and provided the cover General Montgomery sought in the form of a blizzard.

Storming Quebec

General Montgomery's plan of attack called for an early morning pincer strike against the lower town of Quebec from two directions while a third detachment feigned an attack on the western approaches of Quebec (the Plains of Abraham) to distract the enemy's attention away from the lower town. General Montgomery would lead 300 New York troops along the St. Lawrence River to approach the lower town from the south while Colonel Arnold would lead his troops, nearly 600 strong, through the suburbs of Saint Roch and along the St. Charles River to approach the lower town of Quebec from the north.[21] Once the lower town was captured, the united American force would storm the upper town. Since they were significantly outnumbered, the American plan depended on both surprise and decisive execution.

Early in the morning of December 31st, with a fierce winter storm raging, the American army formed for battle. The attack began at 5:00 a.m. when Colonel James Livingston, in command of one of the diversionary detachments of Canadian militia volunteers, fired three signal rockets outside the western wall of Quebec. Livingston's troops, and a second detachment slightly to the north, advanced towards the wall and opened fire with small arms while a third detachment a bit further to the north fired mortars into Quebec.[22]

---

[21] Brendan Morissey, *Quebec 1775: The American invasion of Canada*, (Osprey, 2003), 54-55
[22] Desjardin, 171

While all of this occurred and Quebec's defenders raced to their alarm posts, General Montgomery led his detachment from the Plains of Abraham down to Wolf's Cove and then along the St. Lawrence River towards the lower town. When his column encountered what appeared to be an abandoned guardhouse, General Montgomery led a charge straight at it. A blast of grapeshot erupted from the guardhouse and smashed into the charging Americans, killing General Montgomery and several of his officers and men. The shock of the blast, coupled with the loss of Montgomery, unnerved the surviving officers and they hastily aborted the attack and withdrew, abandoning Colonel Arnold and his detachment to their fate.[23]

Colonel Arnold's column approached the lower town of Quebec through the northern suburbs and along the St. Charles River. Arnold accompanied a 30 man advance guard at the head of the column. A single six pound brass cannon on a sled followed, its crew struggling to move it through the snow. The remainder of Arnold's force, with Captain Morgan and his rifle company in the lead, followed. Virginian Charles Porterfield was with Captain Morgan and described the march to the lower town in his diary:

> We paraded at 4 o' clock, A.M....The signal given, with shouts we set out. In passing by the Palace gate, they fired, and the bells rung an alarm. We marched with as much precipitancy as possible, sustaining a heavy fire for some distance, without the opportunity to return it, being close under the wall.[24]

Pennsylvania rifleman John Joseph Henry provided a bit more description of the approach through the storm:

---

[23] Lt. Col. Strange, "Historical Notes on the Defence of Quebec in 1775," *The Centenary Fete of the Literary and Historical Society of Quebec*, 1876, 23-24

[24] "Diary of Colonel Charles Porterfield," *Magazine of American History*, Vol. 21, (April 1889), 318-319

> Covering the locks of our guns with the lappets of our coats, and holding down our heads, (for it was impossible to bear up our faces against the imperious storm of wind and snow,) we ran along the foot of the hill in single file...we received a tremendous fire of musketry from the ramparts above us. Here we lost some brave men, when powerless to return the salutes we received, as the enemy was covered by his impregnable defences. They were even sightless to us – we could see nothing but the blaze from the muzzles of their muskets.[25]

Arnold's detachment continued on through the storm until it reached an enemy barricade protected by a two gun battery of artillery. The original plan called for the six pound American field piece to be brought forth to blast the barricade. Dragging the heavy cannon through the deep snow, however, proved too difficult and it was abandoned along the route. Complicating matters further, much of Arnold's force, which had become spread out in the difficult march, went astray in the blinding storm and narrow streets of Saint Roch and the lower town. As a result, when Colonel Arnold and the American advance party reached the first barricade, their only immediate support was Captain Morgan's company of riflemen. Despite this, the Americans charged headlong towards the barricade. Virginian Charles Porterfield described what happened:

> Coming to the barrier of the entrance of the lower town, guarded by a captain and 50 men, with two pieces of cannon, one of which they discharged and killed two men, we forced them from the cannon, firing in at the portholes, all the time exposed to the fire of the musketry from the bank above us in the upper town. Here, Colonel Arnold was wounded in the leg and had to retire. The scaling ladders being brought up, if there was any honor in being first over the barrier, I had it. I was immediately

---

[25] Roberts, ed., "John Joseph Henry's Journal, 1 January, 1775" 375-376

followed by Captain Morgan. Upon our approach the guards fled, and we followed close to the guard-house, when, making a halt till some more men should come up, we sallied through into the street. We took thirty men and a captain...[26]

A slightly different account of the assault, told by the Reverend William Hill, a friend of Daniel Morgan's who presumably learned the details from Morgan himself, claimed that with Colonel Arnold wounded in the leg and out of action, Captain Morgan assumed command and led a charge against the enemy barricade. According to Reverend Hill

When ready to scale the walls, Morgan ordered one of his men first to mount the Ladder, but seeing him hesitate, he took the ladder himself & as soon as he [Morgan] raised his head over the wall a musket was fired in his face, the ball missed him, but he was badly burned by the powder, some grains of which he carried in his face to his grave, & by the shock was thrown back at the feet of the ladder.[27]

Undeterred by this close call, Captain Morgan scrambled to his feet and up the ladder again, passing over the barricade.

A third account of the assault on the first barricade was actually provided by Morgan himself many years after the attack. In it he omitted his fall from the ladder, but corroborated Charles Porterfield's account of the assault with one significant difference. Captain Morgan claimed that he was the first over the barricade, followed by Porterfield and the rest of his riflemen. The way Morgan remembered it

---

[26] "Diary of Colonel Charles Porterfield," *Magazine of American History*, Vol. 21, (April 1889), 319
[27] William Hill Notes

I had to attack a two-gun battery, supported by Captain M'Leod and 50 regular troops. The first gun that was fired missed us, the second flashed, when I ordered the ladder, which was on two men's shoulders, to be placed; (every two men carried a ladder.) This order was immediately obeyed, and, for fear the business might not be executed with spirit, I mounted myself, and was the first man who leaped into the town, among M'Leod's guard, who were panic struck, and, after a faint resistance, ran into a house that joined the battery and platform. I [landed] *on the end of a heavy piece of artillery, which hurt me exceedingly and perhaps saved my life, as I fell from the gun upon the platform, where the bayonets were not directed. Charles Porterfield, who was then a Cadet in my company, was the first man who followed me; the rest lost not a moment, but spring in as fast as they could find room; all this was performed in a few seconds. I ordered the men to fire into the house, and follow up their fire with their pikes (for besides our rifles we were furnished with long espontoons) this was done, and the guard was driven into the street. I went through a sally-port at the end of the platform; met them in the street; and ordered them to lay down their arms, if they expected quarter; they took me at my word and every man threw down his gun.*[28]

---

[28] Dawson, "General Daniel Morgan: An Autobiography," *The Historical Magazine and Notes and Queries Concerning the Antiquities, History and Biography of America, 2nd Series,* Vol. 9, 379-380

Lower Town

Photo by the Author

Whatever version of the assault is most accurate, the fact remained that Arnold's detachment, with Captain Morgan leading the way, captured the first barricade. But in doing so, Arnold's troops were scattered about the lower town in disarray. A delay in the assault ensued as the officers with Morgan decided to wait for their men to reform and for General Montgomery and his detachment to arrive from the other side of the Lower Town.

Unwilling to stand idle, Captain Morgan advanced ahead of the stalled Americans to reconnoiter the second barricade. He observed that

> *The sally-port through the barrier* [of the second barricade] *was standing open; the guard left it; and the people came running, in seeming platoon, and gave themselves up, in order to get out of the way of the confusion that was likely to ensue. I went up to the edge of the upper town, with an interpreter, to observe what was going on, as the firing had ceased. I found no person in arms at all.*[29]

Morgan returned and called a council of war. He urged an immediate advance on the second barricade with the men that they had (approximately 200).[30] Morgan bitterly remembered that

> *I was overruled by hard reasoning; it was stated that, if I went on, I would break an order, in the first place; in the next place, I had more prisoners than I had men; that if I left them, they might break out, retake the battery, and cut off our retreat; that General Montgomery was certainly coming down the River St. Lawrence, and would join us in a few minutes, so that we were sure of conquest if we acted*

---

[29] Ibid., 380

[30] Ibid. and "Diary of Colonel Charles Porterfield," *Magazine of American History,* Vol. 21, (April 1889), 319

with caution. To these arguments I sacrificed my own opinion and lost the town.[31]

Nearly an hour passed before the attack was finally resumed.[32]

During this delay, the British rushed men to the second barrier. Lieutenant Colonel Henry Caldwell, the commander of the British militia in Quebec, described what he found there when he arrived with reinforcements from the upper town:

> *The enemy had got in* [the Lower Town] *at the Sault-au-Matelot,* [first barricade] *but neglecting to push on, as they should have done, were stopped at the second barrier which our people got shut just as I arrived.*[33]

Caldwell's timely arrival at the second barricade bolstered the spirits of its defenders. Caldwell posted men inside buildings overlooking the barricade (and Sault-au-Matelot Street, the only avenue of approach for the Americans) and placed a detachment at the foot of the barricade with fixed bayonets, ready to fall upon any rebel who dared scale the twelve foot high wall.[34]

As daylight approached, Arnold's detachment finally advanced down Sault-au-Matelot Street towards the second barricade, some 300 yards away.[35] As they rounded a curve,

---

[31] Dawson, "General Daniel Morgan: An Autobiography," *The Historical Magazine and Notes and Queries Concerning the Antiquities, History and Biography of America, 2nd Series,* Vol. 9, 380

[32] "Diary of Colonel Charles Porterfield," *Magazine of American History,* Vol. 21, (April 1889), 319

[33] J.M. LeMoine, "Col. Caldwell to Gen. James Murray, Spring, 1776," *The Centenary Fete of the Literary and Historical Society of Quebec,* 1876, 62

[34] Ibid., and Roberts, ed., "John Joseph Henry's Diary, 1 January, 1775," 378

[35] Roberts, ed., "John Joseph Henry's Diary, 1 January, 1775," 377

Lower Town

Photo by the Author

Captain Morgan, at the head of the column, was hailed by a detachment of the enemy that had sallied forth from the second barricade. Captain Abner Stocking recorded what happened in his journal:

> *We...were proceeding to the second barrier, when on turning an angle in the street, we were hailed by a Captain Anderson who had just issued from the gate with a body of troops to attack us. Captain Morgan who led our little band in this forlorn hope, answered the British Captain by a ball through his head, his soldiers drew him within the barricade and closed the gate; a tremendous fire from the windows of the buildings and port holes of the wall was directed against [us].*[36]

Virginian Charles Porterfield, still with Captain Morgan, described the heavy fire the Americans faced at the second barricade:

> *On approaching the second barrier, [the enemy] hailed us. We immediately fired; they returned it with a shower of shot. Being planted in houses on the opposite side of the barrier, a continual fire ensued for some time, while we rushed up to the barrier, set up our ladder, and, at the same instant, Captain Morgan mounted one, I the other, to force our way, spear in hand, but we were obliged to draw back. Here we were at a disadvantage. Our guns being wet, could not return the fire we were subject to; [we] were obliged to retreat into the street.*[37]

Pennsylvania rifleman George Morison also described the assault on the second barricade:

---

[36] Roberts, ed., "Abner Stocking's Journal," 565
[37] "Diary of Colonel Charles Porterfield," *Magazine of American History*, Vol. 21, (April 1889), 319

> *The ladders are laid to the wall – our gallant officers are mounting followed by several men when a furious discharge of musketry is let loose upon us from behind houses; in an instant we are assailed from different quarters with a deadly fire. We now find it impossible to force the battery or guard the port-holes any longer. –We rush on to every part, rouse the enemy from their coverts, and force a body of them to an open fight, some of our riflemen take to houses and do considerable execution. We are now attacked by thrice our number; the battle becomes hot, and is much scattered; but we distinguish each other by hemlock springs previously placed in our hats. All our officers act most gallantly. Betwixt every peal the awful voice of Morgan is heard, whose gigantic stature and terrible appearance carries dismay among the foe wherever he comes.*[38]

Despite Morgan's bold leadership and effort, the American situation was critical. "*Confined in a narrow street hardly more than twenty feet wide, and on the lower ground, scarcely a ball, well aimed or otherwise, but must take effect upon us,*" recalled John Joseph Henry.[39] American losses quickly mounted. Lieutenant William Humphreys, Morgan's friend and first lieutenant, fell as did Captain William Hendricks, both mortally wounded. Bodies of dead and wounded men littered the narrow street before the barricade. Those who were unhurt sought shelter in nearby buildings and fought on, encouraged by Captain Morgan who, "*stormed and raged,*" at both his men and the enemy.[40] Charles Porterfield found cover inside one such building with fellow Virginian Peter Bruin and seven or eight other men.

---

[38] Roberts, ed., "George Morison's Journal," 537
[39] Roberts, ed., "John Joseph Henry's Diary, 1 January, 1775," 378
[40] Ibid.

We fired...from the windows," recalled Porterfield, *determined to stand it out or die...Upon seeing Colonel Green and others give up their arms, we held a council what to do, Bruin declaring to the men that, if they thought proper to risk it, he was willing to fight our way out – that he should stand or fall with them.*[41]

Inside one building that comprised part of the barricade, the struggle became hand to hand as combatants from both sides entered simultaneously, the Americans through the front door and the British via a ladder through an upstairs window. The British emerged victorious in this clash, driving the Americans back into the street.[42]

While the fight raged on at the second barrier, hundreds of enemy troops recaptured the first barricade and advanced on the Americans from the rear. Trapped in the lower town between two strong enemy forces, the Americans fought on, hoping that General Montgomery's detachment would arrive to relieve them. By 10:00 a.m., however, it was evident that Montgomery was not coming and that the attack had failed. With no hope of holding on until nightfall and a promise of good treatment from their captors, Arnold's men surrendered.

Captain Daniel Morgan was one of the last to do so, reportedly weeping with anger as he handed his sword, not to the enemy, but to a local clergyman.[43] The battle of Quebec ended in defeat for the Americans. Ahead lay eight months of captivity for Captain Morgan and his men.

---

[41] "Diary of Colonel Charles Porterfield," *Magazine of American History,* Vol. 21, (April 1889), 319

[42] J.M. LeMoine, "Col. Caldwell to Gen. James Murray, Spring, 1776," *The Centenary Fete of the Literary and Historical Society of Quebec,* 1876, 62

[43] Graham, *Life of General Daniel Morgan,* 103

Chapter Five

Captivity, Promotion, Morgan's Rifle Corps: 1776-77

Over four hundred Americans were captured in the attack on Quebec. Another hundred were killed or wounded.[1] The British lost only a handful of men. Yet, Governor Carleton refused to press his advantage and remained behind the city's walls. Colonel Arnold, who was seriously wounded in the leg, assumed command of the remnants of the American army outside of Quebec. Although he could not breach the walls of Quebec, he could still disrupt Carleton's communication and the commerce of the town. While his battered force did so, Arnold slowly recovered from his leg wound and brazenly dared Carleton to attack.

Inside Quebec, Captain Morgan and his fellow captives faired reasonably well. Great kindness and consideration were initially shown the American officers and men. Lieutenant William Heth, of Morgan's company, noted in his diary that,

> Many of the [enemy] Officers waited upon us -- & promis'd to give what assistance they could...His Excellency [Governor Carleton] made us a Compliment of a Hogshead of exceeding good Porter...Rev. John Oliver Brian...presented us with 2 Hhds [hogsheads or barrels] Spanish wine, 6 Loav's sugar & 12 lb. Tea.[2]

Efforts were made by the captors to turn their captives away from the American cause. For the prisoners born in England and Ireland, coercion was applied in the form of a threat to send

---

[1] Higginbotham, 50
[2] B. Floyd Flickinger, ed., "Diary of Lieutenant William Heth while a Prisoner in Quebec, 1776", *Annual Papers of Winchester Virginia Historical Society*, Vol. 1, (1931), 39-40

them to England to face treason charges unless they enlisted in the British army.³ American born prisoners were also encouraged to enlist and escape imprisonment. A number of captives accepted Carleton's offer, but when several deserted their post at the first opportunity and returned to the American army outside Quebec, Governor Carleton suspended this approach and returned most of the new "recruits" to captivity.⁴

In the spring, the British uncovered an elaborate plot among the American enlisted men that involved seizing one of the gates to the city and opening it to allow Colonel Arnold's troops, who were still deployed outside of Quebec, into the city. Foiled at the very last minute, the favorable treatment of the American troops ended and the men were held in chains for the next two months.⁵

Captain Morgan and the other American officers were held separately from their men and were not involved or even aware of the plot, so they did not receive the harsh treatment. Efforts to persuade the American officers to abandon their cause were also attempted. Captain Morgan, whom many of the British officers respected for his bold conduct in battle, was frequently visited by a particular British officer and encouraged to join the British side.⁶ On one such visit Morgan was offered a colonel's commission in the British army if he would agree to withdraw from the Americans and join the British.⁷ Morgan rejected this offer with disdain and declared that

> *He hoped* [the British officer] *would never again insult him in his present distressed and unfortunate situation, by making him offers which plainly implied that he thought* [Morgan] *a rascal!*⁸

---

³ Graham, 110
⁴ Ibid.
⁵ Ibid., 110-111
⁶ William Hill Notes
⁷ Ibid.
⁸ Ibid.

This was not the only incident experienced by Morgan while in captivity. He had several violent encounters with some of his fellow officers during their imprisonment. The chief cause of these affairs appeared to be Captain Morgan's extreme dislike of Captain William Goodrich of Massachusetts, a sentiment possibly provoked by Goodrich's insubordinate conduct towards Colonel Arnold during the brief siege of Quebec in November and December.

In one particular incident, Captain Morgan, furious at Captain Goodrich for refusing to return a watch to its rightful owner, choked Goodrich until he agreed to relinquish the watch.[9] In a second incident, described by Morgan's fellow Virginian, Charles Porterfield, Captain Morgan scuffled with several allies of the Massachusetts captain. According to Porterfield, Captain Morgan desired to discuss a matter with Major Timothy Bigelow and requested Bigelow's presence. Major Bigelow soon arrived at Morgan's room, trailed by Captain Goodrich who, according to Porterfield, was known to eavesdrop at every opportunity and who was despised by all of the Virginia officers. Porterfield recalled that

> [Goodrich] *no sooner reached the door than Capt. Morgan ordered him out, as having no business here, and took him by the throat to put him out. Immediately came Mr. Andrews and many more, rushing in at the door. Andrews took hold of Capt. Morgan and struck him, while four or five others were holding* [Morgan] *from Goodrich. Goodrich ran out of the room, and most of the party with him....*[10]

---

[9] J. A. Waddell, ed., 'Diary of a Prisoner of War at Quebec, 1776,' *The Virginia Magazine of History and Biography*, Vol. 9 (Richmond, VA: The Virginia Historical Society, July 1901 no. 1), 152
[10] Ibid., 150

Goodrich apparently stayed far away from Captain Morgan after this incident, convinced that Morgan might kill him at their next encounter.[11]

Parole

In August, after eight months of captivity and with American troops long since forced out of Canada by British reinforcements, Governor Carleton paroled Captain Morgan and his fellow prisoners. This meant they could return to their homes on the condition that they not serve in the ongoing conflict until they were officially exchanged for British prisoners captured by the Americans. Morgan and his comrades boarded British transport ships on August 10th and arrived off New York, which faced imminent invasion by General William Howe and his powerful British and German army, in early September.[12]

Much had occurred during Morgan's long captivity. Boston was liberated in March and independence declared by the Continental Congress in July. The war expanded significantly in size and scope in 1776 and the Americans suffered setbacks in Canada in the spring and on Long Island in late August, but these were just the beginning of what would be a very trying fall and winter for the American cause.

For Captain Morgan and his fellow Virginians, however, their parole meant a happy return to their homes after fifteen months away. The war would have to go on, at least temporarily, without them.

General Washington had different wishes for Captain Morgan, however. In late September, the commander-in-chief wrote to Congress to propose the Morgan be given command of a combined rifle battalion composed of riflemen from Virginia,

---

[11] Ibid., 151 and Higginbotham, 53
[12] Graham, 115

Pennsylvania, and Maryland.[13] The unit was originally commanded by Colonel Hugh Stephenson (Morgan's fellow Virginia rifle captain from 1775) but Stephenson died suddenly of an illness in early September. Captain Morgan's timely return from Canada, coupled with his bold leadership in the expedition there, made him the obvious candidate to command the rifle battalion. General Washington said as much in a letter to Congress in late September:

> *As Col: Hugh Stephenson of the Rifle Regiment ordered lately to be raised, is dead...I would beg leave to recommend to the particular notice of Congress, Captain Daniel Morgan, just returned among the prisoners from Canada, as a fit and proper person to succeed to the vacancy occasioned by his Death. The present Field Officers of the Regiment cannot claim any right in preference to him, because he ranked above them as Captain when he first entered the service; His Conduct as an Officer on the expedition with General Arnold last fall, his intrepid behavior in the Assault on Quebec when the brave Montgomery fell; the inflexible attachment he professed to our Cause during his imprisonment and which he perseveres in; added to these his residence in the place Col: Stevenson came from and his Interest and influence in the same circle and with such men as are to compose such a Regiment; all in my Opinion entitle him to the favor of Congress, and lead me to believe, that in his promotion, the States will gain a good and valuable Officer for the sort of Troops he is particularly recommended to command.*[14]

---

[13] Philander D. Chase and Frank E. Grizzard, Jr., eds., "General Washington to John Hancock, 28 September, 1776," *The Papers of George Washington, Revolutionary War Series,* Vol. 6, (Charlottesville: University Press of Virginia, 1994), 421

[14] Chase and Grizzard, Jr., eds., "General Washington to John Hancock, 28 September, 1776," *The Papers of George Washington, Revolutionary War Series,* Vol. 6, 421

Morgan's status as a parolee complicated the issue, prompting Washington to add

> Should Congress be pleased to appoint Capt. Morgan...I would still beg leave to suggest the propriety and necessity of keeping the matter closed and not suffering it to transpire until he is exonerated from the parole he is under.[15]

General Washington worried that should the British learn of Morgan's promotion to the rank of colonel before he was exchanged, they might demand an officer of equal rank for Morgan. Washington informed Congress that high ranking enemy officers were something, "*of which we have but very few in our hands and none that I recollect of that rank* [colonel]."[16] John Hancock, the President of the Congress, assured Washington that the position would be quietly reserved for Morgan. Events soon transpired, however, that made the issue mute.

The second half of 1776 was a disaster for General Washington and the American army. Routed on Long Island in late August and chased from New York City in mid-September, Washington and his army dug in at Harlem Heights on the northern end of Manhattan Island. When British General William Howe threatened to trap the Americans on Manhattan by landing his army on the mainland above Manhattan in October, Washington marched the bulk of his troops off the island, unwisely leaving a garrison behind at Fort Washington (overlooking the Hudson River). In mid-November General Howe unexpectedly marched his army back to Manhattan and attacked Fort Washington whose defenders included the riflemen of the late Colonel Hugh Stephenson's Battalion. After a brief engagement, in which the riflemen fought very

---

[15] Ibid.
[16] Ibid.

well, the entire American garrison at Fort Washington, nearly 3,000 men, surrendered. Whether Daniel Morgan would have eventually commanded Stephenson's riflemen is unclear, for at about the same time Fort Washington fell, Virginia's new government authorized the formation of six additional regiments (on top of the nine regiments that were already formed). Morgan was selected to command one of the new regiments, but as he had not yet been formally exchanged, his involvement in military activities was still restricted. This changed in January when notification arrived that Morgan had officially been exchanged.[17]

Command of the 11th Virginia Regiment

Colonel Daniel Morgan assumed command of the 11th Virginia Regiment in January 1777 and was joined by some of his comrades from the Quebec expedition, including Christian Febiger and William Heth who were appointed Lieutenant Colonel and Major of the regiment, respectively. Febiger had not actually been a member of Morgan's original rifle company but he earned Morgan's respect as a volunteer member of the expedition and followed Morgan to Virginia after their release. In recognition of their conduct at Quebec, Peter Bruin and Charles Porterfield were also given appointments as company captains in the regiment.

The authorization of six new regiments brought Virginia's total to 15 in 1776-77. Regiments raised a year earlier in Virginia consisted of seven musket and three rifle companies and five of the six new regiments were likely organized in similar fashion.[18] Daniel Morgan's 11th Virginia was different, however. Half of the regiment (five of its ten companies) consisted of independent rifle companies raised in Virginia during the summer of 1776, months before the 11th Regiment

---

[17] Alexander Purdie's Virginia Gazette, 7 February, 1777," 1
[18] William Hening, *The Statutes at Large Being a Collection of all the Laws of Virginia,* Vol. 9 (Richmond: J & G Cochran, 1821), 76

was formed.[19] Unfortunately, four of these companies were captured at Ft. Washington in mid-November. Thus, they were part of the 11th Virginia in name only. Just one of the original five independent rifle companies assigned to Morgan's regiment actually joined the unit. The company was commanded by Captain William Blackwell of Fauquier County whose first lieutenant was twenty year old John Marshall, future Chief Justice of the U.S. Supreme Court.

The other half of Morgan's 11th Virginia consisted of a company from Prince William County and two companies each from Loudoun County and Frederick County. The two Frederick County companies were rifle companies commanded by veterans of Morgan's original rifle company, Peter Bruin and Charles Porterfield.[20] Two additional independent rifle companies raised in the summer of 1776, one from Virginia under Captain Gabriel Long and the other from Pennsylvania under Captain James Calderwood, were attached to Morgan's regiment in the spring of 1777, presumably as partial replacements for the four captured rifle companies lost at Fort Washington.[21]

The abundance of riflemen in Morgan's regiment, along with Morgan's long association with riflemen, contributed to the long held belief that the 11th Virginia Regiment was solely a rifle regiment. This appears to be inaccurate, however. Although Captains Blackwell, Porterfield, Bruin, Long, and Calderwood commanded rifle companies, the two Loudoun

---

[19] H.R. McIlwaine, ed. *Journals of the Council of the State of Virginia*, Vol. 1, (Richmond: Virginia State Library, 1931), 321
[20] W.T.R. Saffell, *Records of the Revolutionary War, 3rd Ed.*, (Baltimore: Charles Saffell, 1894), 260
And
  E.M. Sanchez-Saavedra, *A Guide to Virginia Military Organizations in the American Revolution, 1774-1787*, (Westminster, MD: Willow Bend, 1978),
[21] Saffell, 256, 268

county companies and the Prince William company were probably made up of musket-men.

Several points support this conclusion. First, the 11th Virginia was never referred to, in contemporary sources, as a rifle regiment. In fact, at least two pension applications from members of the 11th Virginia, refer to the unit as, *"Morgan's musket regiment."* In 1818 Eden Clevenger, a former rifleman in Captain Porterfield's company, claimed that he served, *"in the 11th Virginia Regiment, generally called Col. Morgan's musket regiment."*[22] His claim was supported by Thomas Stothard, who declared that, *"he went out with Eden Clevenger in the regiment of musket men in the same company and messed with him all the time of service."*[23]

The fact that some of Morgan's men marched north unarmed and were supplied with weapons (probably muskets) when they arrived in camp also supports the view that there were musket-men in the 11th Virginia. Lastly, when General Washington formed a corps of riflemen in June of 1777 to serve as light infantry, most of the members of the 11th Virginia remained with the regiment and many of the riflemen who stayed had to exchange their rifles for muskets per order of General Washington.[24]

So while Daniel Morgan's 11th Virginia did indeed have a higher proportion of riflemen in its ranks compared to other Virginia regiments (five out of eight companies) it was not solely a rifle regiment.

Recruitment of the five new companies of Colonel Morgan's regiment occurred over the winter of 1776-77. Each company was authorized to raise sixty-eight men, but it is doubtful that

---

[22] John Frederick Dorman, ed., "Eden Clevenger Pension Application," *Virginia Revolutionary Pension Applications,* Vol. 20, (Washington, D.C., 1972), 9

[23] Ibid. 10

[24] Frank E. Grizzard, Jr., ed., "General Orders, 13 June, 1777," *The Papers of George Washington Series*, Vol. 10, (Charlottesville: University Press of Virginia, 2000), 20

they all reached that number. General Washington, desperate for reinforcements, urged the states to send men as quickly as possible, regardless of whether their units were complete or not.[25] The first company from the 11th Virginia to head north was Captain Blackwell's. It departed sometime in January before it was even assigned to Morgan's regiment. When the company arrived in Philadelphia they immediately underwent inoculation for small pox. Although inoculations would better prepare the American army for the upcoming campaign, their immediate impact was to decrease the number of troops available for service to General Washington. As a result, the American commander-in-chief repeated his appeal to the states for more men.

Virginia's leaders responded to General Washington's appeals by ordering Colonel Morgan to, *"...forthwith march to Head Quarters, to join the Army under the Command of His Excellency, General Washington."*[26] Colonel Morgan and his officers, however, found recruiting in the third year of the war much harder than at the outbreak and had few troops to send. It took three more weeks for Morgan to partially comply with the instruction. In late February Lieutenant Colonel Febiger led three companies of the regiment northward and announced his arrival in Philadelphia in a letter to General Washington on March 6th.

> *I have the honor of informing your Excellency of my Arrival in this City with the first Company of our Regiment, two Companies more being on their March and hourly expected, those men, who are in Town are under Inoculation and recovering fast, as soon as they*

---

[25] Frank E. Grizzard, Jr., ed., "General Washington to Colonel George Weedon, 9 January, 1777*,"The Papers of George Washington, Revolutionary War Series,* Vol. 8, (Charlottesville, University Press of Virginia, 1998), 15-16

[26] McIlwaine, 324

can be cloathed and arm'd, I shall march them to Camp.[27]

The shortage of clothing was, in part, the result of the small pox inoculation the men underwent. The process, which typically took a few weeks, required that the men's old clothes be thoroughly washed and smoked before they left camp.[28] Of course, General Washington preferred that new clothing be issued to the men, but there simply wasn't enough to go around.

Febiger also updated General Washington on the status of the rest of Colonel Morgan's regiment:

> *"Of the 5 new Companies allotted to us by the Government of Virginia, Capt. Bruin of Frederick and Gallihue of Prince William are hourly expected with full Companies, having been some Time on their March. Captains Wm. Johnson and Smith of Loudon will come in a Short Time under the Major and Colonel Morgan will come with the last whom I don't know, as it was not determin'd whether we should have the Forquair or Dunmore Company, when I left Winchester."*[29]

It appears that the last company to march north was actually Captain Charles Porterfield's, accompanied in all likelihood, by Colonel Morgan.

---

[27] Grizzard Jr., ed., "Lt. Col. Christian Febiger to General Washington, 6 March 1777," *The Papers of George Washington,* Vol. 8, 520
[28] Grizzard Jr., ed., "General Washington to Major General Horatio Gates, 28 January, 1777," *The Papers of George Washington,* Vol. 8, 172
[29] Grizzard Jr., ed., "Lt. Col. Christian Febiger to General Washington, 6 March 1777," *The Papers of George Washington,* Vol. 8, 520

Morgan's Regiment in New Jersey

By the spring of 1777, the bulk of Colonel Morgan's regiment, numbering less than half its authorized strength, was posted near Bound Brook, New Jersey.[30] Inoculated against smallpox, Morgan's troops joined the growing American army in central New Jersey, which had swelled to over 8,000 men by May.[31] The large influx of soldiers (which was largely the result of Washington's stunning winter victories at Trenton and Princeton a few months earlier) prompted General Washington to re-organize his army. Morgan's 11th Virginia Regiment was brigaded with the 3rd, 7th, and 15th Virginia Regiments under General William Woodford.[32] Woodford had commanded one of Virginia's first regiments in 1775, the 2nd Virginia, and was victorious at a significant battle in southern Virginia that helped drive the Royal Governor, John Murray, the Earl of Dunmore, from Virginia.

Although the growth of the American army was eagerly welcomed by General Washington, he still declined to risk battle with the British in the open field, away from his strong position in the Watchtung Mountains of New Jersey. Washington thus waited for General William Howe to make the first move and kick off the military campaign of 1777. Howe was inexplicably slow to act, however, and the American army remained encamped in the Watchtung Mountains through June.

---

[30] Charles H. Lesser, ed., "A Return of the Troops…Under Command of Maj. Gen. Lincoln, May 3, 1777," Benjamin Lincoln Papers, Massachusetts Historical Society, *The Sinews of Independence: Monthly Strength Reports of the Continental Army*, (Chicago: The University of Chicago Press, 1976), 45

[31] "Report on Virginia Battalions, 17 May, 1777," *George Washington Papers at the Library of Congress, 1741-1799: Series 4*, Image 943 (Online)

[32] Philander D. Chase, ed., "General Orders, 22 May, 1777," *The Papers of George Washington, Revolutionary War Series*, Vol. 9, (Charlottesville: University Press of Virginia, 1999), 495

Colonel Morgan used the time in camp to improve his regiment. He issued frequent orders to practice the manual of arms and the evolutions (marching). Morgan also stressed the need to keep the regimental camp, arms, and men, as clean as possible.[33]

Morgan's strict orders and expectations for his troops challenge the popular belief held by many that American riflemen in the Revolution were rowdy, undisciplined, frontier soldiers who rarely followed orders. Some undoubtedly were, especially in 1775, but Colonel Morgan, the severe disciplinarian from Arnold's expedition, clearly expected his men, both musket-men and riflemen, to be well trained and well disciplined, so he made no distinction between the different companies in his regimental orders. Line and rifle troops of the 11th Virginia drilled together, and in doing so, improved their military skills and discipline.

Colonel Morgan's command of the 11th Virginia was temporarily suspended in mid-June when he was selected by General Washington for a new command. Morgan's experience, leadership, and reputation, made him the perfect choice to command a newly formed "picked" corps of riflemen that General Washington had decided to create for the upcoming campaign.

Morgan's Rifle Corps

Although General Washington was encouraged by the number of men who joined his ranks in 1777, he still had a few glaring shortfalls to address. One was the need for an effective body of light infantry. The British used their light infantry as

---

[33] Orderly Book of Major William Heth of the Third (sic) Virginia regiment, May 15 – July 1, 1777 in *Virginia Historical Society Collections, New Series, 11* (1892)
Accessed via the website: RevWar75.com
Note: The author contends that this orderly book has long been misidentified as belonging to the 3rd Virginia Regiment when in fact, it pertains to the 11th Virginia Regiment

flankers and skirmishers. They often combined these soldiers with German jaegers (riflemen) and British dragoons for reconnaissance activities.

General Washington largely relied on militia troops for such duty in 1776 and found them ineffective. Washington's orders for June 1st, 1777, suggest that he had settled on a replacement for the militia:

> *The commanding officer of every Corps is to make a report early tomorrow morning...of the number of Rifle-men under his command—In doing which, he is to include none but such as are known to be perfectly skilled in the use of these guns, and who are known to be active and orderly in their behaviour.*[34]

Two weeks later, on June 13th, Washington formed a new, independent rifle corps and appointed Colonel Daniel Morgan to command it. Washington informed Colonel Morgan that

> *The corps of Rangers newly formed and under your command, are to be considered as a body of light infantry, and are to act as such, for which reason they will be exempted from the common duties of the line.*[35]

An apparent shortage of rifles caused Washington to order:

> *Such rifles as belong to the States, in the different brigades, to be immediately exchanged with Col. Morgan for musquets...If a sufficient number of rifles (public property) cannot be procured, the Brigadiers are*

---

[34] Chase, ed., "General Orders, 1 June, 1777," *The Papers of George Washington,* Vol. 9, 578

[35] Frank E. Grizzard, Jr., ed., "General Washington to Colonel Morgan, 13 June, 1777," *The Papers of George Washington, Revolutionary War Series,* Vol. 10, 31

requested to assist Col. Morgan, either by exchanging, or purchasing those that are private property.[36]

General Washington also made arrangements for the riflemen to receive spears as a defense against mounted troops. He informed Colonel Morgan that,

> *I have sent for Spears, which I expect shortly to receive and deliver you, as a defence against Horse; till you are furnished with these, take care not to be caught in such a Situation as to give them any advantage over you.*[37]

The spears arrived a week later. General Washington was pleased, but recommended a few adjustments to suit the riflemen:

> *The Spears have come to hand, and are very handy and will be useful to the Rifle Men. But they would be more conveniently carried, if they had a sling fixed to them, they should also have a spike in the butt end to fix them in the ground and they would then serve as a rest for the Rifle. The Iron plates which fix the spear head to the shaft, should be at least eighteen inches long to prevent the Shaft from being cut through, with a stroke of a Horseman's Sword.*[38]

It is unclear how long the riflemen actually used the spears. No further reference to them appears after June 20th, which suggests the cumbersome weapons were possibly discarded by the riflemen.

---

[36] Grizzard, Jr., ed., "General Orders, 13 June, 1777," *The Papers of George Washington*, Vol. 10, 20

[37] Grizzard, Jr., ed., "General Washington to Colonel Morgan, 13 June, 1777," *The Papers of George Washington*, Vol. 10, 31

[38] Grizzard, Jr., ed., "General Washington to Richard Peters, 20 June, 1777," *The Papers of George Washington*, Vol. 10, 88

Morgan's corps consisted of riflemen from Virginia and Pennsylvania (500 in all), and the unit was immediately employed in the field. General Washington's orders to Morgan on the first day of the corps' formation demonstrates the American commander's intended use of the rifle corps.

> *Take post at Van Vechten's Bridge, and watch, with very small scouting parties (to avoid fatiguing your men too much...) the enemy's left flank...In case of any movement of the enemy, you are instantly to fall upon their flanks, and gall them as much as possible, taking especial care not to be surrounded, or to have your retreat to the army cut off.*[39]

The next day, General Howe sent a large detachment towards the American lines. Morgan's rifle corps skirmished with them for much of the day, but little came of the engagement and the British broke off contact at nightfall.[40] They remained in the field, however, which prompted General Washington to re-iterate his orders to Colonel Morgan:

> *You will continue to keep out your active parties carefully watching every motion of the enemy; and have your whole body in readiness to move without confusion, and free from danger....*[41]

The British held their position near the Americans for nearly a week and skirmished daily with Morgan's riflemen. When General Howe finally withdrew, Morgan's rifle corps, along with troops under General Nathanael Greene of Rhode Island and General Anthony Wayne of Pennsylvania, pursued them all

---

[39] Grizzard, Jr., ed., "General Washington to Colonel Morgan, 13 June, 1777," *The Papers of George Washington*, Vol. 10, 31

[40] Grizzard, Jr., ed., "General Washington to General Sullivan, 14 June, 1777," *The Papers of George Washington*, Vol. 10, 40

[41] Grizzard, Jr., ed., "Richard Meade to Daniel Morgan, 16 June, 1777," *The Papers of George Washington*, Vol. 10, 40

the way to Piscataway. Washington noted that, "*In the pursuit, Colo. Morgans Rifle Men exchanged several sharp Fires with the Enemy, which it is imagined did them considerable execution."*[42] Captain Thomas Posey of Virginia commanded one of Morgan's rifle companies and provided a detailed account of the engagement in his biography:

> *The* [rifle] *regiment was posted in a thick wood somewhat swampy near the rode, & when the main body of the enemy passed, & the rear guard came on, Morgan ordered the regiment to attack and indeavour to cut it off. The order was promptly obeyed, & the action was warmly contested on both sides; in the course of the action Capt. Posey was ordered with his company across a causeway, being through a considerable swamp to gain the front of the enemy which was promptly executed & a sharp conflict took place, but the light Infantry of the enemy surrounded his company, and was near cutting him off* [when] *he, perceiving his situation, ordered a well directed fire upon a particular part of the enemy, which opened a passage for him to retreat through.*[43]

General Washington believed that his rifle corps had soundly thrashed the enemy:

> *I fancy the British Grenadiers got a pretty severe peppering yesterday by Morgan's Riffle Corps – they fought it seems a considerable time within the distance of, from twenty to forty yards...more than a hundd of them must have fallen.*[44]

---

[42] Grizzard, Jr., ed., "General Washington to John Hancock, 22 June, 1777," *The Papers of George Washington,* Vol. 10, 104-105
[43] "*A Short Biography of the Life of Governor Thomas Posey*," Thomas Posey Papers, Indiana Historical Society Library, Indianapolis, IN (Referred to henceforth as Posey's Biography)
[44] Grizzard, Jr., ed., "General Washington to Joseph Reed, 23 June, 1777,"

Four days later, General Howe renewed his efforts to draw Washington out of his fortified lines with a sudden march towards the American left flank. This movement surprised the Americans and was nearly a disaster for Colonel Morgan and his rifle corps. Captain John Chilton of the 3rd Virginia Regiment, described what happened:

> *Col. Morgan with the Rifle Regmt. was on the Mattuchin lines at the time and our main army had come down into the Plains. The Enemy unexpectedly stole a march in the night of the 25th and had nearly surrounded Morgan before he was aware of it. He with difficulty saved his men and baggage and after a retreat, rallied his men and sustained a heavy charge until reinforced by Major Genl. Ld. Stirling, who gave them so warm a reception that they* [the British] *were obliged to retreat so precipitately that it had like to have become a rout. But being strongly reinforced he* [Stirling] *was obliged to retreat with the loss of 2 pieces of Artillery.*[45]

Although Morgan's Rifle Corps and other American advance parties were surprised by the British and forced to retreat in this engagement, the main American position remained secure. General Howe, discouraged by his failure to draw the American army away from its strong position and into an open engagement, withdrew to New York and Staten Island to develop a new plan of attack.

The Papers of George Washington, Vol. 10, 115

[45] Lyon Tyler, "John Chilton to his brother, 29 June, 1777", *Tyler's Quarterly Historical and Genealogical Magazine,* Vol. 12, (Richmond, VA: Richmond Press Inc., 1931), 118

Tour of the Jerseys

General Howe's actions in late June baffled General Washington. With a 7,000 man British army under General John Burgoyne marching from Canada, it was possible that General Howe intended to move up the Hudson River to cooperate with Burgoyne and effectively sever New England from the other states. General Washington made preparations to march the army north into New York to assist General Philip Schuyler and the American northern army, but first Washington had to be sure that Howe intended to move north. He confided to a fellow officer that

> *Were we to proceed with our Whole force to Peeks Kill leaving* [Howe] *on Staten Island, he might turn about…and push to Philadelphia.*[46]

Washington added that it was also risky to remain encamped in central New Jersey, so he shifted the army a bit northward from Bound Brook to Morristown and waited for more detailed intelligence on Howe's intentions.[47]

In early July, General Washington became aware that a large portion of Howe's force in New York, including General Howe himself, had boarded British ships. Their destination was a mystery, but Washington feared Howe planned to unite with General Burgoyne on the Hudson River in New York so as a precaution Washington ordered the American army to march northward towards the Hudson River.[48]

---

[46] Grizzard, Jr., ed., "General Washington to General William Heath, 4 July, 1777," *The Papers of George Washington,* Vol. 10, 189
[47] Ibid.
[48] Grizzard, Jr., ed., "General Washington to John Hancock, 10 July, 1777," *The Papers of George Washington,* Vol. 10, 241

Colonel Morgan and the rifle corps were ordered to screen the army's right flank on its march north.[49] Over the next ten days, Washington slowly moved his troops into New York. On July 19th, Colonel Morgan was ordered to take post at Haverstraw, New York, on the Hudson River, *"to observe the motions of the Enemy, & if they land...oppose* [them]".[50] Before he arrived, Morgan was ordered to halt either in Paramus, New Jersey, or if he had not reached that village, wherever he was (which was Hackensack) and await further instructions.[51] Apparently new intelligence suggested to General Washington that Howe was not destined for the Hudson River as he had long assumed. The American commander-in-chief halted his movement north for several days in southern New York and anxiously waited for updated intelligence on General Howe's mysterious fleet.

It arrived on July 23rd and suggested that General Washington had grievously miscalculated; General Howe's true destination was somewhere south of New York, probably Philadelphia via the Delaware River or Chesapeake Bay. With his army significantly out of position to intercept Howe's army, Washington commenced a forced march back towards Philadelphia on July 24th. Colonel Morgan, who was busy trying to gather intelligence in Hackensack for General Washington, received his marching orders the same day:

The Enemy's Fleet having left Sandy Hook & gone to Sea, you are, immediately on receipt of this, to march with the Corps under your Command to the City of Philadelphia & there receive Orders from the Commanding Officer – You will proceed as expeditiously, as you can by the shortest

---

[49] Grizzard, Jr., ed., "General Orders, 11 July, 1777, Footnote 2," *The Papers of George Washington,* Vol. 10, 247
[50] Grizzard, Jr., ed., "Colonel Morgan to General Washington, 19 July, 1777, Footnote," *The Papers of George Washington,* Vol. 10, 340
[51] Ibid.

Routs – You will take no Heavy Baggage with you, but leave it to follow with an Officer and a proper Guard.[52]

Two days into the march, Colonel Morgan was ordered to halt in Trenton and await further orders, unless he received authentic information of the enemy fleet in the Delaware River. If that were the case, Morgan was to march on to Philadelphia.[53] With no such information forthcoming, Morgan halted his rifle corps on the banks of the Delaware River in Trenton. Behind him came the bulk of the American army, exhausted from a 100 mile four day forced march in the summer heat. Captain John Chilton of the 3rd Virginia Regiment described some of the hardship the troops underwent in his diary:

> *As our March was a forced one & the Season extremely warm the victuals became putrid by sweat & heat – the Men badly off for Shoes, many being entirely barefoot.*[54]

Fortunately for Washington's troops the army briefly halted at the Delaware River, then crossed and encamped in the village of Germantown, just outside of Philadelphia, and waited for General Washington to make sense of sketchy intelligence reports on the British fleet. On two occasions during this long halt Washington concluded that Howe's naval movement was actually a feint to draw the American army away from the Hudson River. He feared that the enemy fleet had sailed just beyond the horizon, out of sight of the Americans, and then doubled back to sail up the Hudson River. Each time Washington reached this conclusion, new information arrived that suggested that the British fleet was still at sea, heading

---

[52] Grizzard, Jr., ed., "General Washington to Colonel Morgan, 24 July, 1777," *The Papers of George Washington,* Vol. 10, 390

[53] Grizzard, Jr., ed., "General Washington to Colonel Morgan, 26 July, 1777," *The Papers of George Washington,* Vol. 10, 427-428

[54] Tyler, "Chilton Diary, 27 July, 1777," *Tyler's Quarterly,* 284

south. Thus, Washington remained about a day's march outside of Philadelphia and waited for further word.

Unbeknownst to Washington, Howe's fleet encountered contrary winds while at sea which significantly delayed its voyage to the Chesapeake Bay and thoroughly confused General Washington. Although he still felt that Howe would attempt to join General Burgoyne in New York, the repeated sightings of portions of the British fleet heading south prompted Washington to keep most of his army in Pennsylvania until he could definitively determine Howe's destination. After the long marches back and forth across New Jersey, Washington's troops welcomed the opportunity to rest.

Colonel Morgan and the rifle corps' respite was cut short, however. In mid-August, General Washington ordered Morgan to march his rifle corps north, back to New York. Morgan and his riflemen were to reinforce General Philip Schuyler's northern army against yet another powerful British army of 7,000 regulars and 1,000 Indians driving south through New York from Canada.

Chapter Six

"Morgan...Poured Down Like a Torrent From the Hill"

Saratoga : 1777

For much of the summer of 1777 General Washington had received disturbing reports from General Philip Schuyler in New York about a large British army under General John Burgoyne advancing unhindered down Lake Champlain and the Hudson River Valley from Canada. Burgoyne's objective was Albany, from which he hoped to sever New England from the rest of the colonies with an army of 7,000 men, aided by one thousand Indians who spread terror along their march.

In early August, while Washington and his army were encamped outside of Philadelphia, General Schuyler lamented that he was powerless to halt Burgoyne's advance through New York in part because fear of the Indians had infected his troops:

> *The most unaccountable panic has seized the Troops...A few shot from a small party of Indians has more than once thrown them into the greatest Confusion – The Day before Yesterday three hundred of our Men...came running in, being drove by a few Indians, certainly not more than fifty.*[1]

Schuyler also complained that he lacked enough troops to stop Burgoyne:

---

[1] Grizzard, Jr., ed., "General Philip Schuyler to General George Washington, 1 August, 1777," *The Papers of George Washington,* Vol. 10, 482-483

> *We have not one Militia from the Eastern States & under forty from this – Can it therefore any longer be a matter of Surprise that we are obligated to give way and retreat before a vastly superior force daily increasing in numbers....* [2]

General Washington responded to Schuyler's appeals in mid-August and sent reinforcements, including Colonel Morgan's Rifle Corps, to New York specifically to counteract the Indians. Washington expressed his high regard of Morgan and his men in his orders to Colonel Morgan:

> *You will march...with [your] corps to Peekskill, taking with you all the baggage belonging to it. When you arrive there, you will take directions from General Putnam, who, I expect, will have vessels provided to carry you to Albany. The approach of the enemy in that quarter has made a further reinforcement necessary. I know of no corps so likely to check their progress, in proportion to its number, as that under your command. I have great dependence on you, your officers and men, and I am persuaded you will do honor to yourselves, and essential services to your country.* [3]

General Washington also expressed his confidence in Morgan's Rifle Corps to New York Governor George Clinton:

> *I am forwarding as fast as possible, to join the Northern army, Colonel Morgan's corps of riflemen, amounting to about five hundred. These are all chosen men, selected from the army at large, well acquainted with the use of*

---

[2] Grizzard, Jr., ed., "General Philip Schuyler to General George Washington, 13 August, 1777," *The Papers of George Washington*, Vol. 10, 606

[3] Grizzard, Jr., ed., "General Washington to Colonel Daniel Morgan, 16 August, 1777," *The Papers of George Washington*, Vol. 10, 641

rifles, and with that mode of fighting, which is necessary to make them a good counterpoise to the Indians; and they have distinguished themselves on a variety of occasions, since the formation of the corps, in skirmishes with the enemy. I expect the most eminent services from them, and I shall be mistaken if their presence does not go far towards producing a general desertion among the savages.[4]

Colonel Morgan's orders were slightly adjusted during his march north to New York. Congress removed General Schuyler from command of the northern army in mid-August and installed General Horatio Gates in his place. Morgan was instructed to report directly to General Gates, a fellow resident of the Shenandoah Valley and former officer in the British army who had settled in Virginia in 1773 after leaving the army.

General Gates, who was encamped with the northern army a few miles north of Albany, was very pleased to hear of the rifle corps' transfer and expressed his satisfaction in a letter to General Washington:

I cannot sufficiently thank your Excellency for sending Colonel Morgan's corps to this army; they will be of the greatest service to it, for until the late successes this way, I am told the army were quite panic-struck by their Indians, and their Tory and Canadian assassins in Indian dresses.[5]

---

[4] Grizzard, Jr., ed., "General Washington to George Clinton, 16 August, 1777," *The Papers of George Washington,* Vol. 10 , 636

[5] Philander D. Chase and Edward G. Lengel, eds., "General Gates to General Washington, 22 August, 1777," *The Papers of George Washington, Revolutionary Ware Series,* Vol. 11, (Charlottesville: University Press of Virginia, 2002), 38

The "late successes" that Gates referred to included the defeat of a British detachment near Fort Stanwix along the Mohawk River (that was cooperating with General Burgoyne's invasion) and the stunning American victory near Bennington, Vermont where 2,000 New Hampshire and Vermont militia overwhelmed a 900 man foraging party from Burgoyne's army.[6] These victories significantly improved American morale in late August, which in turn led to an increase in militia turnout for General Gates. By the time Morgan and his riflemen joined Gates in early September, they found an American army that had surpassed Burgoyne's in size.[7]

Unfortunately, Morgan's corps was not at full strength when it reached camp. Three months of active service and the long journey north took a toll on the rifle corps. Less than 400 riflemen arrived with Colonel Morgan fit for service.[8] General Gates partially alleviated Morgan's manpower shortage by drafting fifteen of the most hardy musket-men from each regiment in his army to serve in a corps of light infantry.[9] They were led by Major Henry Dearborn of New Hampshire, a veteran of Arnold's expedition to Quebec and an officer whom Morgan respected. The addition of 250 hand-picked musket-men with bayonets greatly enhanced the fighting effectiveness of Morgan's riflemen. Morgan's combined corps had both long range and close combat capabilities and would soon have the

---

[6] Mark M. Boatner III, ed., *Encyclopedia of the American Revolution, 3rd. ed.* (Stackpole Books, 1994), 75

[7] Lesser, ed. "A General Return of the Continental Troops Under the Command of Major General Horatio Gates, 7 September, 1777," (Gates Papers) *The Sinews of Independence: Monthly Strength Reports of the Continental Army*, 49

[8] General James Wilkinson, "A Return of Colonel Morgan's detachment of Riflemen, 3 September, 1777," *Memoirs of My Own Times,* Vol. 1 (Philadelphia: Abraham Small, 1816) Appendix C
   Reprinted by AMS Press Inc., :NY, 1973

[9] Graham, "General Gates to Colonel Morgan, 29 August, 1777," *The Life of General Daniel Morgan,* 138

opportunity to demonstrate these capabilities on the battlefields of Saratoga.

Battle of Saratoga: Freeman Farm

With the influx of reinforcements swelling his ranks, General Gates advanced north with his army, halting on September 12th, upon Bemis Heights, an excellent defensive position overlooking the Hudson River. Most of the American troops spent the next week erecting fortifications. Colonel Morgan's corps had a different task, reconnaissance. With General Burgoyne and his army just a few miles to the north preparing for a final push on Albany, General Gates wanted as much intelligence on them as possible. Frequent patrols by Morgan's troops helped provide that intelligence.

General Burgoyne also desired intelligence on the Americans, but the departure of most of his Indians in late August hampered his ability to collect it. Dissatisfaction with the campaign and their treatment by Burgoyne caused most of natives to leave, and with them went Burgoyne's best scouts. The British general knew that a large enemy force lay to his front somewhere north of Albany, but he was unsure of its strength and placement. This uncertainty of what awaited him in the woods to his south did not halt Burgoyne's march on Albany, he boldly divided his army into three columns and marched south towards the Americans on September 19th.[10]

General Burgoyne's left column, commanded by General Friedrich von Riedesel, comprised approximately 3,000 men.[11] It included most of the artillery and a large baggage train protected by four German regiments and the 47th British regiment. This column slowly marched along the river road

---

[10] James Baxter, ed., *The British Invasion from the North: Digby's Journal of the Campaigned of Generals Carleton and Burgoyne from Canada, 1776-1777*, (New York : De Capa Press, 1970), 267

[11] John Luzader, *Saratoga: A Military History of the Decisive Campaign of the American Revolution,* (New York: Savas Beatie, 2008), 230

towards the Americans at Bemis Heights, stopping several times to repair small bridges destroyed by the Americans. General Burgoyne's right column, approximately 2,550 troops under General Simon Fraser, was tasked to screen the British right flank and probe the American left flank.[12] To do this, Fraser marched nearly three miles west, away from the river, and then swung south towards the Americans.

General Burgoyne marched southwestward into the woods with his center column, moving in a diagonal direction from the river. This column totaled 1,600 men from the 9th, 20th, 21st, and 62nd British regiments and was commanded by General James Hamilton. Four pieces of artillery were also part of this column.[13]

The three columns began their march around 9:00 a.m. on September 19th, and were quickly observed by American scouts. Word reached General Gates in the American camp that the enemy was on the move. Colonel James Wilkinson, an aide to General Gates, recalled that General Gates

> *Ordered Colonel Morgan to advance his corps, who was instructed, should he find the enemy approaching, to hang on their front and flanks, to retard their march, and cripple them as much as possible.* [14]

Morgan's light corps, numbering around 600 men, advanced in a narrow column through the thick woods towards Burgoyne's center detachment, the riflemen ahead of the light infantry.[15] They marched about a mile and a half and emerged

---

[12] Ibid.
[13] Richard M. Ketchum, *Saratoga,: Turning Point of America's Revolutionary War*, (NY: Holt & Co., 1997), 357
[14] Wilkinson, 236
[15] Wilkinson, Appendix E   and   Joseph Lee Boyle, ed., "From Saratoga to Valley Forge: The Diary of Lt. Samuel Armstrong," *The Pennsylvania Magazine of History and Biography*, Vol. 121 No. 3 (July 1997), 245
 (Henceforth referred to as Lieutenant Armstrong's Diary)

Freeman Farm
Adapted from Library of Congress

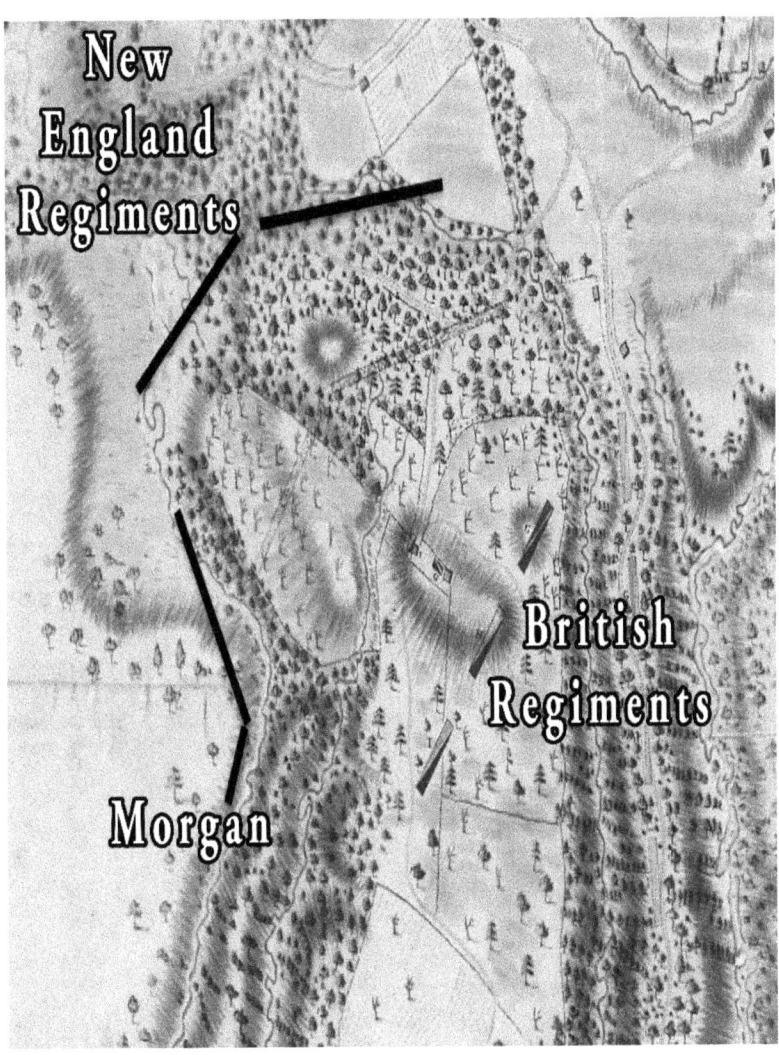

at the edge of an abandoned farm. The clearing was dotted with tall grass, dead trees and stumps. Two small buildings (described as cabins by many eyewitnesses) sat on a rise of ground about 300 yards away. The opposite wood line was only 150 yards beyond the cabins. Morgan's corps arrived at the southern end of the clearing just as an enemy advance party attacked the American picquet guard posted in the cabins. Samuel Armstrong, a member of Major Dearborn's light infantry, described the encounter:

> [At] *about 12 Oclock we were Alarm'd by the firing of two or three Musketts from the Enemies Scouts, upon which the Riffle and Light Infantry Battalions were Ordered off to Scour the Woods. We forwarded down to our Picquet Guard where we had no sooner got Sight of than we saw the Enemy surrounding them.* [16]

The American pickets in the cabins quickly dispersed and fled Freeman's Farm in the face of the approaching enemy.[17] As the British skirmishers pushed past the cabins and approached Morgan's position in the southern wood line they collided with the advance of Morgan's light corps. British Lieutenant William Digby described what happened:

> *A little after 12 our advanced picquets came up with Colonel Morgan and engaged, but from the great superiority of fire received from him – his numbers being much greater – they were obliged to fall back, every officer being either killed or wounded except one.*[18]

---

[16] Boyle, ed., "Lieutenant Armstrong's Diary," 245

[17] John Burgoyne, *A State of the Expedition from Canada*, (New York Times & Arno Press, 1969), 68

Note: This account is supported by the observation of American Lieutenant Colonel James Wilkinson, who saw British bodies lying around the cabins after the initial engagement, but prior to the resumption of battle.

[18] Baxter, ed., "Digby's Journal," 272

The British skirmishers, outnumbered and outgunned, retreated under a deadly barrage of fire from Morgan's men. Advance elements of Morgan's corps pursued the fleeing skirmishers across the field and into the woods beyond. Their pursuit abruptly ended when the Americans discovered the main body of General Burgoyne's center column. These soldiers, deployed in the opposite wood line from which Morgan's men emerged, startled the Americans with a volley that hit friend and foe alike.[19]

The result was chaos for Morgan's corps. Already somewhat disorganized by the unauthorized charge across the open field, Morgan's corps disintegrated on contact with the main body of the enemy. Men ran in all directions to escape. The sudden emergence on their left flank of two British companies and a field piece from General Fraser's column added urgency to the flight of Morgan's men.[20]

Appalled by the turn of events, Colonel Morgan struggled to reorganize his shattered corps. He used an uncommon military tool to do so, a turkey whistle. Lieutenant Colonel James Wilkinson an aide to General Gates, appeared on the scene at this time and observed Morgan's efforts to reform his riflemen:

> *My ears were saluted by an uncommon noise, which I approached, and perceived Colonel Morgan attended by two men only, who with a turkey call was collecting his dispersed troops. The moment I came up to him, he burst into tears, and exclaimed, 'I am ruined, by G—d! Major Morris ran on so rapidly with the front, that they were beaten before I could get up with the rear, and my men*

---

[19] Horatio Rogers ed., *Hadden's Journal and Orderly Book: A Journal Kept in Canada and Upon Burgoyne's Campaign in 1776 and 1777*, (Boston: Gregg Press, 1972), 163

[20] Sydney Jackman, ed., *With Burgoyne from Quebec: An Account of the Life at Quebec and of the Famous Battle at Saratoga,* (Toronto: Macmillan of Canada, 1963), 72
    (Henceforth referred to as Anburey's Journal)

are scattered God knows where.' I remarked to the Colonel that he had a long day before him to retrieve an inauspicious beginning, and informed him where I had seen his field officers, which appeared to cheer him.... [21]

One of the field officers that Lieutenant Colonel Wilkinson met prior to Morgan was Major Joseph Morris. Morris led the charge against the fleeing British pickets and gave Wilkinson a detailed account of the engagement:

From him [Major Morris] *I learnt that the corps was advancing by files in two lines, when they unexpectedly fell upon a picket of the enemy, which they almost instantly forced, and pursuing the fugitives, their front had as unexpectedly fallen in with the British line; that several officers and men had been made prisoners, and that to save himself, he had been obliged to push his horse through the ranks of the enemy, and escaped by a circuitous route.* [22]

Wilkinson also encountered Lieutenant Colonel Richard Butler, the rifle corps' second in command. He confirmed Morris's account:

I [Wilkinson] *crossed the angle of the field, leapt the fence, and just before me on a ridge discovered Lieutenant-colonel Butler with three men, all tree'd; from him I learnt that they had 'caught a Scotch prize,' that having forced the picket, they had closed with the British line, had been instantly routed, and from the suddenness of the shock and the nature of the ground, were broken and scattered in all directions.*[23]

---

[21] Wilkinson, 238
[22] Ibid. 237
[23] Ibid.

Fortunately for Colonel Morgan, the British did not pursue his scattered troops and a pause in the engagement allowed Morgan to re-organize most of his riflemen in the woods to the south of Freeman's Farm, their front protected by a deep ravine.[24] To Morgan's left, reinforcements in the form of three continental regiments from New Hampshire from General Enoch Poor's brigade deployed westward. Major Dearborn's light infantry, which had become separated from Morgan and his riflemen in the initial engagement, covered the far left flank of the American line and fought the rest of the day detached from Morgan and his riflemen.

The battle at Freeman's Farm resumed around mid-afternoon when General Hamilton's troops emerged from the far woods and advanced across Freeman's field towards the Americans. The British deployed on a small ridge just beyond the cabins. Lieutenant James Hadden, a British artillery officer, described the action:

> *The Enemy being in possession of the wood almost immediately attacked the Corps which took post beyond two log Huts on Freemans Farm...I was advanced with two Guns to the left of the 62nd Regt and ye two left companies being formed en potence* [refused or bent to protect the flank] *I took post in the Angle...In this situation we sustained a heavy tho intermitting fire for near three hours....*[25]

The American fire, enhanced by the accuracy of Morgan's riflemen (some of who climbed trees to get better shots) was especially hard on the British artillerymen. Lieutenant Hadden lost 19 out of 22 men and all of his horses. The 62nd regiment lost nearly half of its men.[26]

---

[24] Rogers ed., *Hadden's Journal and Orderly Book: A Journal Kept in Canada and Upon Burgoyne's Campaign in 1776 and 1777*, 164
[25] Ibid. 165
[26] Ibid.

Hadden's position was not the only hot spot for the British. The battle raged all along the line. British Lieutenant William Digby noted that he had never seen anything like it:

> *Such an explosion of fire I never had any idea of before, and the heavy artillery joining in concert like great peals of thunder, assisted by the echoes of the woods, almost deafened us with the noise.*[27]

British corporal Roger Lamb gave a similar account:

> *The conflict was dreadful; for four hours a constant blaze of fire was kept up, and both armies seemed to be determined on death or victory...Men, and particularly officers, dropped every moment on each side. Several of the Americans placed themselves in high trees, and as often as they could distinguish a British officer's uniform, took him off by deliberately aiming at his person.*[28]

The impact of American marksmanship, no doubt enhanced by Colonel Morgan's riflemen, was also noted by Colonel James Wilkinson, who observed that it repeatedly drove the British from the Freeman house ridge:

> *The fire of our marksmen from this wood was too deadly to be withstood by the enemy in line, and when they gave way and broke, our men rushing from their cover, pursued them to the eminence, where having their flanks protected, they* [the enemy] *rallied and charging in turn drove us back into the wood, from whence a dreadful fire would again force them to fall*

---

[27] Baxter, ed., "Digby's Journal," 237
[28] Roger Lamb, *An Original and Authentic Journal of Occurrences During the Late American War from Its Commencement to 1783*, (Dublin: Wilkinson & Courtney, 1809), 159
   Reprinted by Arno Press, 1968

> back; and in this manner did the battle fluctuate, like waves of a stormy sea, with alternate advantage for four hours without one moment's intermission. The British artillery fell into our possession at every charge, but we could neither turn the pieces upon the enemy, nor bring them off...The slaughter of this brigade of artillerists was remarkable, the captain and thirty-six men being killed or wounded out of forty-eight.[29]

Even General Burgoyne acknowledged the impact of Morgan's riflemen:

> The enemy had with their army great numbers of marksmen, armed with rifle-barrel pieces; these during an engagement, hovered upon the flanks in small detachments, and were very expert in securing themselves, and in shifting their ground. In this action many placed themselves in high trees in the rear of their own line, and there was seldom a minute's interval of smoke, in any part of our line without officers being taken off by single shot. It will naturally be supposed, that the Indians would be of great use against this mode of fighting. The example of those that remained after the great desertion proved the contrary, for not a man of them was to be brought within the sound of a rifle shot. [30]

As sunset approached, the British were in serious trouble. The 62nd regiment was shattered, and the other regiments were barely holding on. Suddenly, drums were heard in the woods beyond Morgan's right flank. German reinforcements from the river column under General Riedesel emerged from the woods to Morgan's right and onto the field to relieve Hamilton's

---
[29] Wilkinson, 241
[30] Burgoyne, 39-40

wavering center column. A German artillery officer, Captain George Pausch, recalled

> *I had shells brought up and placed by the side of the cannon and as soon as I got the range, I fired twelve or fourteen shots in quick succession into the foe who were within good pistol shot distance.*[31]

The targets of the German shelling included Morgan's riflemen, who had been on the scene for over six hours.

The arrival of the German reinforcements revived the spirits of General Hamilton's battered British troops and they rallied one more time. Captain Pausch noted

> *The firing from muskets was at once renewed, and assumed lively proportions, particularly the platoon fire from the left wing of Riedesel. Presently, the enemy's fire, though very lively at one time, suddenly ceased. I advanced about sixty paces sending a few shells after the flying enemy, and firing from twelve to fifteen shots more into the woods into which they had retreated. Everything then became quiet; and about fifteen minutes afterwards darkness set in....*[32]

One of the most intense battles of the Revolutionary War was over, and the carnage was appalling. The field was littered with dead and wounded men who remained unattended all night. British lieutenant William Digby described the scene:

> *During the night we remained in our ranks, and tho we heard the groans of our wounded and dying at a small distance, yet could not assist them till morning, not knowing the position of the enemy, and expecting the*

---

[31] George Pausch, *Journal of Captain Pausch, Chief of the Hanau Artillery During the Burgoyne Campaign*, Translated by William L. Stone, (Albany, NY: Joel Munsell's Sons, 1886), 137-138
[32] Ibid. 138

action would be renewed at day break. Sleep was a stranger to us...
20th. At day break we sent out parties to bring in our wounded, and lit fires as we were almost froze with cold, and our wounded who lived till the morning must have severely felt it. [33]

British ensign Thomas Anburey had the misfortune to command a burial party the next day:

The day after our late engagement, I had as unpleasant a duty as can fall to the lot of an officer, the command of the party sent out to bury the dead and bring in the wounded...They [the wounded] had remained out all night, and from the loss of blood and want of nourishment, were upon the point of expiring with faintness; some of them begged they might lie and die, others again were insensible, some upon the least movement were put in the most horrid tortures, and all had near a mile to be conveyed to the hospitals; others at their last gasp, who for want of our timely assistance must have inevitably expired. These poor creatures, perishing with cold and weltering in their blood, displayed such a scene, it must be a heart of adamant that could not be affected at it.[34]

Although the British kept the field, it was at a heavy cost; they suffered twice as many casualties as the Americans. Some of the British, like Thomas Anburey, questioned the value of the victory:

Notwithstanding the glory of the day remains on our side, I am fearful the real advantage resulting from this hard fought battle will rest on that of the Americans, our

---

[33] Baxter, ed., "Digby's Journal," 274
[34] Jackman, ed., "Anburey's Journal," 176

> army being so weakened by this engagement as not to be of sufficient strength to venture forth and improve the victory, which may, in the end, put a stop to our intended expedition; the only apparent benefit gained is that we keep possession of the ground where the engagement began. [35]

General Burgoyne, in a letter to Lord George Germain, reached a similar conclusion about the victory:

> It was soon found that no fruits, honour excepted, were attained by the preceding victory, the enemy working with redoubled ardour to strengthen their left, their right was already unattackable.[36]

Despite their retreat from the field, the attitude in the American camp was far from defeatist. In fact, most American accounts bragged about punishing the enemy and attributed the retreat merely to darkness. Major Henry Dearborn's observation was typical:

> On this Day has Been fought one of the Greatest Battles that Ever was fought in America, & I Trust we have Convinced the British Butchers that the Cowardly yankees Can & when there is a Call for it, will, fight...The Enimy Brought almost their whole force against us, together with 8 pieces of Artillery. But we who had Something more at Stake than fighting for six Pence Pr Day kept our ground til Night Closed the scene, & then Both Parties Retire'd.[37]

---

[35] Ibid. 175

[36] Burgoyne, "General Burgoyne to Lord Germaine, 10 October, 1777," *A State of the Expedition,* Appendix, 88

[37] Lloyd Brown and Howard Peckman, ed., *Revolutionary War Journals of Henry Dearborn, 1775-1783*, Freeport, NY: Books for Libraries Press, 1939, 106

Many of the British did indeed change their opinion of the Americans after the battle. Ensign Thomas Anburey's comments were typical:

> The courage and obstinacy with which the Americans fought were the astonishment of everyone, and we now become fully convinced they are not that contemptible enemy we had hitherto imagined them, incapable of standing a regular engagement, and that they would only fight behind strong and powerful works.[38]

Colonel Morgan's riflemen were some of the combatants that Anburey referred to. They engaged the British for approximately six hours and inflicted heavy losses on them. They, in turn, suffered only sixteen casualties (seven killed and nine wounded).[39] The extended range of rifles, which allowed Morgan's men to fire from beyond musket distance, contributed to the low rifle casualties. In contrast, Major Dearborn's light infantry battalion, armed with smoothbore muskets, had the highest number of unit deaths, with eighteen. Twenty-two of his men were wounded.[40] An official count of American casualties listed 321 in all, with 65 killed, 218 wounded, and 38 missing.[41]

Although the Americans believed they had dealt Burgoyne a significant blow, they realized that his army was still very dangerous and braced themselves for another attack. Fortunately for the Americans -- who were very low on ammunition -- it never materialized.

General Burgoyne actually planned to resume his advance the next day, but canceled at the last minute to rest his troops. While they rested, Burgoyne received news that General Henry Clinton was leading a British detachment northward from New

---

[38] Jackman, ed., "Anburey's Journal," 175
[39] Wilkinson, Appendix D
[40] Ibid.
[41] Ibid.

York City to attack the American posts in the New York Highlands and draw some of the American troops with General Gates away from Bemis Heights. Although Clinton's force was too small to fight its way to General Burgoyne, both generals hoped that Clinton's presence would force General Gates to send some of his troops south and give Burgoyne a better chance to break through to Albany.

General Burgoyne decided to fortify his position and wait for Clinton's advance to have the desired effect. Unfortunately for Burgoyne, few Americans left Bemis Heights. In fact, during the seventeen day pause, the American army swelled to over 10,000 men.[42]

With time on his side, the ever cautious Gates waited behind his fortified lines. Every passing day saw Burgoyne's supplies dwindle and his situation grow more desperate. Colonel Morgan's light corps added to Burgoyne's discomfort by constantly harassing his lines and foraging parties. General Burgoyne acknowledged Morgan's impact in a letter:

> *From the 20th of September to the 7th of October, the armies were so near, that not a single night passed without firing, and sometimes concerted attacks upon our advanced picquets; no foraging party could be made without great detachments to cover it; it was the plan of the enemy to harass the army by constant alarms, and their superiority of numbers enabled them to attempt it without fatigue to themselves.*[43]

The value of Colonel Morgan and his rifle corps was highlighted in an exchange of letters between General Washington and General Gates. On September 24th, General Washington, who had suffered a significant defeat against

---

[42] Wilkinson, "A General Return of the Army of the United States, commanded by the Hon. Major-General Horatio Gates, 4 Oct. 1777," Appendix E
[43] Burgoyne, 168

General Howe at the Battle of Brandywine in Pennsylvania, congratulated Gates on his success at Freeman's Farm. He then requested the return of Morgan's rifle corps to the main army:

> *This Army has not been able to oppose General Howe's with the success that was wished, and needs a Reinforcement. I therefore request, if you have been so fortunate, as to Oblige General Burgoyne to retreat to Tyconderoga—or If you have not and circumstances will admit, that you will Order Colo. Morgan to Join me again with his Corps. I sent him up when I thought you materially wanted him, and if his services can be dispensed with now, you will direct his return immediately.*[44]

The fact that Washington requested only the Rifle Corps return is a testament of his high regard for the unit. General Gates's response was equally telling of his esteem and reliance on Morgan and his riflemen:

> *Since the Action of the 19th Instant, the Enemy have kept the Ground they Occupied the Morning of that Day, And fortified their Camp. The Advanced Centrys of my picquets, are posted within Shot, And Opposite the Enemy's; neither side have given Ground an Inch. In this Situation, Your Excellency would not wish me to part with the Corps the Army of General Burgoyne are most Afraid of.*[45]

General Gates added that with British provisions dwindling it was only a matter of days or weeks before Burgoyne either risked another battle or withdrew to Ticonderoga. Gates was confident of success and informed Washington that he hoped to

---

[44] Chase and Lengel, eds., "General Washington to General Gates, 24 September, 1777," *The Papers of George Washington,* Vol. 11, 310

[45] Chase and Lengel, eds., "General Gates to General Washington, 5 October, 1777," *The Papers of George Washington,* Vol. 11, 392

soon send far more than just Morgan's riflemen southward to reinforce Washington.[46]

The day after he wrote to Washington, General Gates ordered Colonel Morgan to reconnoiter the enemy's lines with his light corps. They circled around to the rear of the British and captured several prisoners.[47] Major Dearborn, who nearly forty years later would gently criticized Morgan in his memoirs as, "*a brave officer in action,* [but] *too cautious as a partisan,*" recorded in his diary on October 6th, that they got lost, due to heavy rain and the darkness of the night, on their way back to camp and were forced to spend the night in the woods.[48]

While Morgan, Dearborn, and the light troops endured a miserable night in the field, the critical British supply situation finally forced General Burgoyne to act. Unwilling to accept the defeat of his plans against Albany, Burgoyne decided to advance and probe the American position on Bemis Heights with a large detachment in hopes of discovering a weak spot.

Battle of Bemis Heights

General Burgoyne's reconnaissance force numbered over 1,500 men and ten cannon.[49] Although nearly all of the army's units contributed men, the bulk came from the right wing of Burgoyne's line. Two redoubts anchored this position. One was manned by British light infantry under Lieutenant Colonel Alexander Balcarress. The other was defended by German grenadiers under Lieutenant Colonel Heinrich Breymann. Since the march route of the British detachment placed this force between the Americans and the redoubts, General

---

[46] Ibid.
[47] Brown and Peckman, ed., "Dearborn's Journal," 108
[48] Ibid.
[49] Eric Schnitzer, "Battling for the Saratoga Landscape," *Cultural Landscape Report: Saratoga Battle, Saratoga National Park,* Vol. 1 (Boston, MA: Olmsted Center for Landscape Preservation), 44

Burgoyne drew heavily from these fortifications, leaving them lightly manned.[50]

Burgoyne led his troops out of camp around noon and slowly advanced toward the American left wing. His skirmishers drove off American picquets less than a mile into their march. Burgoyne halted in a wheat field and posted his men in a long line facing south, towards Bemis Heights. The British right flank, composed of light infantry troops, rested on a ridge just east of a wooded hill. German troops, supported by artillery, held the center of the line, and the left was defended by British grenadiers and artillery.[51]

General Burgoyne tried to observe the American fortifications from the wheat field, but the woods obscured his view. Ironically, as Burgoyne and his staff struggled to peer through the woods, they were observed by an American officer.

When reports of Burgoyne's advance reached American headquarters, General Gates dispatched his aide, Lieutenant Colonel Wilkinson, to investigate. Wilkinson reported that the enemy was on the move, at which General Gates sent Wilkinson to Colonel Morgan with instructions to *"begin the game."* Wilkinson recalled

> *I waited on the Colonel,* [Morgan] *whose corps was formed in front of our centre, and delivered the order; he knew the ground, and inquired the position of the enemy: they were formed across a newly cultivated field, their grenadiers with several pieces on the left, bordering on a wood and a small ravine...their light infantry on the right, covered by a worm fence at the foot of the hill...thickly covered with wood; their centre composed of British and German*

---

[50] Henry Dearborn, "A Narrative of the Saratoga Campaign – Major General Henry Dearborn, 1815," *The Bulletin of the Fort Ticonderoga Museum*, Vol. 1, No. 5, January, 1929, 7
and
Dearborn's Journal, 108
[51] Luzader, 52

battalions. Colonel Morgan, with his usual sagacity, proposed to make a circuit with his corps by our left, and under cover of the wood to gain the height on the right of the enemy, and from thence commence his attack, so soon as our fire should be opened against their left.[52]

According to Major Wilkinson, General Gates approved Morgan's proposal and ordered General Benedict Arnold to send General Poor's brigade against Burgoyne's left flank and General Learned's brigade against the center of Burgoyne's line.[53] Arnold accompanied his troops into battle.

Colonel Morgan's corps was still moving into position along a wooded ridge overlooking Burgoyne's right flank when fighting erupted on the British left. It was General Poor's men, followed by General Learned's troops, and the intensity of the engagement caused some in Morgan's corps to worry that their comrades were losing. Major Dearborn recalled,

---

[52] Wilkinson, 268.

[53] Note: Historians have long reported, based largely on the memoirs of Major Wilkinson, that General Benedict Arnold had relinquished command of his division after the Battle of Freeman Farm following a heated dispute with General Gates over the lack of credit Arnold received in General Gates's report to Congress and the removal of Colonel Morgan's light corps from Arnold's command. The long held belief was that Arnold was preparing to leave the army and present his grievances about General Gates to Congress when, upon learning of Burgoyne's advance towards the American lines, Arnold mounted a horse (some claim while intoxicated) and rode out of camp (without the authorization or approval of General Gates) to assume command of his old brigades. The recent discovery of a letter written on October 9, 1777 from Nathaniel Bacheller, an adjutant in a New Hampshire militia battalion attached to Learned's brigade, claims that General Arnold sought and received permission from General Gates to lead troops against Burgoyne.
See:
Nathaniel Bacheller Letter, 9 October, 1777, Copy on file at Saratoga National Historical Park

> *Our light troops moved on with a quick step in the course directed, and after ascending the woody hill to a small field about 500 yards to the right of the Enemies main line, we discovered a body of British light Infantry handsomely posted on a ridge 150 yards from the edge of the wood where we then were. At this time the fire of the two main armies was unusually heavy and we were apprehensive from the fire that our line was giving way.*[54]

Colonel Morgan rushed his men towards the enemy flank. Captain Thomas Posey of Virginia described what happened:

> *They* [the enemy] *had repulsed* [General] *Arnold twice before Morgan made his attack, which was on the right wing of* [the] *enemy – the* [rifle] *regiment had march'd under cover of a thick wood, and a ridge, which ridge the enemy were about to take possession of as Morgan gained the summit of it, the enemy being within good rifle shot, the regiment poured in a well directed fire which brought almost every officer on horseback to the ground.*[55]

Lieutenant Colonel Richard Butler noted the impact of Morgan's attack on the battle:

> *I had the Honour to lead the Corps of Riflemen Against their Right wing Under Morgan, Who Commanded in Center of the Whole, our light troops About 1000, & Can say without Ostenation that we saved the day by our timely & vigourous Attack (I believe the Indian Hoop helped A little) as we broke the Right Wing of the Enemy took two 12 Pounders & one six and turned them on them.*[56]

---

[54] Dearborn, "A Narrative of the Saratoga Campaign – Major General Henry Dearborn, 1815," 7
[55] Posey Biography
[56] "Lt. Col. Richard Butler to Col. James Wilson, 22 January, 1778," Gratz Collection, Case 4, Box 11, Historical Society of Pennsylvania

Burgoyne's Initial Deployment On October 7th

Adapted from Library of Congress

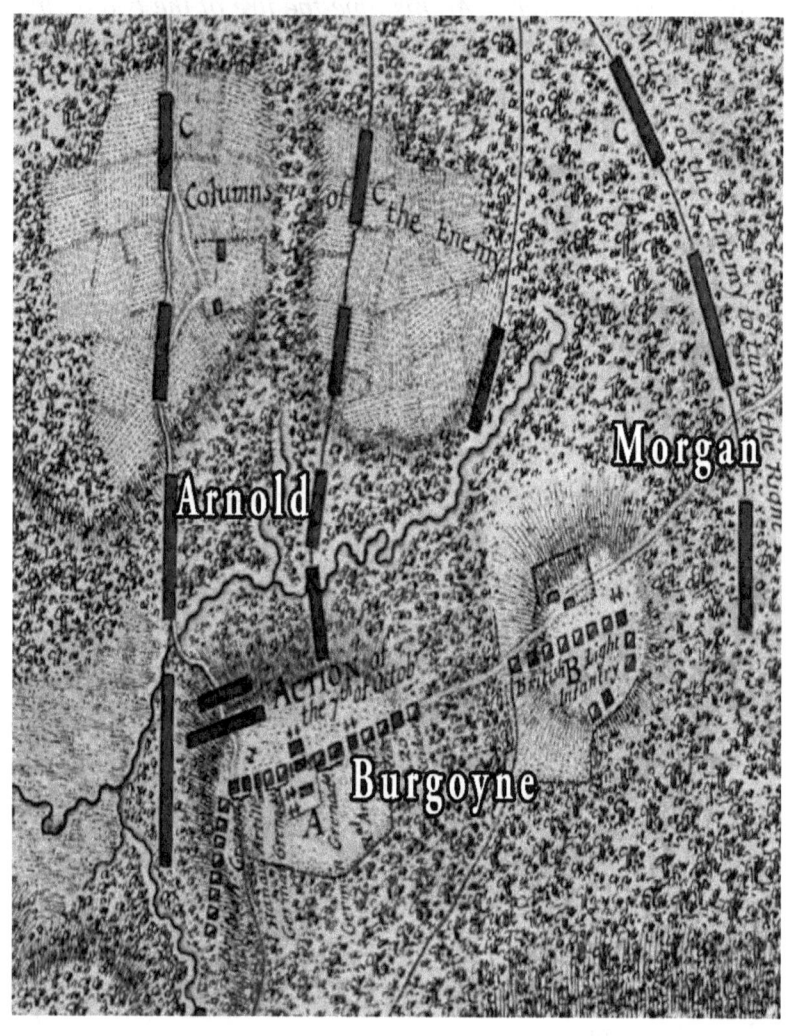

Lieutenant Colonel Wilkinson also credited Morgan's corps with routing Burgoyne's right flank:

> *True to his purpose, Morgan at this critical moment poured down like a torrent from the hill, and attacked the right of the enemy in front and flank. Dearborn at the moment, when the enemy's light infantry were attempting to change front,* [to face the riflemen] *pressed forward with ardour and delivered a close fire; then lept the fence, shouted, charged and gallantly forced them in disorder.* [57]

The situation was no better for Burgoyne on his left flank, where his grenadiers were decimated by General Poor's men.

Despite the collapse of his flanks, Burgoyne's center held firm. Furthermore, the commander of the British right flank, General Fraser, worked hard to restore the line. His efforts abruptly ended, however, when one of Morgan's riflemen shot him from his horse. Several years after the battle, while recounting the Battle of Saratoga to a captured British officer in Winchester, Morgan described his role in Fraser's death. According to the unidentified British officer, Morgan declared

> *Oh we whopped them tarnation well, surelie, said* [Morgan], *rubbing his hands; though to be sure they gave us tough work too…Me and my boys attacked a height that day, and drove Ackland and his grenadiers, but we were hardly on the top when the British rallied, and came on again with such fury that nothing could stop them. I saw that they were led by an officer on a grey horse – a devilish brave fellow; so when we took the height a second time, says I to one of my best shots, says I, you get up into that there tree, and single out him on the white horse. Dang it, 'twas no sooner said than done. On came the British again, with the grey*

---

[57] Wilkinson, 268

horseman leading; but his career was short enough this time. I jist tuck my eyes off him for a moment, and when I turned them to the place where he had been – pooh, he was gone![58]

General Fraser, mortally wounded, was removed to the rear and died the next day in the British camp.

Although both of General Burgoyne's flanks had given ground, the center of his line, defended by his Hessian troops, stubbornly held firm. The pressure on their front and flanks, however, soon proved too great, and they joined the rest of Burgoyne's detachment in retreat. Eight British cannon and scores of men were abandoned on the field. Lt. Colonel Wilkinson described the carnage:

> The ground which had been occupied by the British grenadiers presented a scene of complicated horror and exultation. In the square space of twelve or fifteen yards lay eighteen grenadiers in the agonies of death, and three officers propped up against stumps of trees, two of them mortally wounded, bleeding, and almost speechless.[59]

Most of General Burgoyne's detachment, including 300 German grenadiers who were drawn from Breymann's redoubt, retreated to the Balcarres redoubt. This bolstered the defenders there, but left Breymann's redoubt (on the extreme right of the British line) undermanned and vulnerable. Two fortified cabins between the redoubts were also weakly manned because of the failure of soldiers to return to them.

Initially these vulnerable positions were not a problem for the British because the Americans, led by General Arnold,

---

[58] Maxwell, ed., "A Recollection of the American Revolutionary War," *Virginia Historical Register and Literary Companion,* Vol. 6, (1853) 210

[59] Wilkinson, 270

concentrated their attack on the Balcarres redoubt. British Corporal Roger Lamb recalled,

> *General Arnold with a brigade of continental troops, pushed rapidly forward, for that part of the camp possessed by lord Balcarres, at the head of the British light infantry, and some of the line; here they were received by a heavy and well directed fire which moved down their ranks, and compelled them to retreat in disorder.* [60]

About three hundred yards to the north, Colonel Morgan's corps prepared to storm the Breymann redoubt.

Morgan's men had advanced very close to the redoubt and used a steep hill in their front to protect them from enemy fire.[61] Lieutenant Colonel Wilkinson described the scene:

> *The Germans were encamped immediately behind the rail breast-work, and the ground in front of it declined in a very gentle slope for about 120 yards, when it sunk abruptly; our troops had formed a line under this declivity, and covered breast high were warmly engaged with the Germans.* [62]

Morgan was reinforced by General Learned's brigade, part of which attacked the two sparsely manned fortified cabins between the Breymann and Balcarres redoubts. Major Wilkinson was on the scene and recalled that

> *I had particularly examined the ground between the left of the Germans and the light infantry, occupied by the provincialists, from whence I had observed a*

---

[60] Lamb, 164
[61] Schnitzer, 50
[62] Wilkinson, 272

Barcarres & Breymann Redoubts
Adapted from Library of Congress

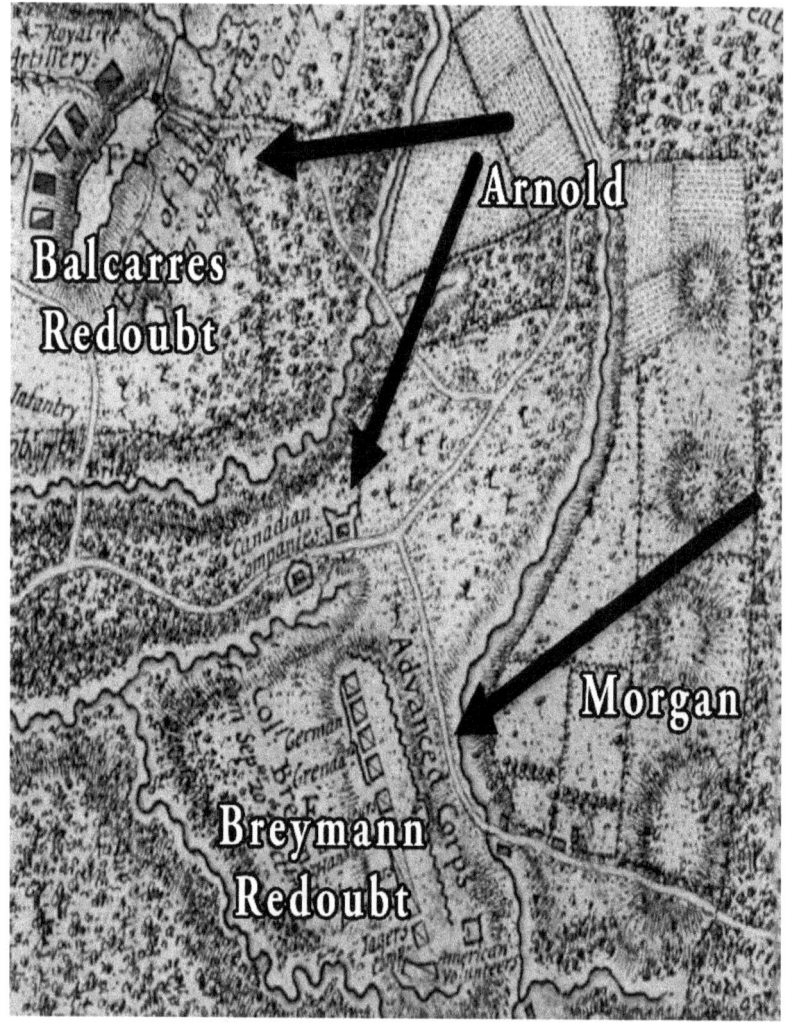

> *slack fire; I therefore recommended to General Learned to incline to his right, and attack at that point: he did so with great gallantry; the provincialists [defending the cabins] abandoned their position and fled; the German flank was by this means uncovered.* [63]

Learned's brigade was joined by General Arnold, who had given up his efforts against the Balcarres redoubt and moved left towards the Breymann redoubt. Colonel Wilkinson recalled that Arnold

> *Dashed to the left through the fire of the two lines and escaped unhurt; he then turned the right of the enemy, as I was informed by that most excellent officer, Colonel Butler, and collecting 15 or 20 riflemen threw himself with this party into the rear of the enemy* [at Breymann's Redoubt] *just as they gave way, where his leg was broke, and his horse killed under him.* [64]

Lieutenant Colonel Richard Butler's account of the assault was similar:

> *Genl. Arnold was the first who Entered,* [Breymann's Redoubt] *one Major Morris with about 12 of the Rifle men followed him on the Rear of their Right Flank while I led up the rest of the Riflemen in front. I was the 3rd officer in* [the redoubt].[65]

Major Dearborn's light infantry also participated in the assault of Breymann's Redoubt. He described it in his memoirs:

---

[63] Ibid.
[64] Ibid., 272
[65] "Lt. Col. Richard Butler to Col. James Wilson, 22 January, 1778," Gratz Collection, Case 4, Box 11, Historical Society of Pennsylvania

> *The assault was commenced by the advance of Arnold with about 200 men through a cops of wood which covered the Enemies right, the appearance of Arnold on the right was the signal for us to advance and assault the front. The whole was executed in the most spirited and prompted manner and as soon as the Enemy had given us one fire, he fell back from his work to his line of tents, and as we entered he gave way and retreated in confusion.*[66]

Whether by design or chance, the assault on Breymann's redoubt was masterfully executed and the Germans were quickly overwhelmed. General Burgoyne's line was breeched, and only nightfall saved the British from further disaster.

General Gates was overjoyed with the day's results, reportedly declaring to Colonel Morgan upon his return to camp

> *Morgan you have done wonders for your country, if you are not promoted I will not serve a day longer myself!*[67]

The American army's work was not yet finished, however. Although General Burgoyne's advance on Albany was clearly over, it remained to be seen whether his retreat to Fort Ticonderoga would succeed.

---

[66] Dearborn, "A Narrative of the Saratoga Campaign – Major General Henry Dearborn, 1815," 8
[67] William Hill Notes, 2

Burgoyne's Retreat and Surrender

Under cover of darkness, General Burgoyne withdrew his army across a deep ravine and established a new position on a steep hill overlooking the Hudson River. The position was called the Great Redoubt, and its location allowed Burgoyne to consolidate his troops and protect the river transports and hospital.

When the Americans realized that Burgoyne had withdrawn across the ravine, they took possession of his old lines and commenced a steady, but ineffectual, bombardment. General Gates sent Morgan's light corps around Burgoyne's position to reconnoiter the enemy's rear and harass them. Major Dearborn participated in this reconnaissance:

> *This morning* [Oct. 8] *the Rifle men & Light Infantry & several other Regiments march'd in the Rear of the Enimy Expecting they ware Retreeting But found they ware Not. there has Been scurmishing all Day...a Large Number of the Enimy Deserted to us to Day.*[68]

General Burgoyne realized that retreat or surrender were the only options left for his army. The former was tremendously difficult, but the latter was still unthinkable. Thus, on the evening of October 8th, Burgoyne began a retreat northward. Over 400 men, too injured or sick to transport, were left under a flag of truce to the care of the Americans. The rest of Burgoyne's army slowly trudged towards the village of Saratoga.

After a few miles, they halted to rest and wait for the boats to catch up. A heavy rain pelted the men all day and when they resumed their march the muddy road slowed the column to a crawl. They arrived at Saratoga after dark and collapsed on the ground in exhaustion. Lieutenant Digby described the scene:

---

[68] Brown and Peckman, ed., "Dearborn's Journal," 109

> *We remained all night under constant, heavy rain without fires or any kind of shelter to guard us from the inclemency of the weather. It was impossible to sleep, even had we an inclination to do so from the cold and rain....* [69]

Ensign Anburey gave an equally distressing account of the British army's first night in Saratoga:

> *The army...arrived at Saratoga, in such a state of fatigue that the men had not strength or inclination to cut wood and make fires, but rather sought sleep in their wet clothes and on the wet ground.* [70]

Despite Burgoyne's slow retreat, the Americans struggled to keep pace. The rain turned the roads into a quagmire of mud, and the size of the American army, over 12,000 strong, was difficult to move in such conditions. Fortunately for the Americans, Burgoyne's retreat ceased at Saratoga.

Over the next few days, as General Burgoyne grappled with his situation, Colonel Morgan's light corps constantly harassed them. A steady American artillery bombardment added to their discomfort. By October 14th, General Burgoyne and his army had had enough. With his officer's consent, Burgoyne asked Gates for terms of surrender. General Gates was generous in his demands and on October 17th, General Burgoyne formally surrendered his army.

The most decisive battle of the Revolutionary War to date was over, and Colonel Daniel Morgan and his riflemen had played a crucial role in the victory. Yet, in General Gates's dispatch to Congress announcing Burgoyne's surrender, no mention was made of Colonel Morgan. It appears that Colonel Morgan had fallen out of favor with General Gates soon after Burgoyne's surrender. Morgan's friend, the Reverend William

---

[69] Baxter, ed., "Digby Journal," 300
[70] Jackman, ed. "Anburey's Journal," 190

Hill, revealed the likely cause for this rupture as it was related to him by Daniel Morgan many years after the battle:

> *Immediately after the surrender of the British army Gates took Morgan aside & apparently in confidence asked Morgan, if he knew that the greatest discontent prevailed in the American army at the Commander in chief* [General Washington] *& that many of the most valuable officers threatened to resign if a change did not take place. Morgan, expecting that Gates meant to make use of the present time, when the recent surrender of Burgoyne's army to him would give him such eclat with Congress, to move the removal of Washington in hopes of getting the place himself, & knowing how little credit was due Gates, who in both days action was not out of his strongly fortified camp replied, 'That he had one favour to ask of him which was never to mention that destestable subject to him again, for under no other man than Washington would he serve as commander in chief.' & suddenly left Gates. From that time all intimacy between them ceased.*[71]

Reverend Hill's recollection also revealed the high esteem that the British officer corps had of Morgan. General Gates hosted a dinner for the British officers soon after their surrender to which Colonel Morgan was conspicuously absent (he was apparently not invited by Gates). Military affairs, however, caused Morgan to seek General Gates at the dinner, after which he departed. Morgan recalled to Reverend Hill that

---

[71] William Hill Notes, 2

The British officers not being introduced to Col. Morgan enquired who he was, & being informed, rose from their seats at table, followed him to the door, & introduced themselves to him, so high an opinion had they conceived of him from their acquaintance they had formed with him on the field of battle.[72]

Colonel Morgan and his riflemen had most certainly lived up to their reputation and high esteem at Saratoga. With the threat of Burgoyne eliminated, it was time for Morgan and his rifle corps to return to General Washington and the main army in Pennsylvania. They marched south within days of Burgoyne's surrender.

---

[72] Ibid.

Daniel Morgan at Saratoga
Source: Library of Congress

Chapter Seven

"[Morgan] is a Brave Officer, and a Well Meaning Man"

1778-1780

General Washington's efforts to defend Philadelphia from General William Howe's 15,000 man army had met with defeat at the battles of Brandywine in September and Germantown in October. Encamped with his weary and demoralized troops less than a day's march north of British occupied Philadelphia, there was little Washington could do to challenge Howe.

Washington remained defiant, however, and eager for Morgan's return to the army, so much so that he sent his aide, Lieutenant Colonel Alexander Hamilton, to New York to expedite Morgan's march. Washington told Hamilton that

> *I expect you will meet Colo: Morgan's Corps on their way down, if you do, let them know how essential their services are to us, and desire the Colo...to hasten their March as much as is consistent with the health of the men....*[1]

Morgan's rifle corps arrived at Washington's camp at Whitemarsh in mid-November significantly understrength; the toil of the Saratoga campaign and the long march from New York took a heavy toll on the men. *"There are not more than one hundred and Seventy of Morgan's Corps fit to march, as they in general want Shoes,"* noted General Washington upon their return.[2]

---

[1] Frank E. Grizzard Jr., and David R. Hoth, eds., "General Washington to Alexander Hamilton, 30 October, 1777," *The Papers of George Washington Revolutionary War Series,* Vol. 12, (Charlottesville: University Press of Virginia, 2002), 61

[2] Grizzard Jr., and Hoth, eds., "General Washington to General Greene, 22 November, 1777," *The Papers of George Washington,* Vol. 12, 349-50

After a brief rest at Whitemarsh, Washington attached Colonel Morgan's riflemen to a large detachment under General Nathanael Greene in New Jersey. Greene's detachment was originally intended to assist the American garrison at Fort Mercer (on the New Jersey side of the Delaware River). This fort, in conjunction with another across the river on Mud Island, were part of the American river defenses that hoped to stop British shipping from reaching Philadelphia. If the forts could resist British attacks and continue to block passage up the river, there was a chance the Americans could starve the British army out of Philadelphia.

The fall of Mud Island to the British on November 15th, however, ended this threat to the British in Philadelphia and eliminated the usefulness of Fort Mercer, so its garrison was evacuated before General Greene's detachment arrived.

General Greene defiantly remained in New Jersey after Fort Mercer was abandoned and skirmished with British foraging parties. The Marquis de La Fayette, a French volunteer in the American army, commanded a portion of Greene's troops in one such skirmish in late November. A detachment of Morgan's riflemen, commanded by Lieutenant Colonel Richard Butler, comprised half of La Fayette's force and greatly impressed him. General Greene noted after the engagement that, *"The Marquis is charmed with the spirited behaviour of the Militia & Rifle Corps."* [3] La Fayette lavished praise on the riflemen in his report to General Washington:

> *I take the greatest pleasure to let you know that the conduct of our soldiers is above all praises – I never saw men so merry, so spirited, so desirous to go on to the enemy what ever forces they could have as the little party was in this little fight. I found the riflemen above even their reputation…I must tell too the riflemen had*

---

[3] Grizzard Jr., and Hoth, eds., "General Greene to General Washington, 26 November, 1777," *The Papers of George Washington*, Vol. 12, 409

been the whole day running before my horse without eating or taking any rest. [4]

General Greene marched the bulk of his force back to Whitemarsh on November 28th, but Morgan's corps and a detachment of Virginian cavalry under Captain Henry Lee of Virginia remained in New Jersey a while longer to bolster the local militia and harass the enemy.[5] After another week of skirmishing with the British, Morgan and his riflemen rejoined Washington's army at Whitemarsh just in time to help fend off General Howe's last major operation of the year.

Battle of Whitemarsh

On the night of December 4th, over 10,000 British troops marched from Philadelphia towards the American camp at Whitemarsh.[6] The American army, about 12,000 strong, was alerted and manned their fortifications among the hills of Whitemarsh in anticipation of an attack.[7] General Howe halted at Chestnut Hill, about three miles south of Whitemarsh to assess Washington's defenses and determine his next move. During this pause, General Washington sent two detachments of Pennsylvania militia, (some 1,600 strong) and a regiment of

---

[4] Grizzard Jr., and Hoth, eds., "General LaFayette to General Washington, 26 November, 1777," *The Papers of George Washington,* Vol. 12, 418-419
[5] Grizzard Jr., and Hoth, eds., "General Greene to General Washington, 28 November, 1777," *The Papers of George Washington,* Vol. 12, 428
[6] David Martin, *The Philadelphia Campaign, June 1777 – July 1778,* (Da Capa Press, 1993), 160
[7] Lesser, "A General Return of the Continental Army…Dec. 3, 1777," 53

Philadelphia and Vicinity
Adapted from Library of Congress

Connecticut continentals forward towards Chestnut Hill to skirmish with Howe's advance parties and obstruct his reconnaissance.[8] Unfortunately, despite a determined but brief stand by the Connecticut continentals, Washington's skirmishers were easily dispersed by General Howe's troops. Yet, the British commander remained stationary for the next two days, reluctant to attack the strong American position in the hills to his front, but determined to strike one last blow against the rebels.

General Howe made his move early in the morning of December 7th. Under cover of darkness he shifted his army several miles to the east in two columns in an effort to flank Washington.[9] General Cornwallis commanded the main column that was to flank the Americans while General Charles Grey commanded a second column that was to distract Washington and his troops by threatening a direct frontal attack. Howe's plan was similar in design to the movements that brought him victory over Washington at Long Island in 1776 and Brandywine in September. This time, however, the American commander anticipated Howe's movement and placed Colonel Morgan's rifle corps, supported by a detachment of Maryland militia, on his far left flank to guard against just such a move.

The engagement that ensued was fierce and costly to both sides. Captain Johann Ewald, of the German Jaegers, recalled,

> *The light infantry fell into an ambuscade which the American Colonel Morgan and his corps of riflemen had laid in a marshy wood, through which over fifty men and three officers were killed.*[10]

---

[8] Thomas McGuire, *The Philadelphia Campaign: Germantown and the Roads to Valley Forge*, Vol. 2. (Stackpole Books, 2007), 241

[9] Grizzard Jr., and Hoth, eds., "General Washington to Patrick Henry, 10 December, 1777," *The Papers of George Washington,* Vol. 12, 590

[10] Ewald, 109

General Howe acknowledged the success of Morgan's ambush, reporting to Lord George Germain after the engagement that

> *The thickness of the wood where the rebels were posted, concealing them from the view of the light infantry, occasioned a loss of one officer killed, three wounded, and between twenty and thirty men killed and wounded from the first fire.*[11]

General Washington's brief description of the engagement to Governor Patrick Henry of Virginia also noted the heavy casualties Morgan's corps inflicted on the enemy:

> *As soon as they* [Howe's troops] *began to move* [against the American left flank] *Colo. Morgan with the light Corps under his command and the Maryland Militia attacked their right flank, and I am informed did them a good deal of damage....*[12]

One of General Washington's aides, Major John Laurens of South Carolina, described a similar scene:

> *Upon hearing they* [the British] *were advancing in two columns Morgan's corps and the Maryland militia were ordered to harass their right flank; there was some very smart firing in consequence, between Morgan's and the British light infantry.*[13]

---

[11] Grizzard Jr., and Hoth, eds., "General Orders, 8 December, 1777," Note 1 "General Howe to Lord George Germain, 13 December, 1777," *The Papers of George Washington,* Vol. 12, 573

[12] Grizzard Jr., and Hoth, eds., "General Washington to Patrick Henry, 10 December, 1777," *The Papers of George Washington,* Vol. 12, 590

[13] Dixon and Hunter, "Extract of a letter from an officer in camp, Dec. 16, 1777," *Virginia Gazette,* 26 December, 1777, 1

Major Laurens learned from Colonel Morgan himself about the effectiveness of the riflemen, adding that,

> *Col. Morgan, who has no need of boasting to establish the reputation of his corps, says the British light infantry lost a great many in their skirmish with him.*[14]

A British officer's account of the engagement confirmed the intense fire of Morgan's men. "*Their fire was more destructive for the time & number than had happened* [in] *the War*," wrote Lieutenant Frederick Wetherall.[15]

These accounts of Morgan's bold conduct at Whitemarsh were contradicted by another British officer who claimed that the British light infantry commander, Colonel Robert Abercromby, routed Morgan's riflemen with an aggressive new tactic. Colonel George Hager, who served with the German Jaegers, claimed:

> *The moment* [the riflemen] *appeared before* [Abecromby], *he ordered his troops to charge with the bayonet, not one* [rifleman] *out of four, had time to fire, and those who did, had no time to load again, they did not stand three minutes*;[16]

This bold tactic of immediately charging at Morgan's riflemen upon contact with them might help account for the high casualties suffered by Morgan's corps. Twenty-seven riflemen reportedly fell at Whitemarsh, including Major Joseph Morris of New Jersey.[17] This distinguished rifle officer was struck in the head and mortally wounded; his loss was severely felt by Colonel Morgan and the rifle corps.

---

[14] Ibid.
[15] McGuire, "Lt. Wetherall Journal," 251
[16] McGuire, 251 quote from: George Hangar, *To All Sportsmen*, (London, 1814), 199-200
[17] Grizzard Jr., and Hoth, eds., "General Washington to Henry Laurens, 10 December, 1777," *The Papers of George Washington*, Vol. 12, 592

Although by most accounts Morgan's riflemen and the Maryland militia that were with them fought bravely, they could not hold against General Howe's column and were forced to withdraw to the main American line at Whitemarsh. Howe did not pursue, halting on Edge Hill for the night. General Washington expected General Howe to renew his attack the next morning and used the conduct of Colonel Morgan and his rifle corps as an example for the army to emulate, declaring in the next day's general orders that

> *The Commander in Chief returns his warmest thanks to Col. Morgan, and the officers and men of his intrepid corps, for their gallant behavior in the several skirmishes with the enemy yesterday – He hopes the most spirited conduct will distinguish the whole army, and gain them a just title to the praises of their country, and the glory due to brave men....*[18]

The British failed to approach, however, and instead, marched back to Philadelphia. General Howe refused to risk his army in a direct assault on Washington's strong position. Howe's withdrawal marked the end of the 1777 campaign. The British looked forward to a relatively comfortable winter in Philadelphia. Colonel Morgan and his fellow Americans were not as fortunate.

Unlike the previous winter, in which General Washington's army was spread out among New Jersey's Watchtung Mountain, the American commander wanted to keep the army relatively intact. To do this he needed a location that could accommodate the army's needs. Whitemarsh would not work because it was too close to Philadelphia; just a few hours march from the British army. Washington needed someplace further away (to allow for a proper warning if the British did try to

---

[18] Grizzard Jr., and Hoth, eds., "General Orders, 8 December, 1777," *The Papers of George Washington,* Vol. 12, 571

attack over the winter) but also defensible and logistically sustainable. He settled on Valley Forge and marched the army there on December 19th.

Valley Forge

Valley Forge was approximately 25 miles northwest of Philadelphia and provided adequate terrain on which to resist a possible British attack. The Schuylkill River protected the American left flank and a steep hill, called Mount Joy, covered their rear. Although the front and right flank of the encampment possessed few natural barriers, the open terrain made an attack from those directions very hazardous.

General Washington ordered that log huts and earthworks be constructed immediately, but it took nearly a month before the entire army was adequately sheltered. Two lines of earthworks were built. The outer line extended along a ridge from the Schuylkill River to the foot of Mount Joy. Most of the army was stationed along this line in rows of huts behind the fortifications. An inner defense line was built along Mount Joy. It also ran to the river.

For much of their time at Valley Forge, Washington's troops lacked both clothing and provisions, especially at the beginning of the encampment. On December 22nd, General James Varnum of Rhode Island reported to General Washington:

> *Three Days successively, we have been destitute of Bread. Two Days we have been intirely without Meat. –It is not to be had from Commissaries. –Whenever we procure Beef, it is of such a vile Quality, as to render it a poor Succedanium for Food. The Men must be supplied, or they cannot be commanded.* [19]

---

[19] Joseph Lee Boyle, "General Varnum to General Washington, 22 December, 1777," *Writings from the Valley Forge Encampment of the Continental Army*, Vol. 1, (Bowie: Heritage Books Inc., 2000), 2

General Washington forwarded the bad news to Congress:

> *I do not know from what cause this alarming deficiency, or rather total failure of Supplies arises: But unless more vigorous exertions and better regulations take place in that line and immediately, This Army must dissolve.*[20]

While the main army struggled with supply problems, Colonel Morgan and his riflemen guarded the approaches to camp. They were posted a few miles south of Valley Forge near the village of Radnor. The riflemen were joined by parties of cavalry and militia who were briefly detached and then recalled to Valley Forge and engaged in occasional skirmishes with British patrols and forage parties.[21] Colonel Morgan, whose writing skills were far from polished, explained to Washington in a letter written on Christmas Eve that the overcautious enemy made it difficult for his riflemen to attack or capture anyone for the foraging parties.

> *I think thair prencisible* [principle] *view in Coming out, was to get in the hay from the islands, thay have had Nigh a hundred wagons halling hay every day since thay have been out – we keep Close round them, thay don't offer to Come far out side of their pequets* [guards] *so that we have little Chance to take any of them....*[22]

Colonel Morgan and his riflemen spent three long weeks guarding some of the roads to Valley Forge. They were

---

[20] Grizzard Jr., and Hoth, eds., "General Washington to Henry Laurens, 22 December, 1777," *The Papers of George Washington,* Vol. 12, 667
[21] Posey Biography
[22] Grizzard Jr., and Hoth, eds., "Colonel Daniel Morgan to General Washington, 24 December, 1777," *The Papers of George Washington* Vol. 12, 694-695

Valley Forge
Adapted from Library of Congress

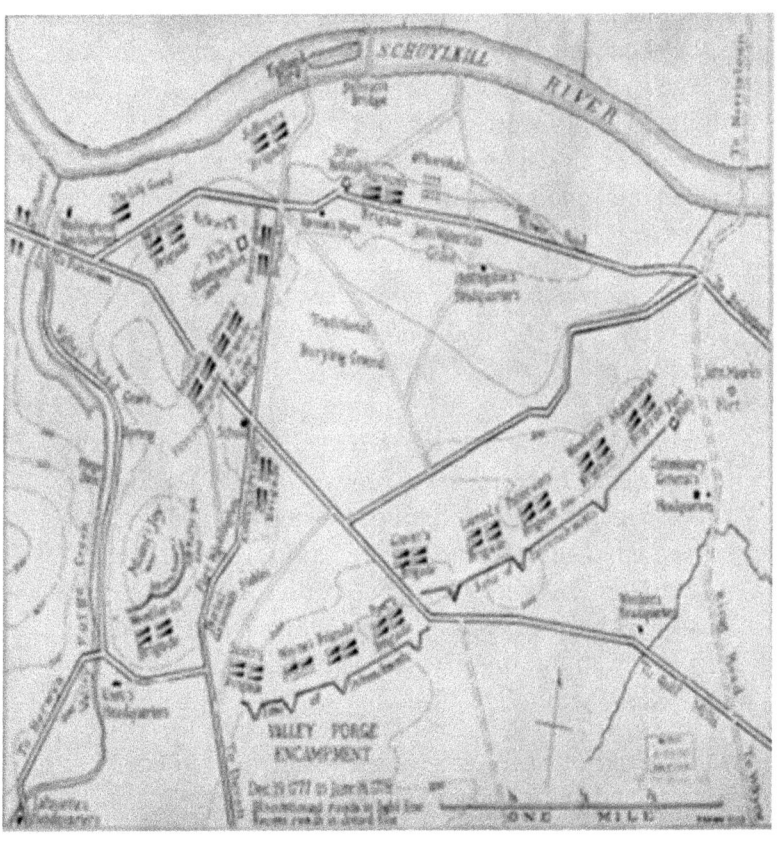

finally relieved in mid-January and reported to the main encampment at Valley Forge.[23]

While Colonel Morgan was in camp, he fell into a heated dispute with Richard Peters, Secretary to Congress's Board of War. Peters had accompanied a delegation of the committee to Valley Forge and Colonel Morgan was under the impression that Peters was involved in a scheme to remove General Washington from command and replace him with General Horatio Gates. Morgan confronted the 34 year old Peters, who described his encounter with Morgan a few days after the incident:

> *I was drawn into an unprovoked Dispute with Col. Morgan of Virginia, which proceeding to the last Extremity convinced me that the Col. Has little understanding & notwithstanding his Character as a Soldier by no means satisfied me of the Soundness of his Spirit. He told me I was spoken of at Camp as concerned in a Party against General Washington, & misconceiving something I said or designedly mistaking it, offered to turn out as Champion for the General's Character. On my denying that charge & agreeing to put our Dispute upon a personal Footing the Col. Declined the Matter.*[24]

It isn't clear how Morgan meant to champion Washington's character, perhaps through fisticuffs, perhaps through a duel (which was forbidden by the Articles of War). Peters' denial of Morgan's accusation seemed to satisfy Morgan and he dropped the matter, but it appears that Peters took great umbrage at Morgan's charges and apparently challenged the rifle

---

[23] Philander D. Chase, ed., "General Orders, 12 January, 1778," *The Papers of George Washington*, Vol. 13, (Charlottesville, VA: University Press of Virginia, 2003), 204

[24] Smith, ed., "Footnote 1, Richard Peters to Robert Morris, 21 January, 1778," *Letters of Delegates to Congress*, Vol. 8, 650-661

commander to a duel himself on personal grounds. Having successfully defended Washington's honor, Morgan refused Peters' challenge.

Within days of this incident, Colonel Morgan was granted a furlough to return to Virginia. Morgan biographer James Graham claimed the rigors of previous campaigns had taken a toll on Morgan's health and he needed time at home to recover and attend to personal affairs.

While Colonel Morgan rested and regained his health in Virginia, he tried to recruit more men for his rifle corps (whose troop strength had declined considerably since its formation). Unfortunately, three years of war had dramatically dampened the martial spirit of Morgan's neighbors, and despite his reputation and high regard in Frederick County, Colonel Morgan gathered few recruits.

Colonel Morgan Returns to the Army

The advent of spring brought improved conditions for the Americans at Valley Forge and a change in the routine of camp life, thanks largely to the efforts of a recently arrived German volunteer named Friedrich Wilhelm Steuben. Baron von Steuben had been an officer in the Prussian army during the Seven Years War (French and Indian War) and had retired from service over a decade earlier. Yet, Congress believed that he could be of some use to General Washington so he reported to the American commander-in-chief in February.

After several discussions with Steuben (in which the German officer identified the army's shortcomings and offered solutions) General Washington appointed Steuben Inspector General of the army and ordered him to retrain the troops. General Steuben strove to replace the several different military drills in use among the units with a new, uniform system written by Steuben himself. As a result, the troops spent countless hours learning Steuben's new drill. Gradually, a more professional army developed, one that undoubtedly caught Colonel Morgan's attention when he returned to the army in May.

Something else that likely attracted Morgan's attention was joyous news of an alliance between America and France. American commissioners in France had long sought official recognition by the court at Versailles, but France had hesitated, in part because of its uncertainty about America's chances for victory. News of the American victory at Saratoga convinced King Louis XVI and his ministers to openly support America with an alliance.

When news of this alliance reached Valley Forge, General Washington ordered a celebration. The task of guarding the army during this joyous event fell in part on Colonel Morgan and his rifle corps. An aide to General Washington informed Morgan on the eve of the celebration that

> *His Excellency desires that you will towards Evening send out patrols under vigilant officers to keep as near the Enemy as they possibly can. They are to continue out all Night and until 10 O Clock tomorrow. The Reason of this is, that the Enemy may think to take Advantage of the celebration of this day. The troops must have more than the common quantity of liquor and perhaps there will be some little drunkenness among them.*[25]

Colonel Morgan and his riflemen spent the rest of May on the outskirts of Valley Forge, watching the British closely as they prepared to leave Philadelphia.

The loss of Philadelphia in the fall of 1777 did not bring the Americans to the bargaining table as the British expected. In fact, in June 1778, Congress spurned British peace overtures that effectively gave America everything it demanded before

---

[25] Edward Lengel, ed., "Tench Tilghman to Colonel Morgan, 5 May 1778," *The Papers of George Washington*, Vol. 15, Note 6, 41

1776. Parliament renounced its right to tax, or even rule over the colonies, except on issues of trade.[26]

The lack of progress in the conflict cost General Howe his command; he returned to Britain in May, replaced by General Henry Clinton. General Clinton realized that the entry of France into the conflict presented significant challenges. French money, arms, and possibly troops and ships might enter the fray at any moment and Britain's other global possessions were now at risk and had to be protected. This stretched British resources and drew much needed men and supplies away from America. As a result, General Clinton, concerned that his forces in America were overextended, decided to abandon Philadelphia and consolidate the army around New York.

Preparations for Philadelphia's evacuation began in May and were noticed by Colonel Morgan, who reported the activity to General Washington. By mid-June, Clinton's army, along with hundreds of loyalist civilians, were on the move.

A portion of the army, and many of the loyalists, departed the city by ship. The remainder, numbering over 10,000 men, marched across New Jersey.[27] Their destination was Sandy Hook, on the Jersey shore, where they intended to rendezvous with the British navy and sail the rest of the way to New York.

General Washington, with nearly 11,000 men, cautiously pursued General Clinton's column into New Jersey.[28] He sent Colonel Morgan's rifle corps, bolstered to 600 men by the addition of 25 chosen marksmen from each brigade, to harass Clinton's right flank.[29] It is likely that the majority of these

---

[26] William Stryker, *The Battle of Monmouth*, (Princeton: Princeton Univ. Press, 1927), 35

[27] Mark M. Boatner III, *Encyclopedia of the American Revolution, 3rd. Ed.* 716

[28] Lengel, ed., "Council of War, 24 June, 1778," *The Papers of George Washington,* Vol. 15, 520

[29] Lengel, ed., "General Orders, 22 June, 1778," and "General Washington to Colonel Daniel Morgan, 23 June, 1778, *The Papers of George Washington* Vol. 15, 493, 518

reinforcements carried muskets instead of rifles, significantly transforming Morgan's corps. While the new men may have lacked the accuracy of rifles, they brought with them bayonets, a very useful weapon in close combat. Morgan pushed hard to position his force to strike the British, but the terrain and the compactness of Clinton's force, presented few chances to do so. Colonel Morgan reported to General Washington on June 25th from Allentown, New Jersey that,

> *I fell in with the enemy rear – we exchanged a few shot – no harm done – thay drew up on one side of the Creek and we on the other – I sent some parties to scarmish with them when they emmediately made off...toward shrewsberry – I moved my whole party after them about a mile, and then filed off to thair right, I intend to gain thair right this evening if possible I am afraid I shant be able to do them much damage, thay encamp in a body so compact that it is empossible to get any advantage of them – except we ware able to beat thair rear gard which is pretty strong.*[30]

Two days later, Morgan reported to General Washington that he was on the enemy's right flank and harassing them as best he could:

> *I arrived at this place* [Squan Swamp] *Yesterday encamp'd in the woods – sent out small parties – Capt. Long fell in with fifteen Granadeers and made them prisoners – deserters are continually comeing in – I have several parties out – whom I expect something from – I shall continue on the enemies Right till I have orders to the contrary – Thay keep in so compact a*

---

[30] Lengel, ed., "Colonel Morgan to George Washington, 25 June, 1778," *The Papers of George Washington*, Vol. 15, 544

body that it is impossible to do them much damage – However I will annoy them as much as possible.[31]

Battle of Monmouth

While Morgan's corps hung on the right flank of the British column, three larger American detachments under the command of General Charles Lee trailed General Clinton's rearguard. General Lee had recently returned to the American army after 18 months of captivity. In 1776 many Americans had viewed Lee, an experienced British officer who settled in the colonies several years before the war, as the American army's best military strategist, but his capture in December of 1776 and subsequent conduct as a prisoner in New York negated much of his appeal. Exchanged in the spring of 1778, General Lee returned to a much different American army than the one he had been captured from eighteen months earlier. This army was ready to fight, and General Washington ordered General Lee to do so on June 28th, at Monmouth Courthouse.

General Lee's force consisted of three large detachments of continental infantry (approximately 5,000 strong) commanded by Generals Charles Scott, Anthony Wayne and the Marquis de LaFayette. They, along with 1,000 New Jersey militia under General Philemon Dickinson and Colonel Morgan's detachment of 600 light troops, formed the American advance guard. At a council of war a few days earlier, General Lee had joined the majority of officers who warned against triggering a general engagement with the British, but General Washington was determined to strike Clinton and instructed General Lee in the late afternoon of June 27th, to prepare to attack his rearguard.
[32]

---

[31] Lengel, ed., "Colonel Morgan to General Washington, 27 June, 1778," *The Papers of George Washington*, Vol. 15, 564

[32] "Testimony of Various Continental Officers at the Court Martial of General Charles Lee," *The Lee Papers*, Vol. 3, (New York Historical Society, 1873), 2-8

Unfortunately, General Lee provided little guidance to his commanders on how to proceed with the attack; he claimed it was best to react to occurrences as they developed during their advance on the enemy in the morning.[33] Lee did send a message to Colonel Morgan early in the morning of June 28th, instructing Morgan to, *"advance with the troops under his command near the enemy, and to attack them on their first movement."*[34] Other than this directive, Lee offered little insight to his commanders on how he planned to attack the enemy.

For some unknown reason, Colonel Morgan never initiated Lee's requested attack. It is possible that Morgan was still out of position when Lee's other detachments made contact with the British rearguard at 9:30 a.m. and that by the time Morgan was able to strike, Lee's attack had broken down and his force was in full retreat. If this was the case it would have been reckless for Morgan to attack the British flank with no support, especially as British troops from General Clinton's main body rushed back to reinforce the rearguard.

This unexpected support of the British rearguard presented a much different situation for the Americans. General Lee had based his movements on the assumption that the British rearguard was isolated from the main body and vulnerable to envelopment. He also assumed his forces outnumbered Clinton's rearguard. Instead, the arrival of British reinforcements from Clinton's main body brought the two sides to roughly equal strength.

To make matters worse, Lee's commanders had no idea what General Lee's strategy was and thus, no idea how to react when British troops swung around and attacked them. Confusion ensued among the Americans and they soon had no choice but to withdraw and regroup.

---

[33] "Testimony of General Wayne and the Testimony of General Charles Lee, at the Court Martial of General Charles Lee," *The Lee Papers*, Vol. 3, 5, 176

[34] "Testimony of Captain Edwards at the Court Martial of General Charles Lee," *The Lee Papers*, Vol. 3, 161

Although Lee's attack on General Clinton's rearguard was a disorganized failure, much fighting was still to be had. The arrival of General Washington upon the scene, ahead of the main body of the American army, halted Lee's retreat west of Monmouth Courthouse and restored some order to the American advance guard. Lee's troops, now led by the commander in chief himself, turned and faced the British, who halted their pursuit in the face of heavy American resistance and massed their artillery in an attempt to drive the Americans further back. General Washington responded with his own cannon and a long range artillery barrage ensued in the afternoon as temperatures soared above 100 degrees. The oppressive heat and humidity created numerous casualties (perhaps even a majority of casualties) on both sides, yet the two armies held their ground until nightfall.

Colonel Morgan and his light corps inexplicably sat on the periphery of the engagement the whole day. Morgan and his men could hear much of the fighting and were only a few miles away, yet, they did not join the fray. Earlier in the morning, during Lee's initial attack upon the British rearguard, Colonel Morgan had sent a dispatch rider to seek orders from General Lee. Why Colonel Morgan did not take the initiative at the sound of battle and advance upon the enemy's flank is a mystery. General Lee believed he had already granted Morgan full discretion to act, so any further guidance from Lee to Morgan was unnecessary. Lee explained his reason for giving Morgan the freedom to act at his own discretion in court martial testimony after the battle:

Monmouth

Source: Library of Congress

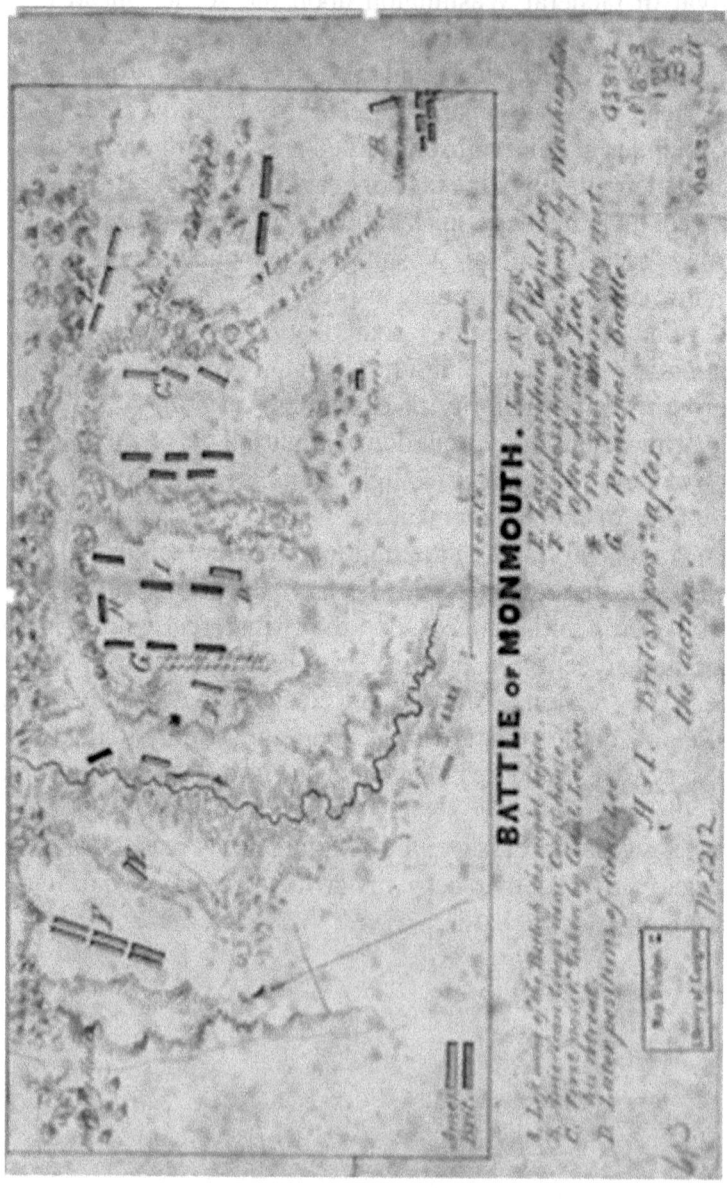

> *Colonel Morgan had received his previous orders to fall on their right flank as his discretion should direct; for to this gentleman, when the general principle had been explained, an almost absolute discretionary power was necessary. It was uncertain, and must be uncertain, on what particular point of the enemy's flank he could be at any moment of the day; to have sent any particular orders, therefore, to him how precisely to conduct himself, would have been idle, impertinent, and vain. In short, from the circumstances of our situation, Colonel Morgan must be left to his own discretion.*[35]

Somewhat uncharacteristically, Colonel Morgan sought further orders from Lee rather than act upon the discretion already granted him by General Lee. It is possible that Morgan was too far out of position to strike the British column at the time that Lee's other detachments advanced, and that the precipitate withdrawal of Lee's main body left Morgan unclear on how to proceed.

Morgan's dispatch rider failed to find General Lee, but came across General Wayne, who commanded one of Lee's detachments, in full retreat. Wayne recalled that

> *I enquired where Colonel Morgan was;* [the rider] *said he was about two or three miles to the left. I told him that he saw our troops were all drawn off; and that Colonel Morgan should govern himself accordingly.*[36]

About two hours later, in the early afternoon, General Washington also received a message from Colonel Morgan (perhaps from the same dispatch rider or perhaps from another

---

[35] "Testimony General Charles Lee, at his Court Martial," *The Lee Papers*, Vol. 3, 195
[36] "Testimony of General Wayne at the Court Martial of General Charles Lee," *The Lee Papers*, Vol. 3, 23

messenger) that sought further guidance on what to do with his light corps. General Washington responded:

> *As your Corps is out of supporting Distance I would have you confine yourself to observing the motions of the Enemy – unless an opportunity offers of intercepting some small Parties – and by no means to come to an Engagement with your whole Body unless you are tempted by some very evident advantage....*[37]

Colonel Morgan and his light corps thus remained where they were, on the right flank of the British column within sound of the heavy fighting but not within view. The gunfire lasted until nightfall, at which time the British disengaged under cover of darkness and continued their march to Sandy Hook.

While the bulk of Washington's forces rested and rejoiced in their apparent victory the next day, Colonel Morgan and his corps trailed the British all the way to Sandy Hook. Morgan congratulated Washington on the victory and lamented his absence in the fight:

> *I congratulate your excellency on the Victory gained over the British army – thay have from every account, had a severe floging – if I had got notice of thair situation – to afell upon them we could have taken most of them I think – we are all very unhappy that we did not share in the glory.*[38]

Although Colonel Morgan may have felt some regret in missing the battle of Monmouth, he could not dwell it. His orders were to stay close to the enemy, prevent them from scouring the

---

[37] Lengel, ed., "General Washington to Colonel Morgan, 28 June, 1778, *The Papers of George Washington*, Vol. 15, 580
[38] Lengel, ed., "Colonel Morgan to General Washington, 30 June, 1778," *The Papers of George Washington*, Vol. 15, 598

countryside for provisions, and encourage General Clinton's troops to desert (which they did in significant numbers.[39]

Colonel Morgan updated Washington on his activities several days after the battle from Middletown, New Jersey:

> *I came to this place early Yesterday Morning – the enemy had left it the night before – thair main body is encamped about three miles from the Town thair rear within a mile, we are in full vew of each other –* [40]

Morgan requested a few horses to better patrol the area. *"Cavalry is the Eyes of the infantry – and without any, my situation must not be very pleasing being, in full Vew of the enemys whole army."*[41] General Washington realized though, that General Clinton's troops were destined for New York, and instructed Morgan and his light corps to return to the army as soon as Morgan determined he could do no further damage to the enemy.[42]

Colonel Morgan remained at Middletown several more days, capturing a few prisoners and attracting a few deserters from the British army. Once the last of Clinton's troops boarded ships at Sandy Hook, Colonel Morgan turned northwestward and marched to join General Washington's main army, which was enroute to the Hudson River and White Plains, New York.

---

[39] David R. Hoth, ed., "General Washington to Henry Laurens, 1 July, 1778," *The Papers of George Washington*, Vol. 16, 6
[40] Hoth, ed., "Colonel Morgan to General Washington, 2 July, 1778," *The Papers of George Washington*, Vol. 16, 12
[41] Ibid.
[42] Ibid., Note 2, 12

Morgan Bids Farewell to the Rifle Corps

With a new phase of the campaign emerging, General Washington needed to re-organize his army. He ordered all of the troops that had been temporarily detached to the several advance guards, including the troops attached to Colonel Morgan's light corps, to return to their original units. This left Morgan's Rifle Corps with a little over 100 riflemen in the ranks, too few to justify Colonel Morgan's command. With no plans to increase the size of the rifle corps, General Washington transferred Colonel Morgan to his original unit, the 11th Virginia Regiment (which was renumbered the 7th Virginia in September). Captain Thomas Posey assumed command of the remnants of Morgan's Rifle Corps and marched the riflemen to the New York frontier as a counter-measure to the hostile Indians that threatened the region.

The 7th Virginia was attached to General William Woodford's brigade, so Morgan fell under the immediate command of Woodford. General Woodford and his men had seen heavy combat at Monmouth, Germantown, and Brandywine, and like most of the units in Washington's army, was only at a fraction of it authorized troop strength. Woodford's troops spent the next few months posted in the vicinity of White Plains, waiting for General Clinton's next move and General Washington's next response.

Not all of Washington's troops remained idle during the summer and fall of 1778. The arrival of a large French naval fleet off Sandy Hook in mid-July produced much excitement for the Americans; they believed they now had a chance to capture New York. Initially, it looked as though the French navy was going to challenge the British navy in New York. Alas, the largest French warships were unable to sail across the sand bar into New York Harbor, so the French redirected their efforts towards Rhode Island, where a combined American-French expedition against a British garrison in Newport met with defeat due largely to poor coordination between the two allied forces.

General Washington received the disappointing news from Rhode Island in late August. Although the defeat was an unpleasant surprise, it was not significant to his overall situation. General Washington's main army remained encamped around White Plains and General Clinton's British forces remained securely in New York.

One troublesome issue that plagued General Washington was the growing disputes among his officer corps over their rank and seniority. General Woodford was a prime player in this drama; he had resigned his colonel's commission in the 2nd Virginia Regiment in the summer of 1776, but had been appointed as one of four brigadier generals from Virginia by the Continental Congress in early 1777. Initially, he was placed as the fourth brigadier, due to his resignation, but he appealed to Congress and they elevated Woodford past the other three Virginia brigadiers. This, of course, upset these gentlemen, who complained to General Washington. Similar complaints from other officers bombarded the commander in chief and caused Washington to appeal to Congress for assistance.

It is not without reluctance that I am constrained, to renew my importunities on the subject of the Committee of Arrangements. The present unsettled state of the Army is productive of so much dissatisfaction and confusion – and of such a variety of disputes, that almost the whole of my time is now employed, in finding temporary and inadequate expedients to quiet the minds of the Officers and keep business on a tolerable sort of footing. Not an hour passes without New applications and New complaints about rank....[43]

---

[43] Hoth, ed.,, "General Washington to Henry Laurens, 3-4, 1778," *The Papers of George Washington,* Vol. 18, 236

Unfortunately, there was little that could be done to resolve these disputes in a way that satisfied all parties, so a number of Washington's officers resigned their commissions in protest.

Colonel Morgan had largely avoided the disputes over rank. As the senior colonel in Woodford's brigade, he assumed command of the brigade upon General Woodford's furlough (to attend to personal matters in Virginia) in October. Although Morgan did not hold the rank of brigadier general, he exercised the authority of that position for the remainder of 1778. As such, Colonel Morgan took on the responsibility of re-enlisting as many of his men as he could (the three year enlistmentss of the old 11th and 15th Virginia Regiments were about to expire). Morgan sheepishly confessed to General Washington that he had little influence over the men and could get very few to re-enlist.

> *For my part I have used every Method in my power, and I thought I had a peculiar turn that way – I made use of active sergeants but to no purpose....*[44]

Morgan reported that only the promise of furloughs for the winter and large bounties from Virginia would induce many of the troops to re-enlist.[45] General Washington agreed to grant furloughs to all those who re-enlisted, but first he had to move the troops into secure quarters for the winter.

General Washington moved his army into winter quarters in late November, splitting his force between posts in Connecticut, New York, and New Jersey. The main body of the army, which included Woodford's brigade under Colonel Morgan, marched to Middlebrook, New Jersey to encamp in the hills of central New Jersey.

---

[44] Hoth, ed., "Colonel Morgan to General Washington, 24 November, 1778," The Papers of George Washington, Vol. 18, 282
[45] Ibid.

Colonel Morgan's stay in Middlebrook was short; like many of his men and fellow officers, he was granted a furlough to return home over the winter to attend to his family.[46] It is unclear how long Morgan stayed in Virginia or what his activities were when he was there, but it is likely that he spent some time trying to recruit new troops for the army.

Upon Morgan's return to the army, sometime in the spring of 1779, he resumed command of his regiment, the 7th Virginia. With less than 200 men in the ranks, it is likely Morgan was less than satisfied with his situation.[47] His attention and interest soon turned to the formation of a brand new unit for the American army, a corps of light infantry.

In the early years of the war, the role of light infantry (namely, to reconnoiter, and protect the flanks and sometimes the advance of the army) was filled by riflemen and, when they were not available, detachments of select men. By 1779, rifles had fallen out of favor with many American commanders, including General Washington, who allowed Morgan's Rifle Corps to disband entirely by 1779. In its place was to be a corps of active, chosen men from throughout the army, armed with muskets and bayonets and modelled after the British army's light infantry battalions.

Colonel Morgan was on furlough in Virginia when the first hints of General Washington's intention to form a light infantry corps appeared. In February, Brigadier-General Anthony Wayne of Pennsylvania formally requested command of the yet to be formed unit.[48] General Washington replied affirmatively a week later:

---

[46] Higginbotham, 94

[47] Charles H. Lesser, "Monthly Return of the Continental Army Under the Command of His Excellency George Washington, For April 1779," *The Sinews of Independence: Monthly Strength Reports of the Continental Army*, 112

[48] Philander Chase and William Ferraro, eds., "General Anthony Wayne to General Washington, 10 February, 1779," *The Papers of George Washington*, Vol. 19, 169

> *I have received your favor of the 10th inst. expressing your desire to have a command in the light Corps – My opinion of your merit will lead me chearfully to comply with your request, as soon as the Arrangement of the army, and other circumstances permit the formation of that Corps.*[49]

Colonel Morgan was likely unaware of Wayne's arrangement with Washington and actively sought command of the light infantry corps soon after his return to the army in the spring.

In mid-May, Washington ordered yet another reorganization of the army, merging some of the depleted Virginia regiments and ordering them, and all of the other regiments of the army, to form eight companies from which men for a ninth company of light infantry for each regiment would be formed.[50] Sixteen light infantry companies (41 men per company) emerged from this restructuring; they comprised the most active officers and men of the army.[51]

Morgan Leaves the Army

News that this light corps of select troops was to be commanded by General Anthony Wayne stung Colonel Morgan severely in late June. He responded with a request to General Washington, which was reluctantly granted, to leave camp and appear before Congress to submit his resignation. On July 19th, Morgan submitted his letter, which began by recounting his many deeds and accomplishments in the war and his success as commander of light troops at Saratoga. Colonel Morgan then declared

---

[49] Chase and Ferraro, eds., "General Washington to General Wayne," 16 February, 1779, *The Papers of George Washington*, Vol. 19, 220

[50] Edward G. Lengel, ed., "General Orders, 12 May, 1779," *The Papers of George Washington*, Vol. 20, 444-445

[51] William Ferraro, ed., "General Orders, 12 May, 1779," *The Papers of George Washington*, Vol. 21, 138-139

> *From these considerations I could not but flatter myself, that if at any time a respectable corps of light troops should be form'd I should be honored with the command of it – my experience as a partisan and the services I had done my country in that way I thought justified my expectations – I am however disappointed, such a corps has been form'd and the command of it given to another.*[52]

Colonel Morgan maintained that people would interpret his absence from command of the light troops as a sign of wrongdoing or worse, a lack of confidence in Morgan by the commander-in-chief or Congress:

> *As it is generally known that I commanded the light troops of our army and that this command is now taken from me, it will Naturally be judged that this change of officers has taken place either on account of some misconduct in me, or on account my want of capacity – I cannot therefore but feel deeply effected with this injury done my reputation, by reducing me from a respectable station in the army...to the Command of a few men.*[53]

Colonel Morgan brushed aside the argument, cited by both General Washington and Congress, that General Wayne was a brigadier-general, a rank appropriate for the light infantry corps, and that he therefore had a proper claim to the command. Morgan reminded Congress that he had answered the call for service in the continental army before Anthony Wayne or Wayne's second in command, Lieutenant Colonel Richard Butler:

---

[52] Ferraro, ed., Footnote, "Daniel Morgan to John Jay, 18 July, 1779," *The Papers of George Washington*, Vol. 21, 306-307
[53] Ibid.

> *It may perhaps be offered that my rank in the army did not intitle me to such a command, to which I beg leave to observe that I am an older officer than either of the gentlemen who have succeeded me – that at the time when thay ware enjoying the sweets of Domestick life – I was engaged in Actual service and undergoing the hardships of war.*[54]

Morgan concluded that he was left with no other choice but to leave the army in protest over the insult his reputation had suffered.

> *I can with sincerity declare that I engaged in the service of my country with a full determination to continue in it as long as my services were wanting – I must conclude from what has happened, that my country has no more occasion for me, I therefore beg leave to retire.*[55]

Colonel Morgan delivered his letter to Congress on July 19th. It was accompanied with a letter from General Washington. The commander in chief hid his displeasure with Morgan's decision and praised his former rifle commander for his long service in the war:

> *Col. Morgan of the Virginia troops, who waits on Congress with his resignation will have the honor of delivering you this – I cannot in justice avoid mentioning him as a very valuable officer who has rendered a series of important services and distinguished himself upon several occasions.*[56]

---

[54] Ibid.
[55] Ibid.
[56] Ferraro, ed., Footnote, "General Washington to John Jay, 30 June, 1779," *The Papers of George Washington*, Vol. 21, 396

Washington revealed his true sentiments on Morgan's actions a year later when the question of Colonel Morgan's rank resurfaced.

> [Morgan] *is a brave Officer, and a well meaning man, but his withdrawing from Service at the time he did last year, could not be justified on any ground; there was not, to my knowledge, the smallest cause for dissatisfaction; and the Season and circumstances were totally opposed to the measure, even if cause had existed, till matters assumed a different aspect than they were at the time of his proffered resignation.*[57]

General Washington's assessment of Morgan's actions would have devastated Colonel Morgan had he been aware of them. Despite his disappointment in being passed over for command of the light corps, there was no man Morgan respected and admired more than General Washington.

Congress found itself in a dilemma on how to react. It had long been plagued by complaints from numerous officers who felt slighted over rank. As a result, many valuable and experienced commanders left the service as Morgan proposed to do. But most members of Congress realized that Daniel Morgan was an exceptional officer and they did not want to lose him. Henry Laurens of South Carolina expressed this sentiment to his son, John Laurens, an aide-de-camp to General Washington:

> *Colonel Daniel Morgan is in Town & has applied to Congress to accept his Commission, he complains of General Wayne's appointment to Command the Corps which should have been continued under him. He is a*

---

[57] John C. Fitzpatrick, ed., "General Washington to Joseph Jones, 22 July, 1780," *The Writings of George Washington,* Vol. 19, (Washington, U.S. Government Printing Office, 1937), 226

good Officer & we will not part with him, if persuasion can prevail.[58]

Complicating the situation was the fact that there was no justification to create a new brigadier generalship in the continental army for Morgan or any other Virginian officer. With three brigadier-generals (Woodford, Scott and Muhlenburg) already in command of the three Virginian brigades that existed in the continental army in 1779, there was no reason to appoint an additional brigadier general from Virginia.

Furthermore, just three days before Morgan submitted his letter of resignation, General Wayne demonstrated his own command abilities with a successful and daring attack upon a British garrison at Stony Point. News of this bold operation, which garnered over 500 British prisoners, electrified Congress and the army and removed any thought that General Washington had chosen wrong for command of the light infantry corps.

Colonel Morgan's letter to Congress was referred to the Board of War who refused to accept Morgan's resignation and instead, granted him an indefinite furlough. Cyrus Griffin, a delegate in Congress, commented on the unique arrangement:

Colonel Morgan is permitted to Virginia without resigning his commission; indeed we could not [permit] such a resignation: I wish some happy [solution] may be found out for his great abilities…I am sorry he is unemployed, and still more sorry should he insist upon resignation.[59]

---

[58] Smith, ed., "Henry Laurens to John Laurens, 23 July, 1779," *Letters of Delegates to Congress,* Vol. 13, 286-287

[59] Smith, ed., "Cyrus Griffin to Burgess Ball, 10 August, 1779," *Letters of Delegates to Congress,* Vol. 13, 345

Colonel Morgan shared his own feelings on Congress's deft decision in a letter to his former brigade commander, General William Woodford:

> *My reasons* [for resigning] *were thought just – but my resignation, was by no means approved of – Congress agree that I have been neglected, but not intentionally – they say the disposing of the light troops were left to General Washington –but all that I have spoke to agree that I ought to have had the command of them – I have been treated with great respect by Congress – they all are desirous to do something for me, and have given me an honorable furlough…till some thing offers – but I don't think I shall ever join the army,* [the] *reasons* [are] *obvious.*[60]

With his pride partially salved by Congress, Colonel Morgan headed to Virginia and a year long furlough at home.

We know little of what occurred with Daniel Morgan during his fifteen month absence from the army. It is safe to assume that he focused much of his attention and energy on his family and small estate.

From time to time Colonel Morgan received word from his associates and friends in the army. Neither General Washington nor General Clinton launched any significant operations in 1779 (aside from the American raid on Stony Point) so much of the news Morgan received centered on camp affairs.

One such report arrived in November from Colonel John Neville, the commander of one of the Virginia regiments under General William Woodford. Colonel Neville claimed that

---

[60] Catesby Willis Stewart, "Daniel Morgan to General William Woodford, 22 July, 1779," *The Life of Brigadier General William Woodford of the American Revolution*, Vol. 2, (Richmond, VA: Whittet & Shepperson, 1973), 1065

Woodford was much disliked by many of the officers under his command, particularly those from Woodford's original brigade. Many wished that Woodford would be promoted to Major General and that Morgan could then take over the brigade as a brigadier general:

> *Then says they for old Morgan a Brig. And we will Kick the world before us. I am not fond of Flattery but I assure you on my word No Mans Ever Leaving the army was more Regretted than yours nor no man Ever wished for More to Return. We saw a letter the other Day from his Excel'cy to you to be forwarded with Speed which Gave the officers Great hope you ware to Return agreeable to your Satisfaction God Send it may be the Case is the Prayer of....*[61]

Morgan undoubtedly appreciated such sentiment, though he may have disagreed with the criticism of his friend, General Woodford. As for the letter referred to by Neville, no such letter from General Washington, if it ever existed (which is doubtful) ever reached Daniel Morgan.

---

[61] "Colonel John Nevill to Colonel Daniel Morgan, 9 November, 1779" Theodorus Bailey Myers Collection, Series 5, #1000, NY Public Library

Chapter Eight

"Morgan's Character as a Soldier is Well Known in America"

Morgan Returns to the Army: 1780

Although military operations among the two main armies in New York decreased significantly after the Battle of Monmouth, this did not mean that the British had ended their efforts to retake their rebellious colonies. Months before Morgan's departure from the army, General Clinton had shifted both his attention and a portion of his army southward in the belief and hope that British success in Georgia and the Carolinas would inspire a legion of Tories (who were reportedly waiting for support) to rise up and help return the southern colonies to British authority. British success in Savannah in late 1778 (and its successful defense against a combined American-French force in 1779) was followed in the spring of 1780 at Charleston, South Carolina, when the bulk of the American southern army (over 5,000 men) surrendered to a British expedition under General Clinton himself.

This tremendous blow to American fortunes in the South prompted Congress to turn to the victor of Saratoga, General Horatio Gates (who had left the army six months before Morgan) and offer Gates command of the remnants of the American southern army. General Gates, who lived in northwestern Virginia, just a day's ride from Colonel Morgan, immediately reached out to Morgan. The two men had reconciled their dispute over Washington's command of the army and had developed a strong relationship during their time off from active service. General Gates informed Morgan that Congress also intended to recall him back to service to the southward (presumably under Gates).[1] Gates wished to meet with Morgan to discuss the particulars.

Colonel Morgan expressed great pleasure at General Gates's appointment, declaring, "*Would to god you'd had it six months ago, our affairs would have wore a more pleasing aspect at this day than they do.*"[2] Morgan was confident that General Gates could rally American forces in the South and give them, "*fresh life.*"[3] He expressed his desire to visit Gates before he departed, but poor health (sciatica, a nerve ailment that Morgan had developed while serving in Arnold's expedition to Canada) prevented him from travelling very far from his home. Instead, Morgan agreed to meet Gates when the general passed through Ashby's Gap on his way to Fredericksburg to gather supplies and troops.

Morgan Returns to the Army

By the time the two men met in late June, the Congressional resolution summoning Colonel Morgan back into active service had arrived. The resolve began with an interesting account of Morgan's departure from the army and clarification of his current status (in the eyes of Congress):

> *That Colo. Danl Morgan (who formerly commanded the rifle corps) on the 18th of July 1779, having...desire to resign...*[due to] *the injury he supposed to be done him in giving the command of the light infantry to another and regretting that so valuable an officer should be lost to the service, proposed to him to accept a furlough, until the*

---

[1] "Horatio Gates to Daniel Morgan, 23 June, 1780," Theodorus Bailey Myers Collection, Series 5, #857, NY Public Library

[2] "Daniel Morgan to Horatio Gates, 24 June, 1780," Horatio Gates Papers, NY Historical Society

[3] Ibid.

Commander in Chief should call for him, or Congress.... To this he agreed and still remains on furlough.[4]

The resolution concluded with a summons for Colonel Morgan to return to active service; he was to report to General Gates in North Carolina for his orders. No reference was made by Congress as to Morgan's rank. It was left unaddressed, which meant that for the time being Morgan remained a colonel.

Although Daniel Morgan was undoubtedly disappointed and perhaps even a bit angry that Congress did not include a promotion to brigadier general with its resolution calling him back into service, he eagerly embraced the opportunity to rejoin the war effort and agreed to return.[5] Morgan's one request to Gates was that he write to Congress on Morgan's behalf to request his desired promotion. General Gates did so in early July on his trek southward and declared his intentions to Congress to give Morgan command of the light infantry troops of the Southern army:

Colonel Morgan requests me to represent to [Congress] *that the State of Virginia have appointed some Junior Officers to himself, Brigadiers General who will take Command of Him, should he take the Field in his present Rank. This is not only a galling Circumstance to so old and deserving an Officer, but must impede, and possibly entirely defeat my Intention, in placing Colonel Morgan at the Head of a Select Corps from whose Services I expect the most brilliant Services. Therefore I humbly entreat* [Congress] *to order a Commission to issue*

---

[4] Worthington C. Ford, ed., "16 June, 1780," *Journal of the Continental Congress,* Vol. 17, 518-519

[5] "General Gates to Congress, 4 July, 1780," *Magazine of American History*, Vol. 5, (New York: A.S. Barnes & Co., 1880), 283

> *immediately, appointing Colonel Morgan a Brigadier General. I am confident the Rank, the Services, and the Experiences of Colo. Morgan is such as will prevent any officer, from thinking Himself aggrieved by His Promotion.*[6]

As eager as he was to rejoin the army, Morgan's health prevented him from taking the field until early September. Morgan explained his delay in a letter to General Gates on August 15th:

> *I have been exceeding ill since I saw you, and Indeed Dispaired of joining the army this fall, but have recovered amasingly, and will without doubt set out in a fortnight. Nothing stops me but a pain in my back & loins, of which I seem to recover fast by means of the cold bath.*[7]

On the very day that Morgan wrote this letter to Gates, the American southern commander approached the enemy outside of Camden, South Carolina. It had been a difficult six weeks for General Gates and his small force. A chronic shortage of provisions left the mixed army of continentals and militia hungry, sick, and demoralized, yet, General Gates marched them into South Carolina in August to challenge the British at Camden. The result was a disaster for General Gates and his army.

---

[6] Ibid.
[7] Walter Clark, ed., "Daniel Morgan to Horatio Gates, 15 August, 1780," *Colonial and State Records of North Carolina*, Vol. 14, (Winston:1896), 558

Battle of Camden

As dawn broke on August 16th, General Gates and his troops waited for battle a few miles north of Camden, South Carolina along both sides of a road. Gates posted his continentals, made up of the 2nd Maryland brigade and the Delaware regiment on the right side of the road under General Johann Baron de Kalb, a Prussian volunteer. Their right flank was protected by an impassable swamp. The North Carolina militia, under General Richard Caswell, held the center of the American line and straddled the road while the left wing of the army was defended by Virginia militia under General Edward Stevens. Their left flank was also protected by a deep swamp. The Americans had roughly 3,300 men, but two thirds were inexperienced militia.[8] Although the British had fewer troops, roughly 2,000, most were battle tested veterans commanded by Britain's best general, Charles Lord Cornwallis.

Advance units from both armies had stumbled into each other a few hours earlier in the pre-dawn darkness and briefly clashed. Lieutenant Colonel Charles Porterfield, who had served under Morgan in his rifle company as well as in Morgan's 11th Virginia Regiment, had led the American advance guard and was grievously wounded in the engagement (succumbing to his wounds a few months later as a prisoner of the British). His force withdrew and reported the clash to General Gates, who chose to hold his position and await daybreak.

When dawn arrived, General Cornwallis marched his army in line of battle straight at the Americans. Before many had even fired a shot, the Virginia militia and much of the North Carolina militia, broke and ran. Garret Watts served with the militia and provided a detailed and personal account of what occurred.

---

[8] Lt. Col. H.L. Landers, *The Battle of Camden, South Carolina: August 16, 1780*, (U.S. Printing Officer, 1929), 45

"*I remember that I was among the nearest to the enemy;...that we had orders to wait for the word to commence firing; that the militia were in front and in a feeble condition at that time. They were fatigued. The weather was warm excessively. They had been fed a short time previously on molasses entirely. I can state on oath that I believe my gun was the first gun fired, notwithstanding the orders, for we were close to the enemy, who appeared to maneuver in contempt of us, and I fired without thinking except that I might prevent the man opposite from killing me. The discharge and loud roar soon became general from one end of the line to the other. Amongst other things, I confess I was amongst the first that fled. The cause of that I cannot tell, except that everyone I saw was about to do the same. It was instantaneous. There was no effort to rally, no encouragement to fight. Officers and men joined in the flight. I threw away my gun, and reflecting I might be punished for being found without arms, I picked up a drum, which gave forth such sounds when touched by twigs I cast it away. When we had gone, we heard the roar of guns still, but we knew not why. Had we known, we might have returned. It was that portion of the army commanded by de Kalb fighting still.*"[9]

All was not lost for General Gates and his army, however. The American continentals and a portion of the militia on the right wing held firm and even pushed the British back. William Seymour, a soldier in the Delaware regiment, described the engagement there.

---

[9] Garret Watts Pension Statement, Revolutionary Pension Roll, in Vol. 14 Sen. Doc. 514, 23rd Cong., 1st sess., 1833-34
 (Accessed via the Documentary History of the Battle of Camden website at http://battleofcamden.org)

> "We advanced...and began the attack from both cannon and small arms with great alacrity and uncommon bravery, making great havock among them, insomuch that the enemy gave way..."[10]

Unfortunately, the loss of the entire left wing of the army spelled disaster for the Americans. General Gates and his officers tried to rally the militia, but they were panic struck and refused to reform. The rout of the militia significantly weakened Gates's army (by over half his force). General William Smallwood's 1st Maryland brigade (the reserve) advanced and engaged in a ferocious fight to protect the left flank of the American line, but it was to no avail. Outnumbered and outflanked, they were soon forced to give ground. Attempts to counterattack and join General De Kalb's continentals, who were two hundred yards to their right, failed.[11]

The British exploited the gap between the two Maryland brigades, driving through it and into the rear of the continentals. General De Kalb's troops were nearly surrounded and the general seriously wounded. Colonel Otho Williams of Maryland, who served as the deputy adjutant general of the American army, described the end.

> *The enemy having collected their corps and directing their whole force against these two devoted brigades, a tremendous fire of musketry was for some time kept up on both sides with equal perseverance and obstinacy, until Lord Cornwallis, perceiving there was no cavalry opposed to him, pushed forward his dragoons, and his infantry charging at the same moment with fixed bayonets put an end to the contest. His victory was complete. All the*

---

[10] William Seymour, "Journal of the Southern Expedition, 1780-1783", *The Pennsylvania Magazine of History and Biography,* Vol. 7, (1883), 288

[11] Landers, 48

artillery and a very great number of prisoners fell into his hands. Many fine fellows lay on the field, and the rout of the remainder was entire. Not even a company retired in any order. Every one escaped as he could.[12]

General De Kalb, who held his position to the end, lay mortally wounded upon the field. The bodies of his men lay all around him. Total American losses were estimated at over 1,000 (250 killed and 800 wounded and/or captured). The British lost only one third that number.[13]

General Gates lost both his army and his reputation at the Battle of Camden. His effort to halt the militia and his subsequent flight northward, first to Charlotte and ultimately to Hillsborough, North Carolina, was ridiculed by many who saw incompetence and cowardice in his actions.

Cornwallis's victory at Camden in August convinced the British commander that it was time to march into North Carolina to support and awaken the large number of loyalists who were reportedly there but afraid to show their support for Britain. Cornwallis believed that strong Tory support in North Carolina would allow him to easily subdue the rebellious province. Unfortunately for the British commander, rampant illness among his troops, which was exacerbated by the hot South Carolina summer, and unexpectedly strong resistance from rebel militia (led largely by General Thomas Sumter and Colonel Francis Marion) delayed Cornwallis's movement into North Carolina until the latter half of September. By the end of that month, however, Cornwallis's advance guard, led by

---

[12] William Johnson, ed., "A Narrative of the Campaign of 1780, by Otho Holland Williams," *Sketches of the Life and Correspondence of Nathanael Greene,* Vol. 1, (Charleston: 1822), 496

[13] John Buchanan, *The Road to Guilford Courthouse: The American Revolution in the Carolinas,* (New York: John Wiley & Sons, Inc., 1997), 170

Lieutenant-Colonel Banastre Tarleton, reached Charlotte, North Carolina against light opposition.[14]

Colonel Morgan Joins the Southern Army

Colonel Morgan arrived at General Gates's encampment at Hillsborough, North Carolina about the same time the British marched into Charlotte. He encountered an army still recovering from the disaster at Camden six weeks earlier. Many of the men were poorly clothed and equipped and General Gates and his officers struggled daily to adequately feed the army.

Colonel Morgan's arrival in camp undoubtedly lifted the spirits of the troops, but his stay in Hillsborough was brief. North Carolina's civil authorities sought to exploit Morgan's stature as a daring military commander to embolden their militia. A member of the North Carolina Board of War wrote directly to Morgan to ask that he accompany General William Smallwood, an experienced continental officer from Maryland whom General Gates had ordered westward to command the American forces along the Yadkin River east of Charlotte:

---

[14] K. G. Davies, ed.,"Major-General Leslie to Lord George Germain, November 27, 1780," *Documents of the American Revolution,* Vol. 18, (Irish University Press, 1978), 235
   and
   Lieut. Col. Banastre Tarleton, *A History of the Campaigns of 1780 and 1781 in the Southern Provinces of North America.*, (North Stratford, NH: Ayer Company Publishers Inc., 1999), 158-159

> *At the request of the Assembly, General Smallwood has agreed to take the command of the Militia of this state, and will set off in a day or two to the Back Country. It would afford me great pleasure for you to accompany the General. [Your] Character as a Soldier is well known in America. I am persuaded your presence would give Spirits to my Countrymen. General Smallwood I expect will have an opportunity of finding Employment suitable to a man of your Rank and Gallantry.*[15]

Out of respect for Morgan's accomplishments and abilities and aware of his sensitivity about rank, the North Carolina Board of War also encouraged its delegation in Congress to support Morgan's promotion to brigadier general.

> *Will it not be a good way for Congress to make Morgan a Brigadier-General? His long Service and Rank will make it exceedingly irksome to him to be commanded by our [militia] Brigadiers.*[16]

Although the American army at Hillsborough was in no condition to march westward to challenge General Cornwallis, General Gates recognized the importance of supporting the few militia that were still in the field, so he gave Colonel Morgan command of some of his best troops, three companies of continental light infantry and a party of riflemen (altogether 200

---

[15] Clark, ed., "Proceedings of the North Carolina Board of War, 30 September, 1780," *The State Records of North Carolina*, Vol. 14, 400

[16] Clark, ed., "Proceedings of the North Carolina Board of War, 2 October, 1780," *The State Records of North Carolina*, Vol. 14, 405

strong) and instructed him to march west to support General Smallwood and the militia along the Yadkin River.[17]

Another 100 continental cavalry under Lieutenant Colonel William Washington were to follow as soon as they could.[18]

Gates ordered Smallwood to assume command of the militia near Salisbury, on the Yadkin River, and establish a secure post there. Smallwood was then to, *"employ Colonel Morgan with all the Riflemen, Cavalry, and Light Troops,"* to suppress and/or harass any enemy advance into central North Carolina.[19]

Morgan and Smallwood's departure from Hillsborough was delayed several days by bad weather. When Colonel Morgan and his troops did finally march, on October 8th, it was ahead of General Smallwood, who had grown ill and needed more time to recover.[20]

While on the march to the Yadkin, news arrived that undoubtedly lifted the spirits of Morgan's men. A detachment of approximately 1,000 American riflemen from the western

---

[17] "General Gates to General Smallwood, 3 October, 1780," Letters from Horatio Gates, *Papers of the Continental Congress*, Record Group 360, Item Number 171, National Archives, 297-298
and
William Seymour, "A Journal of the Southern Experience, 1780-1783," *The Pennsylvania Magazine of History and Biography*, Vol. 7, 290
and
Clark, ed., "Proceedings of the North Carolina Board of War, 7 October, 1780," *The State Records of North Carolina*, Vol. 14, 411

[18] Clark, ed., "Proceedings of the North Carolina Board of War," 7 October, 1781," *The State Records of North Carolina*, Vol. 14, 410

[19] "General Gates to General Smallwood, 3 October, 1780," Letters from Horatio Gates, *Papers of the Continental Congress*, Record Group 360, Item Number 171, National Archives, 297-298

[20] Rev. Joseph Brown Turner, ed., *The Journal and Order Book of Captain Robert Kirkwood*, (Wilmington, The Historical Society of Delaware, 1910), 12 (Henceforth referred to as Kirkwood's Journal)

The Carolinas
Source: Combat Studies Institute: U.S. Army

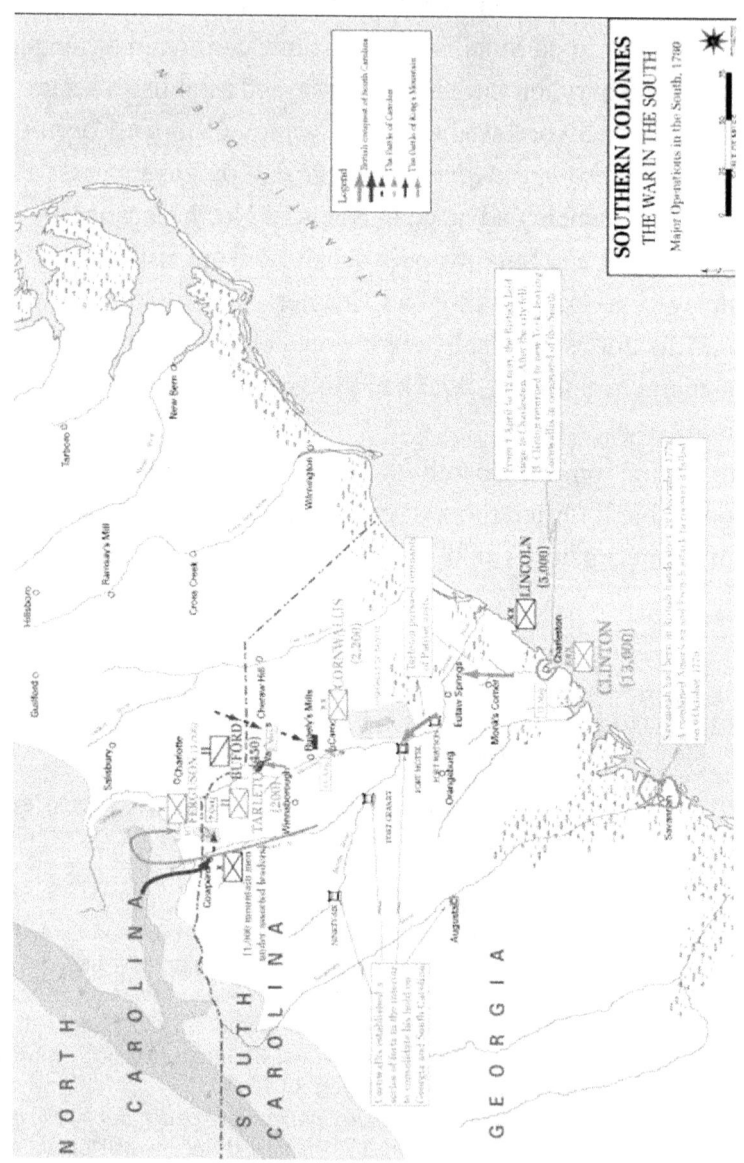

settlements of the Carolinas and Virginia had destroyed an equal sized detachment of southern Tory and provincial troops under British Major Patrick Ferguson at King's Mountain in South Carolina.

Ferguson's force was one of two detached corps (the other being Lieutenant Colonel Banastre Tarleton's British Legion) that served as Cornwallis's advance guard and was a crucial element of Cornwallis's army. Commanded by an exceptional British officer, Major Ferguson's detachment screened Cornwallis's flank on his march into North Carolina.

Ferguson had marched into the western foothills of North Carolina two weeks ahead of Cornwallis to suppress rebel activity and screen Cornwallis's left flank. Instead of suppressing the rebel frontiersmen, however, Ferguson provoked them with threats to lay waste to their country. The result was the loss of Ferguson's entire force (and his death) at Kings Mountain on October 7th.[21]

Ferguson's demise was a stunning turn of events that undermined General Cornwallis's plans to subjugate North Carolina and caused him to abandon Charlotte. Concerned that several British outposts in South Carolina were now vulnerable to rebel attack, General Cornwallis withdrew southward in mid-October to Winnsboro, South Carolina to await reinforcements from the north and establish a winter camp within supporting distance of the threatened British outposts.

Colonel Morgan learned of these developments when he reached Salisbury, on the Yadkin River, on October 15th.[22] Three days later, Morgan marched to Charlotte and by October

---

[21] Lyman C. Draper, *King's Mountain and Its Heroes: History of the Battle of King's Mountain*, (Cincinnati :Peter G. Thomson, 1881), 169
[22] Turner, ed., "15 October, 1780," *Kirkwood's Journal*, 12

22nd, he was encamped with his light infantry 14 miles south of Charlotte at New Providence, along Six Mile Creek. It was there that Morgan received the welcomed news that Congress had finally promoted him to the rank of brigadier-general.[23]

Morgan's promotion was not the only action taken by Congress that October concerning the American southern army. On October 5th, Congress directed General Washington to appoint a replacement for General Gates, who was to face a court of inquiry over his command (particularly at Camden) of the southern army.[24] On October 14th, Washington chose General Nathanael Greene of Rhode Island and informed Congress a few days later that General Greene was, *"an Officer, in whose abilities, fortitude and integrity, from a long and intimate experience of them, I have the most intire confidence."*[25] Greene was an excellent choice to replace Gates and quickly headed south to assume command of the southern army.

General Gates and General Morgan learned of Congress's decision to relieve Gates in early November, but they did not know who his replacement was to be. Morgan attempted to console Gates and assure him of his loyalty:

> *I am informed you are to be recall'd, for which I am sorry and glad both, for I don't think it will be in the power of any gent. Officer who commands in this country to add to his reputation, whatever he may loose from it. I was informed that you was*

---

[23] Turner, ed., "25 October, 1780," *Kirkwood's Journal*, 12

[24] Ford, ed., "October 5, 1780," *Journals of the Continental Congress*, Vol. 18, 906

[25] Fitzpatrick, ed., "General Washington to Congress, 22 October, 1780 *The Writings of George Washington*, Vol. 20, 244

apprehensive I had joined a party against you. I intended to convince you to the contrary by my conduct, and not mention the matter to you; but as you are going away, that will not be in my power; I must therefore tell, on my word and Honor, that I never had the most distant thought of such a thing nor was a thing of that Kind ever mentioned to me, or I would have let you a known it immediately, for I despise party matters as I do the devil.[26]

Morgan remained at New Providence in command of the army's light infantry and a detachment of riflemen. General Smallwood was also at New Providence and commanded all of the American forces there, (militia, Morgan's troops, and a large detachment of light dragoons under Lieutenant Colonel William Washington). The remainder of the American southern army under General Gates marched southward to New Providence from Hillsborough in early November and arrived on November 22nd.

The unification of the army presented logistical challenges for General Gates, namely, an inadequate amount of forage for his army in the vicinity of New Providence. Gates opted to withdraw the bulk of the army northward to Charlotte, which he felt was better suited to supply the army and a better position to defend in case the British advanced into North Carolina again. General Morgan and his light troops were ordered to remain behind at New Providence to screen the main army from the south.

---

[26] Clark, ed., "Gen. Daniel Morgan to Genl. Gates, 9 November, 1780," *The State Records of North Carolina*, Vol. 14, 730

The remainder of November was largely incident free, save for one foraging expedition by Morgan to retrieve a supply of corn and pork reportedly near the Waxhaws settlement. Morgan collected few provisions, but on his return to New Providence he learned of a party of 100 Tories assembled at Colonel Rowland Rugeley's plantation and sent Lieutenant Colonel William Washington and his cavalry ahead to attack. Rugeley had sheltered his force in a fortified barn on his plantation, which was just a few miles north of the Camden battlefield. Washington realized that a direct assault on the barn would be costly to his dragoons, so he instead employed a ruse to convince Rugeley that he had artillery and would smash the barn down around the Tories. Washington's artillery was actually a log placed upon a cannon carriage that from a distance appeared to be a real cannon. The deception worked. Colonel Rugeley knew that his barn could not withstand many blasts of artillery so he agreed to surrender without a shot being fired. [27]

Morgan returned to New Providence where a week later he and the American southern army finally learned who was to take command of the army from General Gates.

---

[27] Richard Showman and Dennis Conrad, eds. "General Smallwood to General Greene, 6 December, 1780," *The Papers of General Nathanael Greene*, Vol. 6, (Chapel Hill, NC: The University of North Carolina Press, 1991), 539

General Greene Takes Command

General Nathanael Greene arrived in Charlotte, North Carolina on December 2, and assumed command of the army from General Gates the following day. He found the condition of the army extremely distressing and wrote to Governor Thomas Jefferson, whose Virginians made up a considerable part of the force, to urge that more be done to properly supply the troops:

> *I find the Troops...in a most wretched Condition, destitute of everything necessary either for the Comfort or Convenience of Soldiers. It is impossible that Men can render any Service...whilst they are starving with Cold and Hunger....No Man will think himself bound to fight the Battles of a State that leaves him to perish for want of Covering, nor can you inspire a Soldier with the Sentiment of Pride whilst his Situation renders him more an Object of Pity than Envy. The Life of a Soldier in its best State is subject to innumerable Hardships, but when they are aggravated by a want of Provision and Cloathing, his Condition becomes intolerable....*[28]

General Greene struggled to supply his men in Charlotte; months of military occupation and operations in the region had largely laid the land to waste. In mid-December, Greene ordered the army to break camp and march east to the Cheraws

---

[28] Showman and Conrad, eds. "General Greene to Governor Thomas Jefferson, 6 December, 1780," *The Papers of General Nathanael Greene*, Vol. 6, 530

region of South Carolina along the Pee Dee River. There was adequate provision for the troops there and the increased distance from the main British army in Winnsboro reduced the threat of a successful surprise attack upon the Americans by Cornwallis.

General Greene worried, however, that his movement east would encourage General Cornwallis to advance back into western North Carolina or, at the very least, dishearten the populace of the region who might see Greene's movement as a retreat before the enemy. As a result, Greene took a bold and unorthodox step; he divided his army in the face of a stronger enemy. General Greene led the bulk of the army eastward to Cheraws as planned, but he formed, *"between 3 and 400 chosen Infantry and Lt. Colonel* [William] *Washington's regiment of Dragoons,"* into a Flying Army under General Morgan and ordered Morgan to march southwestward, across the Catawba River where Greene hoped Morgan's presence would bolster both the morale and number of patriot militia.[29] General Greene's orders to Morgan stated that

> *You are appointed to the command of a Corps of Light Infantry, a detachment of Militia and Lt. Col. Washington's Regiment of Light Dragoons. With these troops you will proceed to the West side of the Catawba River where you will be joined by a body of Volunteer Militia.... This force and such others as may join you from Georgia you will employ against the enemy on the West side of the river, either offensively*

---

[29] Showman and Conrad, eds. "General Greene to Samuel Huntington, President of the Continental Congress, 28 December, 1780," *The Papers of General Nathanael Greene*, Vol. 7, 8

or defensively as your own prudence and discretion may direct, acting with caution and avoiding surprizes by every possible precaution. For the present I give you the entire command in that quarter, and do hereby require all Officers and Soldiers engaged in the American cause to be subject to your orders and command.[30]

General Greene added that the purpose of Morgan's deployment was to, "*give protection to that part of the country and spirit up the people, to annoy the enemy in that quarter.*"[31] In this, Greene expressed his utmost confidence in General Morgan:

Confiding in your abilities and activity, I intrust you with this command, being persuaded you will do everything in your power to distress the enemy and afford protection to the Country.[32]

---

[30] Showman and Conrad, eds. "General Greene to General Daniel Morgan, 16 December, 1780," *The Papers of General Nathanael Greene*, Vol. 6, 589
[31] Ibid.
[32] Ibid.

Chapter Nine

"I Have Given [Tarleton] a Devil of a Whipping"

Cowpens : 1781

After several days of preparation, General Morgan and his small force marched west on December 21st into South Carolina. They halted four days later at Grindall Shoals, a crossing point of the Pacolet River, 45 miles west of Charlotte and 60 miles northwest of General Cornwallis's encampment in Winnsboro. General Morgan established an encampment along the east bank of the Pacolet River upon land owned by Alexander Chesney, a prominent Tory who had been captured at King's Mountain in October but had since escaped and returned to the service of the British.

Reports that approximately 250 Georgia Tories were plundering the inhabitants to the south of Morgan prompted him to send Lieutenant Colonel Washington's cavalry, reinforced by 200 mounted militia, southward on December 29th, to confront the Tories.[1] General Morgan described the engagement that ensued to General Greene:

> *Before* [Washington] *could overtake* [the Tories], *they had retreated upwards of Twenty Miles. He came up with them next day About 12 oClock a.m. at Hammonds Store House About 40 Miles from our Camp. They were alarmed and flew to their Horses.*

---

[1] Showman and Conrad, eds. "General Morgan to General Greene, 31 December, 1780," *The Papers of General Nathanael Greene*, Vol. 7 30-31

> *Washington Extended his Mounted Riflemen on the Wings and charged them in Front with his own Regiment. They fled with the greatest Precipitation without making any Resistance. 150 were killed and wounded & About 40 Taken Prisoners. What makes this success more Valuable is it was Attained without the Loss of a man.*[2]

Not only had Lieutenant-Colonel Washington completely routed a large Tory detachment within a day's march of British forces at Winnsboro and Ninety-Six, but a detachment of his cavalry had continued even further south and burned a fortified plantation on the outskirts of Ninety-Six.[3]

The repercussions of Washington's success extended far beyond the loss of several hundred Tories to the British. General Cornwallis, initially baffled by General Greene's division of forces, was now alarmed for the security of his outpost at Ninety-Six. He moved immediately to protect this important post by ordering twenty-six year old Lieutenant-Colonel Banastre Tarleton to march west with his British Legion and a battalion of infantry from the 71st Regiment to protect Ninety-Six and, *"push* [Morgan] *to the utmost."*[4]

Despite his relative youth, Banastre Tarleton was an experienced field commander and his British Legion, comprised of loyalist American cavalry and infantry, was one of General Cornwallis's most dependable units. Successful engagements during the siege of Charleston, at the Waxhaws

---

[2] Ibid.
[3] Ibid.
[4] Tarleton, "General Cornwallis to Lt. Col. Tarleton, 2 January, 1781," 244

(where Tarleton's men reportedly refused to give quarter to surrendering Virginians) at Camden, and in numerous encounters with rebel militia in South Carolina, helped enhance the British Legion's reputation as a formidable force (and earn their commander the nickname "Bloody Tarleton" from the Americans).

Upon learning of the engagement at Hammond's Store and the destruction of Williams Plantation, General Cornwallis turned to Tarleton and his legion of 550 cavalry and infantry to protect the important British outpost of Ninety-Six. A three pound cannon and a battalion of infantry from the 71st Regiment were attached to Tarleton, bringing his force to approximately 750 men (nearly 300 of which were mounted).[5] Tarleton marched westward from Winnsboro on January 2nd, but soon realized, based on reports that Morgan was still encamped on the Pacolet River, that Ninety-Six was not in danger. Tarleton halted his march about twenty miles west of the Broad River and wrote to General Cornwallis to update him on the situation and propose an operation against Morgan.[6]

Tarleton's proposal was to pursue and destroy Morgan, should Morgan choose to stand and fight Tarleton, or trap him in a vise should Morgan flee from Tarleton's advance. *"When I advance,"* wrote Tarleton to Cornwallis, *"I must either destroy Morgan's corps, or push it before me over the Broad river, towards King's mountain."*[7] Tarleton proposed a coordinated movement with Cornwallis, each leading their troops northward along parallel routes. If Morgan retreated from Tarleton's

---

[5] Tarleton, "Earl Cornwallis to Sir Henry Clinton, 18 January, 1781, 249-250
[6] Tarleton, 211
[7] Tarleton, "Lieutenant-colonel Tarleton to Earl Cornwallis, 4 January, 1781, 245-246

advance and attempted to reunite with General Greene as expected, Cornwallis would be in position to cut off Morgan's escape at Kings Mountain. If Morgan chose to stand against Tarleton, all the better; Tarleton's force would then destroy Morgan. To achieve this, Tarleton asked for reinforcements and received the 7th Regiment Royal Fusiliers, (200 strong) a detachment of cavalry from the 17th Dragoons (50 strong) and another three pound cannon.[8] Tarleton's force, which included a small number of loyalist guides, numbered over 1100 men when he finally proceeded north on January 11th, to push General Morgan.[9]

During all this time, General Morgan sat impatiently at Grindall's Ford, initially unaware of Tarleton's plan. He had proposed a movement into Georgia in the wake of Washington's success at Hammond's Store, but wanted Greene's approval before he proceeded.[10] While he waited for Greene's reply, (which was inexplicably delayed) Morgan prepared to march:

> *I have sent for 100 Swords which I intend to put into the Hands of expert Riflemen to be mounted and incorporated with Lieut. Col. Washington's Corps. I have also Wrote to the Quarter Master to have me one hundred Pack Saddles made immediately.... Pack saddles ought to be procured let our Movements be what they may, for our Waggons will be an*

---

[8] Tarleton, 212

[9] Lawrence E. Babits, *A Devil of a Whipping: The Battle of Cowpens*, (Chapel Hill : The University of North Carolina Press, 1998), 50

[10] Showman and Conrad, eds. "General Morgan to General Greene, 31 December, 1780," *The Papers of General Nathanael Greene*, Vol. 7 30-31

Impediment, whether we attempt to annoy the Enemy, or provide for our own Safety. It is incompatible with the Nature of Light Troops to be encumbered with Baggage.[11]

One hundred and twenty miles to the east, General Greene, unaware of Tarleton's plans but aware that General Cornwallis would soon receive a large reinforcement of troops from New York under General Alexander Leslie, speculated that Cornwallis would soon push north into North Carolina again. If Cornwallis did so, Greene wanted Morgan to strike Cornwallis's left flank and rear. With this in mind, Greene explained to Morgan that he opposed Morgan's movement into Georgia:

> *I have maturely considered your proposition of an expedition into Georgia and cannot think it warrantable in the critical situation our Army is in. I have no small reason to think by intelligence from different quarters that the enemy have a movement in contemplation.... Should you go into Georgia and the enemy push this way your whole force will be useless. The Enemy having no object there but what is secure in their fortifications, will take no notice of your movement.... But if you continue in the neighbourhood of the place you now are and they attempt to push forward you may intercept their communication with Charlestown, or harass their rear, both of which will alarm the enemy not a little.*[12]

---

[11] Ibid.
[12] Showman and Conrad, eds. "General Greene to General Morgan 8 January, 1781," *The Papers of General Nathanael Greene*, Vol. 7

It took a week for Greene's reply to reach Morgan, during which Morgan waited impatiently and grew discouraged at his situation. Provisions remained a problem for Morgan's force, so much so that most of the militia that had joined him (only 200 from South Carolina and Georgia and another 140 from North Carolina) were posted miles from camp in order to obtain enough forage and food for their horses and men.[13] General Morgan received Greene's reply on January 14th, and responded the next day with a pessimistic assessment of his situation and a frustrated appeal for his light corps to be recalled to the army:

> *Upon a full and mature deliberation, I am confirmed in the opinion that nothing can be effected by my detachment in this country which will balance the risks I will be subjected to by remaining here. The enemy's great superiority of numbers and our distance from the main army, will enable Lord Cornwallis to detach so superior a force against me, as to render it essential to our safety to avoid coming to action, nor will this be always in my power. No attempt to surprise me will be left untried by them, and situated as we must be, every possible precaution may not be sufficient to secure us. The scarcity of forage makes it impossible for us to be always in a compact body, and were this not the case, it is beyond the art of man to keep the militia from straggling. These reasons induce me to*

72-73

[13] Showman and Conrad, eds. "General Morgan to General Greene, 15 January, 1781," *The Papers of General Nathanael Greene*, Vol. 7 127-128

request that I may be recalled with my detachment....[14]

General Morgan asserted that the militia under General William Davidson and Colonel Andrew Pickens could remain in the region to restrain the disaffected populous (loyalists) without becoming, "*the object of the enemy's attention,*" the way his force had become.[15]

Despite the pessimistic tone of Morgan's reply, he assured Greene that if he decided not to recall Morgan, "*You may depend on my attempting everything to annoy the enemy, and to provide for the safety of the detachment. I shall cheerfully acquiesce to your determination.*"[16]

There would be no time for Morgan to receive or comply with General Greene's wishes. He had already become aware of the potential pincer movement that was developing against him between Tarleton's and Cornwallis's forces (who were both marching north) and moved his small corps to Burr's Mill on Thicketty Creek (about ten miles north of Grindall's Ford) in response.

When Morgan learned on the morning of January 16th, that Tarleton had crossed the Pacolet River in the evening and was only a few miles to his south, he immediately broke camp and

---

[14] Ibid.
[15] Ibid.
[16] Ibid.

Western South Carolina
Adapted from Library of Congress

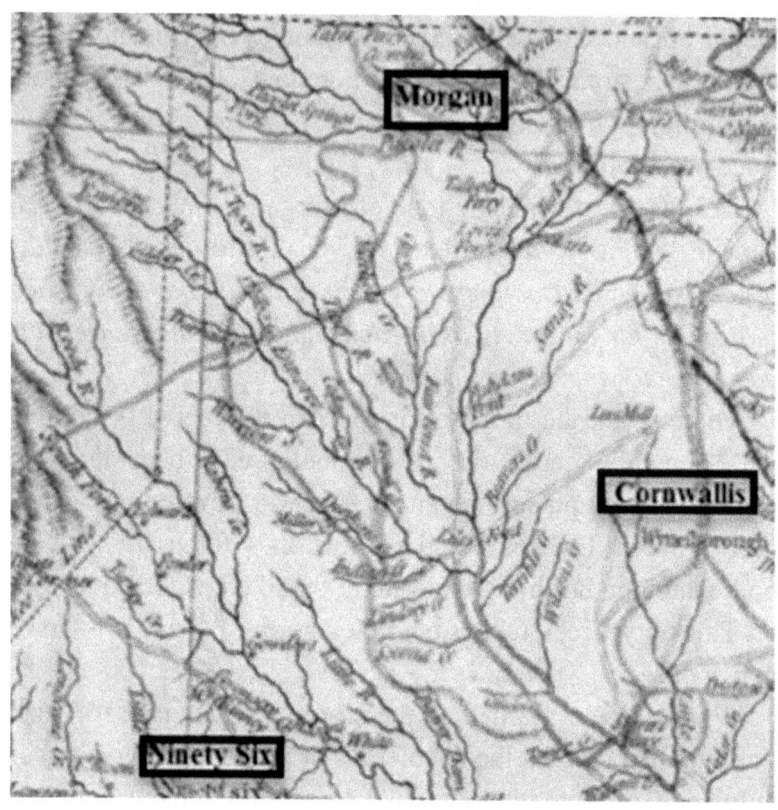

marched towards the Broad River. He halted in the afternoon about five miles from the river in an area known as the Cowpens. It was a flat, lightly wooded area where Carolina farmers grazed their cattle before driving them on to market in the east. Tarleton halted for the evening in Morgan's abandoned camp at Burr's Mill, twelve miles to the south of Cowpens. Tarleton's men, who had been on the move all day and night, welcomed the opportunity to rest and enjoyed the abandoned, half cooked provisions the Americans left behind.[17] Their respite was brief, however, for Banastre Tarleton was determined to catch Morgan, and Tarleton's men were back on the march well before sunrise of January 17th.

Eve of Battle at Cowpens

When General Morgan halted in the late afternoon of January 16th, at Cowpens he did not intend to stand and fight. The ground his men rested on was less than ideal to defend, especially against a force with as much cavalry as Tarleton had. Relatively flat, with open woods, there was little defensible terrain on which to anchor his flanks and prevent Tarleton's cavalry from sweeping around and into his rear. Morgan knew a fight was coming, but his plan was to cross the Broad River early the next morning and post his army on, "*a strong piece of ground and there decide the matter*," against Tarleton.[18]

Fortune seemed to shine on General Morgan at the Cowpens as hundreds of new militia arrived over the course of the day

---

[17] Babitts, 53
[18] "General Morgan to William Snickers, 26 January 1781," Horatio Gates Papers, NY Historical Society

and evening.[19] The American commander spent much of the evening with his troops, hoping to bolster their spirits and prepare them for battle. Moving from campfire to campfire, Morgan spoke encouragingly to the men, particularly the militia, one of whom recalled years later that

> *It was upon this occasion I was more perfectly convinced of Gen. Morgan's qualifications to command militia, than I had ever before been. He went among the volunteers, helped them fix their swords, joked with them about their sweet-hearts, told them to keep in good spirits, and the day would be ours. And long after I laid down, he was going about among the soldiers encouraging them, and telling them that the old wagoner would crack his whip over Ben. [Tarleton] in the morning, as sure as they lived. 'Just hold up your heads, boys, three fires,' he would say, 'and you are free, and then when you return to your homes, how the old folks will bless you, and the girls kiss you, for your gallant conduct!' I don't believe he slept a wink that night!*[20]

If General Morgan did get any rest, it was likely brief, for he received reports in the pre-dawn hours of January 17th, that Tarleton was rapidly approaching and was only five miles away.[21] Morgan recalled his reaction in a letter a week later:

---

[19] Babbits, 53
[20] George F. Scheer and Hugh F. Rankin, "Tarleton Run Down the Road Helter-Skelter: Cowpens, Memoir of Thomas Young", *Rebels and Redcoats,* (Da Capo Press,1957), 428
[21] "General Morgan to William Snickers, 26 January 1781," Horatio Gates Papers, NY Historical Society

> *No time was to be lost, I prepared for Battle, as soon as the day Broke & had just time to form a disposition when they hove in sight.*[22]

General Morgan explained his decision to stand and fight at the Cowpens to John Marshall, the future Chief Justice of the Supreme Court, soon after his return from the southern campaign. Marshall recounted Morgan's justification to stand and fight at Cowpens in his three volume history of the *Life of George Washington*:

> *It was believed that* [Morgan] *might have crossed the Broad River, or have reached a mountainous country which was also near him, before he could be overtaken; and the superiority of his adversary was so decided as to induce his best officers to think that every effort ought to be made to avoid an engagement. But Morgan had great and just confidence in himself and in his troops; he was unwilling to fly from an enemy not so decidedly his superior as to render it madness to fight him; and he also thought that, if he should be overtaken while his men were fatigued and retreating, the probability of success would be much less than if he should exhibit the appearance of fighting from choice.*[23]

So General Morgan formed his troops and prepared to face Tarleton at Cowpens.

---

[22] Ibid.
[23] John Marshall, *The Life of George Washington,* Vol. 3 (Fredericksburg, VA: Citizen's Guild of Washington's Boyhood Home, 1926), 303-304

Morgan's experience told him not to rely too heavily on the militia and he developed a battle plan accordingly. It called for a defense in depth comprising three battle lines. Morgan placed approximately 150 militia riflemen from Georgia and the Carolinas in a skirmish line that extended across the road that Tarleton was expected to approach from.[24] They deployed in loose order behind trees and were ordered to *"bring on the action,"* and, *"feel the enemy as he approached."*[25] Since they were ordered to hold their fire until the enemy was within fifty yards, the riflemen were only expected to fire a shot or two before withdrawing to the flanks of the next American line 150 yards in their rear.

Morgan's second line consisted of 300 North and South Carolina militia, many armed with rifles. It also stretched across the road and was divided into four battalions. Unlike the skirmishers, who fired individually, the militia line fired massed battalion volleys. General Morgan expected each battalion to fire at least two volleys before they retreated to the third and final American line.

Morgan's third line consisted of his best troops, the Maryland, Delaware, and Virginia continentals. They were augmented by two companies of Virginia militia -- many with rifles -- a company of Virginia State troops, and a few North Carolina militia and state troops. The line was formed in two ranks about 150 yards behind the militia and numbered about 550.[26]

---

[24] Mark M. Boatner, III, *Encyclopedia of the American Revolution*, 293

[25] Babits, 81

[26] Note: The number of troops in the militia line has been reported as high as 1,000. See Tarleton, 216; If the bulk of the skirmish line joined the militia line then the number would have approached 450 at the very least. Exact figures for the militia line, as for the entire American force, vary widely. The number above is an approximation based on the literature of Cowpens.

Lieutenant Colonel William Washington commanded about 120 cavalry, two thirds continental and the rest mounted militia.[27] They were held in reserve behind the third line. A few horsemen were posted three miles ahead of the skirmish line as pickets.

Battle of Cowpens

Colonel Tarleton reached Cowpens at dawn and halted to assess Morgan's deployment. The American skirmish line hampered Tarleton's ability to see Morgan's full troop disposition, so he ordered some dragoons forward to drive the riflemen back. The horsemen advanced towards the skirmishers and were met with a scattered, but deadly fire. The riflemen, secure behind trees, did not budge, and it was the dragoons that fell back.[28]

Colonel Tarleton grew impatient and proceeded to attack. His troops dropped their extra gear and formed battle lines across the road. His two three pound cannon were placed in the road and commenced firing, but the guns had little effect against the scattered American skirmishers. Thomas Young, who was posted with Washington's cavalry, recalled that

> *The morning...was bitterly cold...About sunrise, the British line advanced at a sort of trot with a loud halloo. It was the most beautiful line I ever saw. When they shouted, I heard Morgan say, 'They give us the British halloo, boys. Give them the Indian halloo, by G--!' and he galloped along the lines, cheering the men and telling them not to fire until we could see the whites of their eyes.*[29]

---

[27] Babits, 41-42
[28] Ibid., 83
[29] Scheer and Rankin, eds., "Memoir of Thomas Young", 430

Battle of Cowpens : January 17, 1781

Source: Combat Studies Institute, U.S. Army

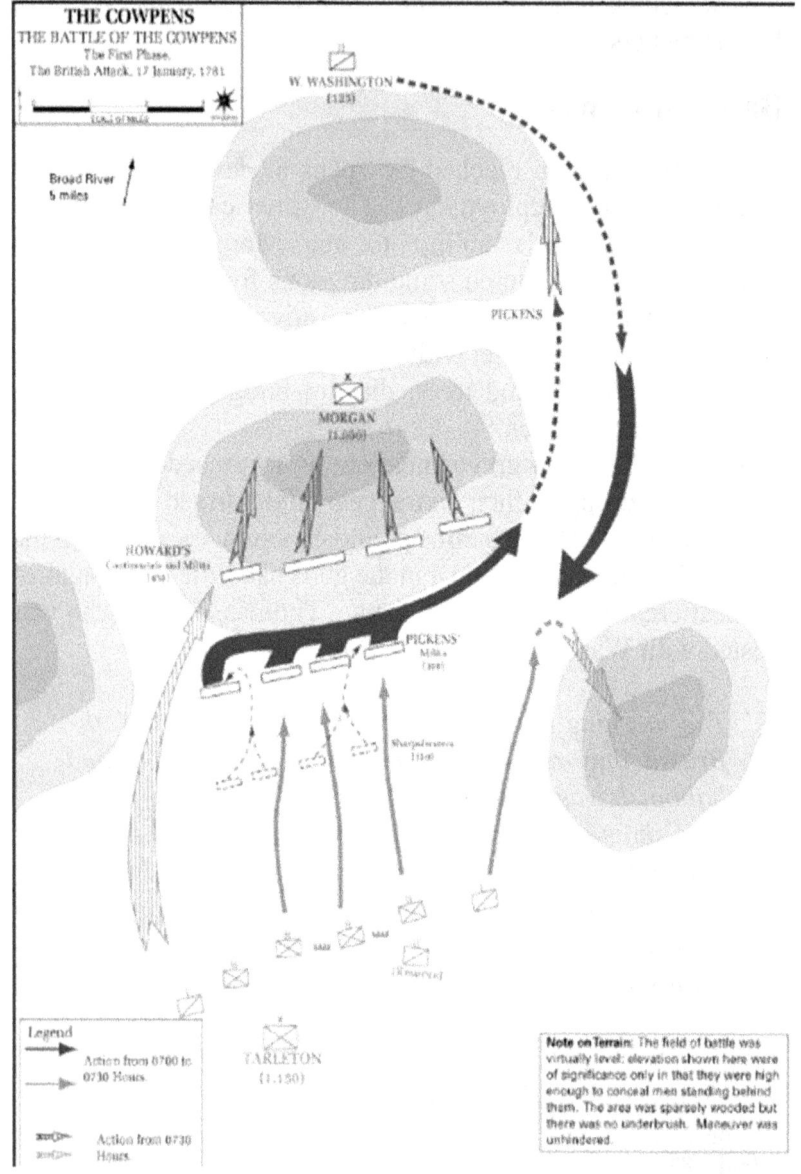

General Morgan noted in a letter to a friend after the battle that Tarleton's troops, *formed into one Line, Raised a Prodigious Yell, and came Running at us as if they Intended to eat us up.*"[30] Morgan and his officers shouted out orders and words of encouragement to the rattled militia, urging them to stand firm. Joseph McJunkin, a South Carolina officer in the militia line, recalled that Morgan

> *Walked behind and through the ranks everywhere, all the time cracking jokes and encouraging the men, and said, 'Boys, squinney well, and don't touch a trigger until you see the whites of their eyes.*[31]

As Tarleton's infantry advanced in open order towards the American skirmish line, Morgan's riflemen peppered them with "*a heavy & galling fire.*"[32] A few inexperienced British soldiers responded with unauthorized shots, but most held their fire and continued forward, driving the riflemen back to the militia line.

General Morgan placed a handful of riflemen a few paces in front of the militia line to begin the action there. One of these riflemen recalled,

> *Morgan had picked out eleven of us who were to fire as a signal for opening the ball, and placed us in front several paces…When they came near enough for us to distinguish plainly their faces, we picked out our man and let* fly.[33]

---

[30] "General Morgan to William Snickers, 26 January 1781," Horatio Gates Papers, NY Historical Society
[31] Babits, 87
[32] Showman and Conrad, eds., "General Daniel Morgan to General Nathanael Greene, 19 January, 1781," *The Papers of General Nathanael Greene,* Vol. 7, 154
[33] Babits, 90

Their shots precipitated a devastating fire upon the British as each militia battalion unleashed a well aimed volley into their ranks. *"The effect of the fire was considerable,"* noted one British officer, *"it produced something like a recoil."*[34] One British company lost two thirds of its strength.[35] Despite the heavy fire, Tarleton's men pressed on and forced the militia to retreat before most had a chance to fire a second time. Their withdrawal was not disorderly, however. A continental officer in the third line observed that the militia,

> *Being overpowered by the superior number of the enemy...retreated, but in very good order, not seeming to be in the least* confused.[36]

The retreating militia sought safety behind the third line but were attacked by a large party of Tarleton's horsemen before they reached it. One soldier recalled that Tarleton's cavalry

> *Overtook us and began to take a few hacks at some...But in a few moments, Colonel Washington's cavalry was among them like a whirlwind, and the poor fellows began to keel from their horses without being able to remount. The shock was so sudden and violent they could not stand it, and immediately betook themselves to flight.*[37]

The timely arrival of Washington's dragoons spared the militia and rallied their spirits. General Morgan did his part to reform them as well, riding up to them with his sword raised, declaring, *"Form, form, my brave fellows! Give them one more*

---

[34] Ibid. 92
[35] Ibid.
[36] William Seymour, "A Journal of the Southern Expedition, 1780-1783," *The Pennsylvania Magazine of History and Biography,* Vol. 7, 294
[37] John M. Roberts, ed., "James Collins", *Autobiography of a Revolutionary Soldier,* (NY: Arno Press, 1979), 57

fire and the day is Ours. Old Morgan was never beaten."[38] Many of the militia did rally and returned to the fight to help decide the battle's outcome.

While Morgan strove to reform the militia, his main line braced for a confrontation with Tarleton. The British briefly halted their advance after breaking the militia line to dress and close ranks. They were well within range of Morgan's riflemen in the third line and endured a warm fire from them. The fight intensified as the British resumed their march. *"When the Enemy advanced to our Line, they received a well-directed and incessant Fire,"* noted Morgan, who had returned to his main line once the panic among the militia had subsided.[39] Thomas Young was especially impressed by the continental volleys from the third line:

> *When the regulars fired, it seemed like one sheet of flame from right to left. Oh! It was beautiful.*[40]

Henry Wells of the Delaware continentals was impressed by General Morgan, whose, *"powerful & trumpet like voice...drove fear from every bosom, and gave new energies to every arm."*[41]

The British responded with their own heavy fire. Lieutenant-Colonel Tarleton observed, *"The fire on both sides was well supported, and produced much slaughter."*[42] Another participant noted that both sides *"Maintained their ground with great bravery; and the conflict...was obstinate and bloody."*[43]

---

[38] Ibid.
[39] Showman and Conrad, eds. "General Daniel Morgan to General Nathanael Greene, 19 January, 1781", *The Papers of General Nathanael Greene,* Vol. 7, 154
[40] Scheer and Rankin, eds., " Memoir of Thomas Young", 430
[41] Babits, 100
[42] Tarleton, 216
[43] C. Stedman, *A History of the Origin, Progress, and Termination of the American War*, Vol. 2, (London: 1794), 321-322

Colonel Tarleton tried to break the deadlock by striking at Morgan's right flank. He recalled,

> *As the contest between the British infantry in the front line and the continentals seemed equally balanced, neither retreating,* [I] *thought the advance of the 71st* [battalion] *into line, and a movement of the cavalry in reserve to threaten the enemy's right flank, would put a victorious period to the action.*[44]

The right flank of the American line was held by Captain Andrew Wallace's company of Virginia continentals. Among the trees on their right, a few yards in advance of them, were North Carolina riflemen under Major Charles McDowell. These were the same riflemen who began the battle on the skirmish line. They were now delivering long range shots into Tarleton's left flank.

In order to turn the American flank, Tarleton had to go through the riflemen and around the Virginia continentals. His dragoons did this, scattering the riflemen and passing around Captain Wallace's right. Just as they were about to cause havoc in the rear, they were intercepted by Colonel Washington's cavalry and forced to retreat.

The American line was still in jeopardy, however, because British troops from the 71st battalion, trailing the British dragoons, flanked the Virginians. Colonel John Howard, commander of the continentals, explained what happened:

> *Seeing my right flank was exposed to the enemy, I attempted to change the front of Wallace's company. In doing this, some confusion ensued, and first a part and then the whole of the company commenced a retreat. The officers along the line seeing this and*

---

[44] Tarleton, 217

supposing that orders had been given for a retreat, faced their men about and moved off.[45]

General Morgan, upset by the unauthorized withdrawal, confronted Colonel Howard, who calmed Morgan by proclaiming that, *"Men were not beaten who retreated in that order."*[46] Morgan described what happened next:

> *We retired in good Order about 50 Paces, formed, advanced on the Enemy & gave them a fortunate Volley which threw **them** into* Disorder.[47]

In truth, Tarleton's men were disordered prior to the American volley. The initial withdrawal of the main American line prompted the British to rush forward. *"They are coming on like a mob,"* Colonel Washington told Howard, *"give them a fire and I will charge them."*[48] Colonel Howard did precisely that, ordering his men, who had reloaded on the march, to face about. *"In a minute we had a perfect line,"* recalled Howard.[49] He continued,

> *The enemy were now very near us. Our men commenced a very destructive fire, which they little expected, and a few rounds occasioned great disorder in their ranks. While in this confusion, I ordered a*

---

[45] Henry Steele Commager and Richard B. Morris, eds., "Lieutenant Colonel John Eager Howard's Account of Cowpens," *The Spirit of Seventy-Six*, (NY: Castle Books, 2002), 1156

[46] Ibid.

[47] Showman and Conrad, eds., "General Daniel Morgan to General Nathanael Greene, 19 January,1781," *The Papers of General Nathanael Greene,* Vol. 7, 154

[48] Babits, 117

[49] Commager and Morris, eds., "Lieutenant Colonel John Eager Howard's Account," *The Spirit of Seventy-Six,* 1156

charge with the bayonet, which order was obeyed with great alacrity.[50]

General Morgan applauded Colonel Howard's leadership and described the impact of the American bayonet charge:

> *Lt. Colonel Howard observing* [the enemy's disorder] *gave orders for the Line to charge Bayonets, which was done with such Address that they fled with the utmost Precipitation, leaving the Field Pieces* [cannon] *in our Possession. We pushed our Advantage so effectually, that they never had an Opportunity of rallying.*[51]

Morgan expressed his great pleasure with the outcome of Lieutenant-Colonel Howard's bold actions, declaring to the commander

> *My dear Howard, you have given me victory and I love and honor you; but had you failed in your charge which you risked without orders, I would have shot you.*[52]

Howard replied, very likely with a smile, "*Had I failed, there would have been no need of shooting me.*"[53]

Morgan's victory at Cowpens was nearly total. Tarleton's force was shattered; he lost over 800 men (killed, wounded, or captured).[54] Only Tarleton and most of his dragoons escaped,

---

[50] Ibid. 1157

[51] Showman and Conrad, eds., "General Daniel Morgan to General Nathanael Greene, 19 January, 1781," *The Papers of General Nathanael Greene,* Vol. 7, 154

[52] Jim Piecuch and John Beakes, "*Cool Deliberate Courage*": *John Eager Howard in the American Revolution*, (Charleston, SC: Nautical and Aviation Publishing, 2009), 65

[53] Ibid.

[54] Babits, 143

the latter in disgrace when they ignored Tarleton's order to assist the infantry and fled.

News of Morgan's victory sparked celebrations throughout the country. Colonel Otho Williams of Maryland, who was with General Greene's army in Cheraws, informed Morgan that

> *We have had a feu de joie* [celebratory gunfire], *drunk all your healths, swore you were the finest fellows on earth, and love you, if possible, more than ever.*[55]

Congress joyously received news of the victory in mid-February and awarded General Morgan a gold medal. Several of his subordinates were also recognized with silver medals and swords.[56] Morgan himself was quite pleased, writing to a friend after the battle:

> *When you left me you remember I was desirous to have a stroke at Tarleton. My wishes are Gratified & I have Given him a devil of a whipping, a more complete victory was never more obtained.*[57]

---

[55] Showman and Conrad, eds., "Colonel Otho Williams to General Daniel Morgan, 26 January, 1781, Footnote 19," *The Papers of General Nathanael Greene,* Vol. 7, 161

[56] Ford, ed.,, "9 March, 1781," *Journals of the Continental Congress,* Vol. 19, 246

[57] "General Morgan to William Snickers, 26 January 1781," Horatio Gates Papers, NY Historical Society

Morgan's Retreat Northward

Chapter Ten

"Nothing Will Help Me But Rest" : 1781

General Morgan had little time to bask in his victory; his troops were still in danger from General Cornwallis and the main British army to the east. Morgan led his troops and the British prisoners able to march northward across the Broad River. His objective was two-fold, to move the hundreds of British prisoners out of reach of Cornwallis and to reunite with General Greene as fast as possible. He left behind at Cowpens scores of wounded men from both sides under the care of local militia and a handful of surgeons.

As Morgan's force marched into North Carolina, most of the Georgia and South Carolina militia that were with him departed. Those that remained turned northeastward on January 23rd, and crossed the Catawba River. Morgan halted at Sherald's Ford, on the east side of the river and sent the British prisoners onwards to Virginia under guard of the Virginia militia, whose time of service had expired. The troops that remained with General Morgan were essentially his original force of less than 300 continentals, Lieutenant-Colonel Washington's 80 odd dragoons, and a handful of North Carolina militia. Hopeful that many more militia would join him at the Catawba, Morgan posted his small force to guard the river crossings and wrote to General Greene for instructions.[1] In a second letter the following day, Morgan included

---

[1] Showman and Conrad, eds., "General Daniel Morgan to General Nathanael Greene, 23 January, 1781," *The Papers of General Nathanael Greene,* Vol. 7, 178

disturbing news; his sciatica had returned and was so painful and debilitating that he feared he could not remain in the field:

> *It is a ciatick pain in my hip, that renders me entirely incapable of active services. I have had it these three wks past, but on getting wet the other day it has ceazed me more violently, which gives me great pain when I ride, and at times when I am walking or standing am obliged to set down in the place it takes me, as quick as if I were shot. I am so well acquainted with this disorder, that I am convinced nothing will help me but rest, and were I to attempt to go through the winters campaign I am satisfied it would Totally disable me from further service.*[2]

Morgan acknowledged the harm his departure would bring to the army but assured General Greene that his condition left him with no other choice but to leave the field to rest and recover.[3]

Despite his poor health, General Morgan remained with the army for three more weeks. The first of these weeks was spent on the east bank of the Catawba River waiting for General Cornwallis to advance.

Hampered by a large baggage train and heavy rains that flooded the numerous creeks and turned the roads into a quagmire, Cornwallis's pursuit of Morgan proceeded at a crawl. In frustration, Cornwallis took the extreme measure of destroying most of his baggage and wagons on January 25th, to

---

[2] Showman and Conrad, eds., "General Daniel Morgan to General Nathanael Greene, 24 January, 1781," *The Papers of General Nathanael Greene,* Vol. 7, 190-191

[3] Ibid.

quicken his march. Heavy rain undermined his efforts and flooded the Catawba River, stranding the British army on the west bank, just out of reach of Morgan, who was posted on the other side. It was not until January 31st that the river receded enough to allow the British to ford the river.

Defending the crossing points against Cornwallis's 2,500 man army were Morgan's 300 continentals and 800 North Carolina militia who had arrived during the week under General William Davidson.[4] A large detachment of these men, led by General Davidson himself, fiercely resisted Cornwallis's late night crossing at Cowans Ford. General Cornwallis described the crossing in a letter to Lord Germain.

> *Full of confidence in the zeal and gallantry of Brigadier-general O' Hara* [and his men] *I ordered them to…* [cross the river and] *not to fire until they gained the opposite bank. Their behavior justified my high opinion of them; for a constant fire from the enemy, in a ford upwards of five hundred yards wide, in many places up to their middle, with a rocky bottom and strong current, made no impression on their cool and determined valour, nor checked their passage.*[5]

Davidson's men inflicted scores of casualties on the British, but failed to halt their crossing. As the British reached the other side of the river, General Davidson's militia fled eastward. They did so without their commander, who was killed in the engagement.

---

[4] Showman and Conrad, eds., "General Daniel Morgan to General Nathanael Greene, 29 January, 1781," *The Papers of General Nathanael Greene,* Vol. 7, 215

[5] Tarleton, "Cornwallis to Lord Germain, 17 March, 1781," 262

The British crossing at Cowans Ford left General Morgan, who had been joined a day earlier by General Greene and a tiny escort of dragoons, with no option but to withdraw northeast through Salisbury and across the Yadkin River. General Greene had already ordered the rest of the southern army on the Pee Dee River to march north to the Yadkin to unite with Morgan. After a difficult march across muddy roads, Morgan and Greene reached the Yadkin and used the handful of boats available to cross. Once again Cornwallis found himself stranded on the opposite side by yet another rain swollen river that could not be forded.

After two days of tense rest and anxiety, General Greene ordered Morgan's flying army to resume its march north, this time to Guilford Courthouse. Greene sent a dispatch rider to re-direct the rest of the army to Guilford, where he hoped to finally unite the two forces and gather more militia. Morgan's troops reached Guilford Courthouse on February 9th, a day after the rest of the army. General Greene held a council of war with General Morgan, General Isaac Huger (who led the main army to Guilford, and Colonel Otho Williams.

Greene informed the officers that the southern army numbered just 1426 men, many who were badly armed and clothed. Another 600 militia were in camp, also poorly armed.[6] General Cornwallis had somewhere between 2,500 to 3,000 troops and was still in pursuit. Greene asked his subordinates a simple question. Should the American southern army stop retreating and risk a battle? The council responded

---

[6] Showman and Conrad, eds., "Proceedings of a Council of War, 9 February, 1781," *The Papers of General Nathanael Greene,* Vol. 7, 261

unanimously, they should avoid a general action and retreat immediately across the Dan River into Virginia.[7]

The council's decision, which General Greene agreed with, precipitated what became known as the Race to the Dan, a four day chase between General Greene and General Cornwallis to the Dan River and Virginia. Greene raced north without his Flying Army commander. Wracked by several ailments, General Morgan was physically unable to continue and was granted a leave of absence from General Greene in the hope that some rest might restore Morgan's health.

Home to Virginia

It took General Morgan several weeks to reach home, his painful condition forced brief stops at General Robert Lawson's residence in Prince Edward County and Carter Harrison's estate in Cumberland County. It was at the latter's residence that Morgan wrote to General Greene with an update on his condition:

> *I have been doctoring these several days, thinking to be able to take the field again. But I find I get worse. My pains now are accompanied by a fever every day.*[8]

General Morgan also offered advice to Greene on how to handle the militia:

---

[7] Ibid., 261-262
[8] Showman and Conrad, eds., "General Daniel Morgan to General Nathanael Greene, 20 February, 1781," *The Papers of General Nathanael Greene,* Vol. 7, 324

I expect Lord Cornwallis will push you until you are obliged to fight him, on which much will depend. You have, from what I see, a great number of militia. If they fight, you will beat Cornwallis; if not, he will beat you, and perhaps cut your regulars to pieces, which will be losing all our hopes. I am informed that among the militia will be found a number of old soldiers. I think it would be advisable to select them from among the militia, and put them in the ranks with the regulars; select the riflemen also, and fight them on the flanks, under enterprising officers who are acquainted with that kind of fighting; and put the militia in the centre, with some picked troops in their rear, with orders to shoot down the first man that runs. If anything will succeed, a disposition of this kind will.[9]

General Greene likely appreciated Morgan's advice and followed much of it at the Battle of Guilford Courthouse in March, but he opted not to post riflemen in the rear of the militia to shoot those who broke ranks. General Edward Stevens, who commanded a brigade of Virginia militia at Guilford, reportedly did post such troops, however. Fortunately, there are no accounts that these picked men fired upon their fellow soldiers. Apparently there was no need to do so as Steven's men fought well at Guilford Courthouse.

For the rest of the spring of 1781 Daniel Morgan's primary focus was to recover his health. Civil unrest in nearby Hampshire County in May over high taxes and Virginia's impressment of supplies for the army hastened Morgan return

---

[9] Ibid.

to the field, albeit locally. He commanded a force of militia to suppress the disturbances and restored order in northwestern Virginia. Once this was accomplished, Morgan hurried home to assist the war effort to in central Virginia.

Spurred on by what amounted to a British invasion of Virginia under General Cornwallis in May, as well as an improvement in his health and a desperate appeal from the Marquis de LaFayette, the newly arrived American commander in Virginia, General Morgan worked hard in Frederick County to raise troops to reinforce LaFayette. The young French commander wrote to Morgan in late May and appealed to his sense of public duty and his ego in an effort to convince the Old Waggoner to retake the field:

> *I do Very Much want Your assistance, and Beg leave to Request it Both as a lover of public welfare and as a private friend of Yours. I Ever Had a Great Esteem for Riflemen and Have done My Best to See them much Employed in our Armies – But in this little Corps they are particularly Wanting, Your influence Can do more than orders from the Executive. Permit me, therefore, My dear Sir, Entirely to depend Upon your Exertions.*[10]

General Morgan spent all of June trying to raise and equip not only a body of riflemen, but also several troops (detachments) of cavalry. He finally joined General LaFayette's army in July, just a day after LaFayette had fallen

---

[10] Stanley J. Idzerda, ed., "General LaFayette to General Morgan, 20 May, 1781," *LaFayette in the Age of the American Revolution*, Vol. 4, (Ithica and London: Cornell University Press, 1981), 117-118

into a trap set by Cornwallis near Jamestown. The Americans managed to avoid a significant defeat on the banks of the James River, but the engagement at Green Spring made clear that General Cornwallis still had the upper hand in the Old Dominion.

Cornwallis concentrated his forces in Portsmouth in July and prepared to implement instructions from his superior, General Henry Clinton in New York, to establish a naval post in the Chesapeake. Cornwallis selected the town of York, on the York River and near the mouth of the bay, and prepared to move his force there. Before they abandoned Portsmouth, Cornwallis sent Lieutenant Colonel Banastre Tarleton and his British Legion on an expedition westward to destroy supply magazines and gather forage.

General Morgan, who was encamped with the American army on the northern bank of the James River at Malvern Hill (about 70 miles upriver from Portsmouth) was given another opportunity to engage Tarleton. Both Morgan and General Anthony Wayne attempted to intercept Tarleton on his way back to Portsmouth, but Tarleton successfully avoided them and returned unscathed.

By the end of July, Morgan's health once again deteriorated to the point that he was compelled to leave the army and return home to rest. Regrettably, he would not return to the army.

While Morgan rested in Frederick County, the military fortunes of the British and Americans shifted significantly. General Washington, who was with the main army in New York, launched a coordinated movement with the French to trap Cornwallis at Yorktown. The allies shifted thousands of troops to the south and, along with a power French naval fleet, bottled up Cornwallis and commenced a siege of their post at

Yorktown. The decisive battle of the Revolutionary War had commenced in Morgan's home state, and he was too ill to join it. About a week before the siege began, with numerous signs pointing to success for the allies, General Morgan wrote a heartfelt letter to General Washington to offer his high esteem for the American commander and his regret that he could not be there to assist:

> *At a time like this, when your excellency's every moment must be devoted to the grand business of America, I know you can have but little leisure for private letters – but the feelings of my heart will not permit me to be silent: I cannot avoid congratulating your excellency on the present favorable appearance of our affairs: I cannot avoid telling your excellency how much I wish you success, and how much I wish that the state of my health would permit me to afford my small services on this great occasion. Such has been my peculiar fate, that during the whole course of the present war, I have never, on any important event, had the honor of serving particularly under your excellency. It is a misfortune I have ever sincerely lamented. There is nothing on earth would have given me more real pleasure than to have made this campaign under your excellency's eye, to have shared the danger, and let me add, the glory too, which I am almost confident will be acquired. But as my health will not admit of my rejoining the army immediately, I must beg leave to repeat to your excellency my most earnest wishes for your success, and for your personal safety.*[11]

---

[11] "General Morgan to General Washington, 20 September, 1781," Theodorus Bailey Myers Collection, Series 5, # 945, NY Public Library

General Washington's reply, on October 5th, expressed his appreciation to Morgan for his *"kind expressions of good wishes"* and his earnest desire for Morgan's quick recovery. It was Washington's praise for Morgan's service to the country that undoubtedly meant the most to Morgan:

> *Surrounded as I am with a great Variety of Concerns on the present Occasion, I can yet find Time to answer your Letter of the 20th ulto., which I have received with much Satisfaction; not only as it is filled with such warm Expressions of Desire for my Success on the present Expedition; but as it breathes the Spirit and Ardor of a Veteran Soldier, who, tho impaired in the Service of his Country, yet retains the Sentiments of a Soldier in the firmest Degree.*
>
> *Be assured, that I most sincerely lament your present Situation, and esteem it a peculiar Loss to the United States, that you are at this Time unable to render your Services in the Field. I most sincerely thank you for the kind Expressions of your good Wishes, and earnestly hope that you may soon be restored to that Share of Health which you may desire, and with which you may again be usefull to your Country in the same eminent Degree, as has already distinguished your Conduct.*[12]

General Daniel Morgan's service in the Revolutionary War effectively ended in the fall of 1781. Washington's victory at Yorktown convinced British leaders to negotiate an end to the war. Military activity in America during the long eighteen

---

[12] Fitzpatrick, ed., "General Washington to General Morgan, 5 October, 1781," *Writings of George Washington*, Vol. 23, 174

month period of negotiations diminished considerably and came to an official close with the adoption of the Treaty of Paris in 1783.

Epilogue

Daniel Morgan was in his mid-forties when the Revolutionary War ended and like most Americans, he was eager to move on from the long struggle. As a prominent and heroic figure in the community, Morgan prospered. He completed construction (reportedly with the help of Hessian prisoners of war) of a two story stone home eleven miles from Winchester in 1782 that he named "Saratoga" and shared ownership of a new grist mill with Nathaniel Burwell, a member of a prominent Tidewater family with extensive land holdings in Frederick County.[13]

Daniel Morgan's military service allowed him to become a prominent landowner as well with thousands of acres of land granted to him in Kentucky. Morgan significantly expanded his holdings into western Virginia and the Northwest Territory with additional land purchases that amounted to over 250,000 acres.[14]

Morgan also reportedly fathered a son, Willoughby, sometime after the war in the mid-1780's. His mother remains a mystery and Morgan himself never formally acknowledged his son, sending him at an early age to be raised in South Carolina.[15]

---

[13] Higginbotham, 172-173, 176-177
[14] Graham, 413
[15] Higginbotham, 183

In 1794 Daniel Morgan briefly returned to military service under the command of President George Washington. Morgan commanded Virginia militia who had been called up by Washington to help suppress the Whiskey Rebellion that had erupted in western Pennsylvania. The arrival of thousands of troops under Washington, as well as Light Horse Harry Lee and Daniel Morgan, quickly ended the unrest and demonstrated that the federal government did indeed have the power to enforce its authority.

Morgan, who was an ardent Federalist, next ran for Congress, losing his first election, but winning a seat in the House of Representatives in 1797. Morgan's tenure in office was brief and relatively uneventful. Declining health caused him to not seek reelection and he returned to private life in Frederick County. By the summer of 1800, Morgan's infirmities caused him to move in with his youngest daughter in Winchester.[16] It was there, on July 6, 1802, that General Daniel Morgan passed away.

---

[16] Graham. 448

Appendix

General Daniel Morgan, "An Autobiography", *The Historical Magazine and Notes and Queries Concerning the Antiquities, History and Biography of America, 2nd Series* **Vol. 9 (1871), 379**

To give my history in the war: I must begin with 1774, when I served a very active and hard campaign under Lord Dunmore. We had beaten the Indians, brought them to order, and confirmed a treat of peace; and on our return home, at the mouth of the river Hockhockin, we were informed of hostilities being offered to our brethren, the people of Boston. We, as an army victorious, formed ourselves into a society, pledging our words of honor to each other to assist our brethren in Boston, in case hostilities should commence, which did on the 19th of April ensuing, at Lexington. I was appointed a captain of riflemen, and march with haste to Boston. In a few days, I raised ninety-six men and set out for Boston – reached that place in twenty-one days from the time I marched, bad weather included, nor did I leave a man behind. I remained at that place inactive for six weeks, as the enemy was shut up in Boston; when with my own consent, detached to Quebec with the command of three rifle companies, viz.: my own, and two from Pennsylvania, under the command of Captains Smith and Hendricks. The latter fell at the attack on the garrison. I was under the command of Gen. Arnold, with whom I marched through the woods and led the van. For a description of that march, I refer to a journal kept by Col. Heth, who was a lieutenant in my company. We reached Canada, I think, on the 3rd of November, in a most shocking condition – destitute of provisions and of every comfort. We marched to Point Levi, recruited the troops, and on the night of the 13th, by the means of some small craft that we found drew up in the guts, and some bark canoes that we purchased from the Indians, crossed the river between two men-of-war, and within point-blank shot, slipping through undiscovered. Here I led the forlorn hope – went up Gen. Wolf's cove, and formed on the plains of Abraham, where I expected to be attacked, but was not discovered. We then proceeded on to Caldwell's house. The enemy had a strong guard in the building, which we attacked and carried sword in hand. Here I also commanded the forlorn hope. We then besieged the place for several days; but finding our ammunition was wet, we raised the siege, and marched to Point Aux Trembles, twenty miles distant from Quebec. Finding there that the rifle powder was dry, I marched back with the three rifle companies under my command, and renewed the siege. On my return, I took several prisoners. I kept up the siege until Gen. Montgomery arrived, when an attack upon the town was determined upon, and in a few days carried into effect. Here I was again appointed to the command of the forlorn hope, on the river St. Charles, under Gen. Arnold. The general having been wounded in the leg while under the walls, and before we got into the town, I sent him off in the care of two of my men, and took his place in the command. For although there were three field officers, they would not take the command, alleging that I had seen service and they had not, which reflected great credit on their judgement. I had to attack a two-gun battery, supported by Capt. McCloud and fifty regular troops. The first gun that was fired missed us – the second flashed, when I ordered the ladders, borne on the shoulders of the men, to be raised. The order was immediately obeyed; and for fear the business might not be executed with spirit, I mounted myself, and leaped into the town. The first man among Capt. McCloud's guard who was panic-struck, made a faint resistance, and run into a house that joined the two-gun batter and platform, where the guard was posted. I lighted on the end of a great gun, which hurt me very much, and perhaps saved my life, as I bell from the gun on the platform, where the bayonets were not directed. Col. Charles Porterfield, who was a cadet in my company, was the first man that followed me, and all the men came after him as fast as they had room to jump down. All this was performed in a few seconds. I ordered the men to fire into the house, and follow up with their pikes (for in addition to our rifles, we were also armed with long espontoons), which they did, and drove the guard into the street. I went through a sally port at the end of the platform; met the retreating guard in the street, and ordered them to lay down their arms if they expected quarters. They took me at my word, and every man threw his arms down. We then made a charge on the battery, and took it sword in hand – and pushing on, took everything that opposed us at the point of the bayonet till we arrived at the barrier gate. Here I was ordered to wait for Gen. Montgomery, and a fatal order it was. It prevented me from taking the garrison, as I had already made half the town prisoners. The sally port through the barrier was standing open; the guard had left it, and the people were running from the upper town in whole platoons, giving themselves up as prisoners, to get out of the way of the confusion which might shortly ensue. I went up to the edge of the upper town…with an interpreter, to see what was going on, as the firing had ceased. Finding no person in arms at all, I returned and called a council of what few officers I had with me, for the greater part of our force had missed their way, and had not got into the town.

Here I was overruled by sound judgement and good reasoning. It was said, in the first place, that if I went on I should break orders; in the next, that I had more prisoners than I had men, and that if I left them they might break out, retake the battery we had just captured, and cut off our retreat. It was further urged that Gen. Montgomery was certainly coming down along the river St. Lawrence, and would join us in a few minutes, and that we were sure of conquest if we acted with caution and prudence. To these good reasons I gave up my own opinion, and lost the town. For Gen. Montgomery, having cut down an out picket, was marching up to the two-gun battery, when an unlucky shot put an end to his existence, killing at the same time Capt. Cheseman, Major McPherson, and some others of his good officers. Upon this Col. Donald Campbell, then quartermaster general, undertook to order a retreat. We were then left to shift for ourselves, but did not yet know the extent of the misfortunes which had occurred, or it was still in our power to have taken the garrison.

Select Correspondence of Daniel Morgan

Frederick County Committee to Captain Daniel Morgan
June 22, 1775

In obedience to a resolve of the Continental Congress, dated 14th of June, 1775, viz.: "That six companies of expert riflemen be immediately raised in Pennsylvania, two in Maryland, and two in Virginia; that each company, as soon as completed, shall march and join the army near Boston; to be there employed as light infantry, under the command of the chief officer of that army –"this committee, reposing a special trust in the courage, conduct, and reverence for liberty under the spirit of the British constitution, of Daniel Morgan, Esq., do hereby certify that we have unanimously appointed him to command a Virginia company of riflemen to march from this county. He is hereby directed to act, by exercising the officers and soldiers under his command, taking particular care to provide them with the necessaries, as the 1st Resolves of Congress directs; and that he is from time to time to follow such directions as he shall receive from the commander-in-chief, or any other of his superior officers of the continental army.

General Washington to Colonel Daniel Morgan
August 16, 1777

Sir:

After you receive this, you will march, as soon as possible, with the corps under your command, to Peekskill, taking with you all the baggage belonging to it. When you arrive there, you will take directions from General Putnam, who, I expect, will have vessels provided to carry you to Albany. The approach of the enemy in that quarter has made a further reinforcement necessary, and I know of no corps so likely to check their progress, in proportion to its number, as that under your command. I have great dependence on you, your officers and men, and I am persuaded you will do honor to yourselves, and essential services to your country.

Daniel Morgan to Congress, 18 July, 1779

From these considerations I could not but flatter myself, that if at any time a respectable corps of light troops should be form'd I should be honored with the command of it – my experience as a partisan and the services I had done my country in that way I thought justified my expectations – I am however disappointed, such a corps has been form'd and the command of it given to another.

As it is generally known that I commanded the light troops of our army and that this command is now taken from me, it will Naturally be judged that this change of officers has taken place either on account of some misconduct in me, or on account my want of capacity – I cannot therefore but feel deeply effected with this injury done my reputation, by reducing me from a respectable station in the army…to the Command of a few men.[53]

It may perhaps be offered that my rank in the army did not intitle me to such a command, to which I beg leave to observe that I am an older officer than either of the gentlemen who have succeeded me – that at the time when thay ware enjoying the

---

[53] Ibid.

sweets of Domestick life – I was engaged in Actual service and undergoing the hardships of war.

I can with sincerity declare that I engaged in the service of my country with a full determination to continue in it as long as my services were wanting – I must conclude from what has happened, that my country has no more occasion for me, I therefore beg leave to retire.

General Morgan to General Gates Nov. 9, 1780

I am informed you are to be recall'd, for which I am sorry and glad both, for I don't think it will be in the power of any gent. Officer who commands in this country to add to his reputation, whatever he may loose from it. I was informed that you was apprehensive I had joined a party against you. I intended to convince you to the contrary by my conduct, and not mention the matter to you; but as you are going away, that will not be in my power; must therefore tell, on my word and Honor, that I never had the most distant thought of such a thing nor was a thing of that Kind ever mentioned to me, or I would have let you a known it immediately, for I despise party matters as I do the devil.[27]

---

[27] Clark, ed., "Gen. Daniel Morgan to Genl. Gates, 9 November, 1780," *The State Records of North Carolina*, Vol. 14, 730

General Morgan to General Greene, January 19, 1781

Dear Sir,

The Troops I had the Honor to command have been so fortunate as to obtain a compleat Victory over a Detachment from the British Army commanded by Lt. Colonel Tarlton. The Action happened on the 17th Instant about Sunrise at the Cowpens. It perhaps would be well to remark, for the Honour of the American Arms, that Altho the Progress of this Corps was marked with Burnings and Devastations & altho' they have waged the most cruel Warfare, not a man was killed during this Contest received so many Lessons of Humanity, I should flatter myself that this might teach them a little, but I fear they are incorrigible.

To give you a just Idea of our Operations it will be necessary to inform you, that on the 14th Instant having received certain Intelligence that Lord Cornwallis and Lt. Colonel Tarlton were both in Motion, and that their movements clearly indicated their Intentions of dislodging me, I abandoned my Encampment at Grendales Ford on Pacolet [River] and on the 16th in the Evening took Possession of a Post, about seven miles from the Cherokee Ford on Broad River. My original Position subjected me at once to the Operations of both Cornwallis and Tarlton, and in Case of a Defeat, my Retreat might easily have been cut off. My Situation at the Cowpens enabled me to improve any Advantages I might gain, and to provide better for my own Security, should I be unfortunate. These Reasons induced me to take this Post at the Risque of its wearing the face of a Retreat.

I received regular Intelligence of the Enemy's Movements from the Time they were first in Motion. On the Evening of the

16th Inst. they took Possession of the Ground I had removed from in the Morning, distant from the Scene of Action about 12 miles. An Hour before Day light one of my Scouts returned and informed me that Lt. Colonel Tarlton had advanced within five miles of our Camp. On this Information I hastened to form as good a Disposition as Circumstances would admit, and from the alacrity of the Troops we were soon prepared to receive them. The Light Infantry commanded by Lt. Colonel Howard and the Virginia Militia, under the command of Maj. Triplette were formed on a rising Ground, and extended a Line in Front. The 3rd Regiment of Dragoons under Lt. Colonel Washington, were so posted at such a Distance in their Rear as not to be subjected to the Line of Fire directed at them, and to be so near as to be able to charge the Enemy, should they be broke. The Volunteers of North Carolina, South Carolina & Georgia under the Command of the brace and valuable Colonel Pickens, were situated to guard the Flanks. Maj. McDowell, of the NC Volunteers, was posted on the right Flank in Front of the Line 150 yards & Major Cunningham with the Georgia Volunteers on the left at the same distance in Front. Colonels Brandon & Thomas of the S Carolinians were posted on the right of Major McDowell and Colonels Hays and McCall of the same Corps, on the left of Major Cunningham. Capts. Tate & Buchannan with the Augusta Riflemen to support the right of the line.

The Enemy drew up in single Line of Battle 400 yards in Front of our advanced Corps. The first Battalion of the 71st Regt. Was opposed to our Right; the 7th Regt. To our Left. The Infantry of the Legion to our Center. The Light Companies on their Flanks. In Front moved two Pieces of Artillery. Lt. Colonel Tarlton with his Cavalry was posted in the Rear of his Line. The Disposition of Battle being thus formed, small

Parties of Riflemen were detached to skirmish with the Enemy, upon which their whole Line moved on with the greatest Impetuosity shouting as they advanced. McDowell & Cunningham gave them a heavy & galling Fire & retreated to the Regiments intended for their Support. The whole of Colonel Picken's Command then kept up a Fire by Regiments retreating agreeable to their Orders. When the Enemy advanced to our Line, they received a well-directed and incessant Fire, but their Numbers being superior to ours, they gained our flanks, which obliged us to change our Position. We retired in good Order about 50 Paces, formed, advanced on the Enemy & gave them a fortunate Volley which threw them into Disorder. Lt. Colonel Howard observing this gave orders for the Line to charge Bayonets, which was done with such Address that they fled with the utmost Precipitation, leaving the Field Pieces in our Possession. We pushed our Advantage so effectually, that they never had an Opportunity of rallying, had their Intentions been ever so good.

Lt.. Colonel Washington having been informed that Tarlton was Cutting [down] our Riflemen on the left Flank pushed forward & charged them with such Firmness that instead of attempting to recover the Fate of the Day, which one would have expected from an officer of his Splendid Character, broke and fled.

The Enemy's whole Force were now bent solely in providing for their Safety in Flight. The List of their killed, wounded and Prisoners, will inform you with what Effect. Tarlton, with the small Remains of his Cavalry & a few scattering Infantry he had mounted on his Waggon Horses made their Escape. He was Persued 24 miles, but owing to our having taken a wrong Trail at first, we never could overtake him.

As I was obliged to move off of the Field of Action in the morning to secure the Prisoners, I cannot be so accurate as to the killed & wounded of the Enemy as I could wish. From the Reports of an officer I sent to view the Ground, there was 100 non Commissioned Officers & Privates. Prisoners independent of the wounded, & the Militia are taking up straglers continually. 29 Commissioned Officers have fell into our Hands. Their Rank ect. Ect. You will see by an enclosed List. The Officers I have paroled. The Privates I am now conveying by the shortest Rout to Salisburrey. Two Standards, two Field Pieces, 35 Waggons, a travelling Forge, & all their Music are ours. Their Baggage, which was immense, they have in great measure destroyed. Our Loss is inconsiderable, which the enclosed Returns will evince. I have not been able to ascertain Colonel Pickens Loss but know it to be very small.

From our Force being composed of such a Variety of Corps, a wrong Judgment may be formed of our Numbers. We fought only 800 men, two thirds of which were Militia. The British with their Baggage Guard, were not less than 1150, & these Veteran Troops. Their own Officers confess, that they fought 1037. Such was the Inferiority of our Numbers that our Success must be attributed to the Justice of our Cause & the Bravery of our Troops. My Wishes would induce me to mention the Name of every private Centinel in the Corps I have the honor to Command. In Justice to their Bravery & good Conduct, I have taken the Liberty to enclose you a List of their officers from a Conviction that you will be pleased to introduce such Characters to the World....

**General Daniel Morgan to William Snickers,
January 26, 1781, Camp Sherelds Ford on Catabaw River
Horatio Gates Papers**

Dear Will,

When you left me you remember I was desirous to have a stroke at Tarleton. My wishes are Gratified, & I have Given him a devil of a whipping, a more complete victory was never more obtained.

When General Greene went to winter quarters at the Cheraw on Pee Dee, he detached me with three hundred Regulars, Major Triplett's corps of Militia, Amounting to one hundred, Colo. Washington's Regt. of Cavalry, Ninety to the west side of the Catabaw River with orders discretionary.

With this detachment I marched over the Broad River and Gained the Left flank of Cornwallis's Army, which you'l think gave him some uneasiness.

The day after I took a position, I had Intelligence of a Body of Two Hundred and fifty Tories, who were on their March to distroy that part of the Country, I detached Colo. Washington with some Militia horse to attack them, we surprised them, Killed and Wounded one hundred fifty, & took forty prisoners without Losing one Man – on this Lord Cornwallis detached Tarleton with Nine hundred Chosen Troops, the flower of his Army, with his Legion, on the west side of Broad River to Attack me in front, while he and General Lesly Marched up on the East side, to Cut off my Retreat. I saw I was pursued by three armies, each vastly superior to mine. I collected about five hundred militia / three of which fought, the others ran away. With this Little Army, I moved up Pacolet River west of

Cornwallis. The three armies followed me like Blood Hounds. Tarleton was foremost in the chase.

On the 17th Inst. my spies came in about two hours before day & told me the enemy was within five miles of me marching very Rapidly. I did not intend to fight that day, but Instead to cross Pacolet [Broad] early that morning to a Strong piece of Ground, & there decide the matter, but as matters were circumstanced, no time was to be lost. I prepared for Battle, as soon as the day Broke & had just time to form a disposition when they hove in sight.

They formed into one Line, Raised a Prodigious Yell, and came Running at us as if they Intended to eat us up, however, we sustained the Charge, the Conflict was severe Indeed, for about forty minutes at which time their over numbers had gained both our flanks, we then had no Alternative left but to Charge them with Bayonets which we did with so much address that we made them give way.

At that time Tarleton was Cuting the Militia on our Left and nearly in our Rear, Colo. Washington with his Regt. Charged the whole of Tarletons Cavalry Amounting to three hundred & thirty seven, & put them to flight, Killed a number of his men. In the meantime we followed up our Blow till we took their field Pieces when every man took to His heels for security – helter skelter -- we were too swift for them.

Killed, wounded & took prisoners One thousand veteran Troops, one thousand Stand of Arms, Two Field pieces, Thirty five Waggons an emense Baggage & entirely Broke up Tarlton's Legion, which is a Great thing Indeed –

Cornwallis and Lesly Joined their forces & attempted to Intercept me with the prisoners, but by a forced March I slipt by the day before he made the push, -- he followed me near a

Hundred Miles, I sent on the prisoners to Salisbury & made a stand at this place, & as my south Militia has all left me, I am falling Trees in the Fords of the River & calling in the North Militia to Join me, they seem to come in very fast.

Cornwallis & Lesly is within Twenty Miles of me – I have Informed General Greene of the Matter – I expect a general Action will take place, if my Lord don't go back. If no body else will fight him & the Militia Turn out well, I'll fight him myself.

Exposing myself so much has given me severe pains particularly the old pain in my Hip, so that I can't ride out of a walk. I shall be obliged to quit the service, for I am determined not to break myself entirely down. You'll see me at home in March, if no Accident happens – I am so much engaged, that I have not time to write to my friends -- Give my Complts. to them, & excuse me – my best comps. to the family.

      With Great Regard, I am…..
            Danl. Morgan

Daniel Morgan Remembered

Notes from Benjamin Berry on Daniel Morgan

Mss7:1M 8214:1
Virginia Historical Society

Benjamin Berry

<u>Notes from the statement made by Benjamin Berry of Berrysville age 83 in relation to General Daniel Morgan.</u>

Morgan has been known to [Berry] since he (Morgan) was about 20 years of age. He came from Pennsylvania about or probably before Braddock's War, and lived for sometime with a Man of the name of Roberts near the place now called Charlestown in Jefferson County, then Frederick where he came to Roberts. Morgan was so poor that he hardly any cloaths and was employed by him as a grubber, after sometime he was employed by John Ashby as a Waggoner, Ashby being then an overseer for Burwell and lived near Berry's Ferry. Morgan afterwards was employed by Ballandine as Mr. Berry supposes about having hired himself and his wagon & Team by the year. After this he went into the Army and was wounded in the face sometime during Braddock's War but Mr. Berry does not know in what character he acted in the Army. During the Time of his being there he has understood that Morgan received 500 lashes for having struck a British officer.

From the time of his first knowing Morgan for many years he was frequently engaged in affrays and was often beaten but would nevertheless renew the combat with those who had just before beaten him.

Some years after Braddocks War he kept a Waggon & Team which for some time he drove himself and at length purchased a small farm at the Place now called Saratoga which he purchased of a Mr. Blackburn. He Seems to have been engaged in gaming drinking quarreling and fighting from that time until the American War came or and made some addition to his property. Altho he would drink [heavily] at times he was never so much addicted to this Vice as to be considered a Drunkard. The place now called BattleTown (Berryville) was frequently the theater in which he carried on his riotous adventures and it has been said to have derived the name from a great pitched battle in which Morgan was a Leader, but Mr. Berry says that it was known by the name before Morgan came.

Mr. Berry supposes that Morgan was about 68 years old at the time of his death for a year or two before which he had become very infirm.

Sketch of Daniel Morgan by Rev. William Hill

Notes
Mss7:1M 8214:1
Virginia Historical Society

I shall [share]… some things which I know to be facts & these facts were partly learned from credible witnesses who were Morgan's companions & partly from himself.

He was raised in the state of New Jersey & sprung from very obscure parentage. He came to Frederick county Virginia when a young man & was employed as a day labourer. He is known by many persons now living to have been employed in grubbing. Attending a sawmill, & driving a wagon, in the last mentioned business he was engaged for a number of years.

It was whilst acting as a waggoner to the army, he was sentenced to receive five hundred lashes for insubordination to an officer, (perhaps he struck him) which he actually received at Fort Chisel. He used frequently afterwards to say in a jocular way, that King George was indebted one lash yet for the drummer miscounted one & he knew in when he did it, so that he only received 499 when he had promised him 500.

He was in his youth after embroiled in quarreling & engaged in fighting & bullying, with the Davis's, Stinson's, Isaac & Darks (one of whom was afterwards Genl. Dark) a set of the stoutest & strongest men perhaps this county ever produced: and from these their riotous & disorderly meetings the chief place of their rendezvous was called Battletown, which name it bears to this day.

It is a fact perhaps not generally know that Genl. Morgan in the latter part of his live became a very altered man. He evidenced great penitence for his former misspent life – became a member of the Presbyterian Church – was a constant & regular attendant upon worship & died in full communion in the church.

The following is a statement of an occurrence which took place while Morgan was a prisoner in Quebec, which the Genl related to me about 2 years before his death.

While in confinement in Quebec he was visited by a British officer to him unknown, but from his dress & uniform he appeared to belong to the navy & to be an officer of some distinction. This officer appeared to commiserate in his… situation. He one day asked Morgan if he did not begin to conclude that the Americans had embarked in a wild…scheme? He endeavoured to convince him that their undertaking was inpracticable & advised him to drop all thoughts of breaking the connection between the Colonies & the mother Country. He said he admired Morgan for the spirit & enterprize he had manifested, a spirit he said worthy of a better cause. And if he would agree to withdraw from the Americans & join the British he was authorized to promise him, the commission rank & enlistment of a Colonel in the British Army. This Proposal was rejected with disdain, with this reply.

"That he hoped he would never again insult him in his destroyed and unfortunate situation, by making him offers which plainly implied that he thought him a rascal." In consequence the offer was never repeated....

When ready to scale the walls, Morgan ordered one of his men first to mount the Ladder, but seeing him hesitate, he took the ladder himself, & as soon as he raised his head over the wall a musket was fired in his face, the ball missed him, but he was badly burned by the powder, some grains of which he carried in his face to his grave, & by the shock was thrown back at the feet of the ladder. He arose & took the ladder a second time and as soon as he was high enough he sprung over the wall landing upon a cannon, he was thrown upon his back under its muzzle which no doubt saved his life, for there were several bayonets thrust at him at that moment which struck the cannon but missed him in consequence of his being thrown upon the ground. But by the time he arose his men came pouring in after & so diverted the attention of those around him that he escaped, & presently took all that part of the town prisoners....

I shall now mention the rise of the difference between Gates & Morgan which took place immediately after the surrender of Burgoyne, as related to me by Genl. Morgan. Immediately after the surrender of the British army Gates took Morgan aside & apparently in confidence asked Morgan, if he know that the greatest discontent prevailed in the American army at the Commander in chief & that many of the most valuable officers threatened to resign if a change did not take place. Morgan expecting that Gates meant to make use of the present time, when the recent surrender of Burgoyne's army to him would give him such eclat with Congress, to move the removal of Washington in hopes of getting the place himself, & knowing how little credit was due Gates, who in both days action was not out of his strongly fortified camp replied," That he had one favour to ask of him which was never to mention that detestable subject to him again, for under no other man than Washington would he sever as commander in chief." & suddenly left Gates. From that time all intimacy between them ceased. A [few] days afterwards when Gates gave a dinner to the British officers, Morgan was not so much as invited, but coming in upon some business, with Gates in time of dinner, the British officers not being introduced to Col. Morgan enquired who he was, & being informed rose from their seats at table followed him to the door, & introduced themselves to him so high an opinion had they conceived of him from their acquaintance they had formed with him on the field of battle....

Hence also we may account for the silence Gates preserved about Morgan in his dispatches to Congress respecting the pursuant actions & surrender of Burgoyne. But his fit tool Wilkenson who was all the time with Gates snug in camp was selected as the favorite messenger & recommended for promotion....

The night after the action Gates met Morgan at the gates of the camp exclaiming, "Morgan you have done wonders for your country, if you are not promoted I will not serve a day longer myself." Yet in his dispatches he does not mention Morgan's name, [which] the rebuff Morgan gave him, when wishing to supplant Washington alone can [account].

William Maxwell, ed., "A Recollection of the American Revolutionary War. By a British Officer, Virginia Historical Register and Literary Companion, Vol. 6, No. 4, (Richmond: 1853), 210-211 (Excerpt)

[Morgan] alluded to [the Battle of Saratoga] with undisguised triumph, and spoke with more volubility, perhaps, than good taste, of his own exploits on the occasion. "*Oh, we whopped them tarnation well, surelie,*" said he, rubbing his hands; "*though to be sure they gave us tough work too. But it was on the 7th of October that the rifles settled the business. Me and my boys attacked a height that day, and druv Ackland and his grenadiers; but we were hardly on the top when the British rallied, and came on again with such fury that nothing could stop them. I saw that they were led by an officer on a grey horse – a devilish brave fellow; so when we took the height a second time, says I to one of my best shots, says I, you get up into that thre tree and single out him on the white horse. Dang it, 'twas no sooner said than done. On came the British again, with the grey horseman leading; but his career was short enough this time. I jist tuck my eyes off him for a moment, and when I turned them to the place where he had been – pooh, he was gone!*"

I knew at once that he spoke of General Fraser, who rode that day a grey horse, and fell from a rifle ball through the body. But Morgan did not confine his loquacity to communications like this. He told us that the British owed him a lash; that he drove one of the wagons which accompanied General Braddock's army, and being a giddy young man, that he had, on a certain occasion, knocked down a sentinel; for that offence he had been condemned to receive four hundred lashes, of which only three hundred and ninety-nine were inflicted – "*I counted them myself*," continued he, laughing, "*and am sure that I am right; nay, I convinced the drum-major of his mistake, but they wouldn't tie me up again; so I am still their creditor to the amount of one last.*"

Rev. William Hill's Sermon at General Morgan's Funeral From the Winchester Gazette

The following is the concluding Address, or Biographical Remarks, of the Rev. William Hill's sermon, upon the death of Gen. Daniel Morgan:

We have now, my brethren, been considering death in a general point of view, or as it concerns us all alike. It may not be amiss for us, at present, to exercise a few thoughts upon the particular instance of death before us. The present case confirms the truth…that "it is appointed unto all men once to die." He that could expose himself time after time on the ensanguined plain, amidst the roar of cannon and the clash of arms – where the death bearing bullets flew like hail stones, and come off unhurt – he, whose iron constitution, and firm [strength] of body enabled him to survive the deadly wound inflicted by the sure aim of a savage marksman*, must at last yield to nature's stern degree.

(Note: * This refers to a wound he once received from an Indian. The bullet entered the back of his neck about midway, and came out at his left cheek, having knocked out all his jaw teeth on that side.)

But my fellow citizens, can we contentedly resign this ancient Patriot and Hero to the tomb in silence, without testifying our gratitude for the favors he contributed so largely to procure for us, and declaring our opinion of his worth as a public character? The imposing occasion compels me to depart from my usual silence, respecting the dead, and gratitude constrains me to eulogize him whom I esteem so much our benefactor.

As to his private character, I presume it would be needless for me to say much before an audience who were generally much better acquainted with him, than myself; and with this we have but little to do.

If, from an almost total neglect of education in his youth, and his being in that critical season of his life exposed to much loose company, he had contracted some bad habits and vices which were not to be overcome but with great difficulty, these should be touched but lightly, especially as we hope he was in his last days brought to see the impropriety and folly of these things, and sincerely repent of the same.

Notwithstanding, it is but justice to declare, that he was the affectionate Husband, the tender and indulgent Parent, the humane master, the steady Friend and one whose heart could not withstand the face of distress or the lake of woe, but constrained him to grant assistance when needed.

But that for which nature chiefly formed him was the Patriot and the Soldier. When we consider the obscurity from which he rose; the honour and power to which he ascended; the great services which he has rendered his country, we may say he had few, very few equals.

The predominant [possession] of his heart appears to have been the Love of his Country. This together with the Vividus

Impetus of his nature, caused him soon to fly to the standard of his country: And how well he acquitted himself there; let history tell.

In the most dark and gloomy stages of our contest with Britain, his attachment was unshaken. Admitting that he was not insensible to the advantage of riches and affluence, this will serve only to shew more conspicuous regard to the public good. It is well known that he began his career in life low in the world and in this state he was still when taken prisoner at Quebec. At that time the American cause was at a low ebb, and but a gloomy prospect presented itself to us. It was in such a state, while in close confinement, he spurned with indignation the rank and emolument of a Colonels commission for life in the British army though he was then but an American Captain. You may see his universal attachment to his country highly commended by General Washington in his letters to Congress, after his exchange, and urged as a motive why he should be promoted to a Colonel's commission in the American army.

The brave, intrepid and I am sorry to add infamous Arnold, was not as inaccessible when placed in circumstances infinitely more eligible than the prison of Quebec. Whenever his country called, our deceased friend was at hand, against her interest no office of honour or emolument had charms; when she was threatened, no danger could intimidate. And even while he retained any recollection, the welfare of his country was his topic, and appeared to absorb his whole soul.

But as a soldier he has rendered his country most essential service. To retrace his different adventures, escapes and achievements would be to recount almost all the memorable transactions that took place from Quebec to Georgia, and give anew the history of the revolution.

Who has not heard of his memorable exploits in storming the walls if Quebec? After the unfortunate Arnold had fallen, although there were other officers superior in rank to him, they all shrunk back and constrained him to conduct the enterprize. By performing prodigies if valour, and feats of heroism, he forced his way into the heart of the town, where he expected to meet the brave Montgomery: But fortune declared against the arduous attempt, and he, and his brave comrades, were in their turns, made prisoners after defending themselves to the last extremity.

At Saratoga he acquired laurels for his commander in chief. He was the acting officer in the first day's actions – And in the second, he acted in concert with Arnold: But, when he again fell, the command devolved upon Col. Morgan. It is a little mysterious that there is no credit given him for those exploits in the American history of the revolution, while in some of the British accounts, his name is mentioned with great honour and applause. I am still in hopes that this business will be enquired into by some future historian, and justice done to his memory. It is certain we owe the capture of Burgoyne's army more to his exertions, watchfulness, and bravery, than any other man.

Who remembers not the ever memorable action of Cowpens? We have just heard that his actions chiefly contributed to brighten our prospects from the north – Now, when America was all but in despair, our spirits dejected, and our nerves paralyzed, we hear him thundering from the south, and giving the first check to the savages of British insolence in that quarter. Had not this event taken place at that time, I cannot certainly say what might have been the consequence. But it flew from south to north like a shock of electricity, revived our languid hopes, and strung our sinews anew from the contest.

Vast crowds came flocking his standard, to assist in his encumbered retreat.

But I must check myself. – As a soldier he appeared to unite what is seldom found in contact, caution with intrepidity, an entire self possession, with an impetuous ardour and flow of spirits. He was certainly a child of fortune; but his success are not attributable only to a fortunate concurrence of circumstances. There was a wisdom, a sagacity discoverable in all his plans and operations, which evinced the strong energetic mind, that knew how to avail itself of every advantage of situation and time, and bar accidents and surprise.

In camp he was ever vigilant and attentive; he made it a point to be in every place in person, and see that every thing was done in season. He was tender and attentive to all his men, and did what was in his power to render them comfortable – he was foremost in fatigue, and never failed to stimulate by example – he was a strict and exact disciplinarian, and had the happy talent of effecting this without severity. In the field of action he was cool and self possessed, but his _____ would appear to be in every place, and dart along his ranks with _____ and keenness peculiar to himself; and in the attack act the impetuosity of a resistless torment: In fact, he was the complete soldier. I think we may venture to assert, that he has not left another behind him to whom we are so much indebted for our Independence and Liberty.

Whilst we sit each under his own vine and fig-tree, and none to make us afraid – Whilst the liberty he has contributed so largely to procure for us gilds our path through life, gladdens every scene, and makes [yon sun] himself to shine with new luster, the name of Morgan shall be precious to our hearts. Posterity itself shall know thy name, and knowing it, learn to imitate they Patriotism and Bravery. Beloved Patriot and Hero, we bid thee, Farwell.

Daniel Morgan's Last Will and Testament

April 17, 1773

I, Daniel Morgan, of Frederick county, Virginia, being in my proper senses, and calling to mind the uncertainty of life and the certainty of death, do make this my last Will and Testament, hereby revoking and disannulling all former wills and codicils of wills, heretofore made by me the aforesaid Daniel Morgan.

And in the first place it is my will and desire, and I do hereby constitute and appoint my loving and affectionate wife Abigail Morgan, the whole and sole executrix of this my last Will and Testament, of all and every part of my estate, both real and personal.

Item, It is my will and desire that all my just debts be honestly and punctually paid, and that the remainder or residue of my estate (after the discharge of those my debts) be appropriated to the use and for the benefit of the said Abigail, my dear and loving wife; and that the same continue to be at her disposal, during her natural life and widowhood.

Item, It is my will and desire, that after the decease of the aforesaid Abigail (or in case she should intermarry after my decease) that the whole and sole of my estate, both real and personal, be equally divided between her two daughters, named Nancy Morgan and Betsy Morgan; and in case of the decease of either of them, that then the whole and sole of my estate aforesaid be appropriated to the use and benefit of the survivor, or surviving sister.

Item, it is my will and desire, and the intent and meaning of this, is that my loving wife Abigail have the use and benefit of all my estate aforesaid, as aforesaid specified, only excepting against, and prohibiting her from disposing of any part thereof to defraud the two children aforesaid, to wit, Nancy Morgan and Betsy Morgan.

Daniel Morgan's Last Will and Testament
                                                March 17, 1801

I, Daniel Morgan, of Winchester, in the county of Frederic and Commonwealth of Virginia, possessing fully the powers of recollection and all the usual faculties of my mind, but being weak in body and knowing that all men must die, do make this my last Will and Testament, hereby revoking all former Wills or Testaments heretofore made by me, and allowing this only to be my last Will and Testament.

First, I recommend my soul to the Omnipotent Creator of all things, trusting for salvation in his mercy and the atonement of my blessed Lord and Saviour Jesus Christ. I desire that my body may be decently interred at the discretion of my family and as to my worldly affairs I make the following arrangement and distribution.

Having by two deeds of trust bearing date the sixteenth day of March in the present year of our Lord one thousand eight hundred and one, conveyed to certain trustees in the said deeds named the place called Saratoga, containing two hundred and fifty-five acres of land with its appurtenances; and also four hundred and seven acres of land more or less, adjoining the lands of Thomas Bryarly, the heir of John Bell deceased, Richard K. Mead and Alexander Henderson, which I purchased of Nathaniel Ashby; also three hundred and eleven acres of land adjoining Saratoga, which I purchased of Col. Nathaniel Burwell, late of Isle of Wight county, deceased, also one hundred acres of land which I purchased of Nathaniel Burwell, Esq., of Frederic county, adjoining Saratoga, all of the said lands being in the county of Frederick, and Commonwealth of Virginia, also all the stock, slaves, household stuff and furniture, on the said place called Saratoga, and in the mansion house thereon, to hold in trust for the benefit of my well beloved daughter Betsy Heard wife of James Heard, according to the tenor of the said deeds, which it is my desire may be fully executed and complied with in every particular, and in addition to the property aforesaid I now give, devise and bequeath to my said daughter Betsy Heard all my land in the State of Kentucky, whether granted for military services or otherwise, and whether in my own name or procured by purchase, computed to be about ten thousand acres, to hold to her the said Betsy Heard, her heirs and assigns forever; and I do hereby empower and authorize Major James Heard to make sale of the said lands in Kentucky or any part or parcel thereof, and upon such sale being made to make good and sufficient titles to the purchaser, and apply the purchase money to the use of the family, provided my said daughter Betsy shall consent to such sale. I also give, devise and bequeath to my said daughter Betsy Heard five thousand acres of land in the State of Tennessee on Crow Creek, purchased of Major Armstead for five thousand dollars to her, her heirs and assigns forever.

 I give, devise and bequeath to my beloved wife Abigail the tract of land I purchased of Samuel Bell, containing two hundred and seventy-eight acres, to her, her heirs and assigns forever, to be by her sold and the money applied to such uses and purposes as she may think proper.

I desire that my executors hereafter named, may with all convenient speed after my decease collect all debts due to me, and out of the moneys so collected pay all my just debts and funeral charges, and being conscious that I owe no just debts of long standing, I desire that if any such should be brought against my estate the statute of limitations shall be pleaded in bar of such claims. All my military land in the northwestern territory I give, devise and bequeath to Presley Neville, my son-in-law, to be disposed of at his discretion to him, his heirs and assigns forever.

All the rest, residue, and remainder of my estate real, personal or mixed, I give and bequeath unto my beloved wife Abigail, for and during the term of her natural life, and after her decease, I give, devise and bequeath the same to my well beloved daughter Nancy Neville, wife of the aforesaid Presley Neville, to her heirs, executors, administrators, and assigns forever.

And lastly, I do hereby appoint my beloved wife Abigail Morgan and my son-in-law Presley Neville, executrix and executor of this my last Will and Testament.

Codicil to Daniel Morgan's Last Will and Testament, March 17, 1802

…I do hereby ratify and confirm in all and every article thereof, except the alteration hereinafter mentioned in this present writing, which I make and add as a codicil to my said last will and testament, and to be taken as part thereof, that is to say, whereas, in and by the said last will and testament, I did among other things give, devise and beqeath unto my well beloved daughter Betsy Heard, wife of James Heard, all my lands in the State of Kentucky whether granted for military services or otherwise, and whether in my name or procured by purchase, computed to be about ten thousand acres, to hold to her the said Betsy Heard, her heirs and assigns forever, and did empower Major James Heard to make sale of the said lands or any part thereof and apply the money arising from such sale to the use of his family, provided the said Betsy should consent to such sale being made, and I did by the same will to the said Betsy five thousand acres of land in the State of Tennessee on Crow Creek, purchased of Major Armstead for five thousand dollars, to her heirs and assigns forever, now it is hereby declared to be my will and desire that instead of said lands going and being devised as aforesaid, that my four grandchildren Matilda Heard, Nancy Morgan Heard, Daniel Morgan Heard, and Morgan Augustus Heard, children of the said Betsy Heard, have the same to be equally divided among them, share and share alike as to quantity and quality, and I do hereby devise the same to them, the said Matilda, Nancy Morgan, Danial Morgan, and Morgan Augustus Heard, their heirs and assigns forever, to be equally divided as aforesaid.

Bibliography

Primary Sources

Books

Abbot, W.W. ed. *The Papers of George Washington, Colonial Series,* Vol. 3. Charlottesville: University Press of Virginia, 1984.

Albion, Robert and Leonidas Dodson Philip, eds. *Philip Vickers Fithian: Journal, 1775-1776, Written on the Virginia-Pennsylvania Frontier and in the Army Around New York*. Princeton: Princeton University Press, 1934.

Ballagh, James C. ed. *Letters of Richard Henry Lee,* Vol. 1. New York: Macmillan Co., 1911.

Baxter, James ed., *The British Invasion from the North: Digby's Journal of the Campaigned of Generals Carleton and Burgoyne from Canada, 1776-1777.* New York : De Capa Press, 1970.

Boyle, Joseph Lee. *Writings from the Valley Forge Encampment of the Continental Army,* Vol. 1. Bowie: Heritage Books Inc., 2000.

Brown, Lloyd and Howard Peckman, ed., *Revolutionary War Journals of Henry Dearborn, 1775-1783*. Freeport, NY: Books for Libraries Press, 1939.

Burgoyne, John. *.A State of the Expedition from Canada*. New York Times & Arno Press, 1969.

Chase, Philander D. ed. et al. *The Papers of George Washington: Revolutionary War Series,* Vol. 1-20. Charlottesville: University Press of Virginia, 1985-2015

Clark, Walter ed. *Colonial and State Records of North Carolina,* Vol. 14. Winston, NC: 1896.

Commager, Henry Steele and Richard B. Morris, eds. "Lieutenant Colonel John Eager Howard's Account of Cowpens," *The Spirit of Seventy-Six.* NY: Castle Books, 2002.

Davies, K. G. Davies, ed. *Documents of the American Revolution,* Vol. 18-20. Irish University Press, 1978.

Dorman, John, ed., "Peter Bruin Pension Application," *Virginia Revolutionary Pension Applications,* Vol. 12. Washington, D.C.: 1965.

Dorman, John Frederick ed., "Eden Clevenger Pension Application," *Virginia Revolutionary Pension Applications,* Vol. 20. Washington, D.C., 1972.

Fitzpatrick, John C. ed. *The Writings of George Washington,* Vol. 19. Washington, U.S. Government Printing Office, 1937.

Ford, Worthington C. ed. *Journals of the Continental Congress: 1774-1789,* Vol. 2. Washington: Government Printing Office, 1905.

Hening, William ed. *The Statutes at Large Being a Collection of all the Laws of Virginia,* Vol. 9. Richmond: J & G Cochran, 1821.

Henry, John Joseph. *Account of Arnold's Campaign Against Quebec.* New York Times & Arno Press, 1968.
    Originally published in 1877

Idzerda, Stanley J. ed. *LaFayette in the Age of the American Revolution*, Vol. 4. Ithica and London: Cornell University Press, 1981.

Jackman, Sydney, ed., *With Burgoyne from Quebec: An Account of the Life at Quebec and of the Famous Battle at Saratoga.* Toronto: Macmillan of Canada, 1963.

Kirkwood, Robert. *The Journal and Order Book of Captain Robert Kirkwood.* edited by Rev. Joseph Brown Turner, Wilmington, The Historical Society of Delaware,1910.

Lamb, Roger. *An Original and Authentic Journal of Occurrences During the Late American War from Its Commencement to 1783.* Dublin:Wilkinson & Courtney, 1809. Reprinted by Arno Press, 1968

Lee, Charles. "Testimony of Various Continental Officers at the Court Martial of General Charles Lee," *The Lee Papers*, Vol. 3. New York Historical Society, 1873.

Lesser, Charles H. ed. *The Sinews of Independence: Monthly Strength Reports of the Continental Army.* Chicago: The University of Chicago Press, 1976.

McILwaine, H.R. ed. *Journals of the Council of the State of Virginia,* Vol. 1. Richmond: Virginia State Library, 1931.

Pausch, George.*Journal of Captain Pausch, Chief of the Hanau Artillery During the Burgoyne Campaign.* Translated by William L. Stone, Albany, NY: Joel Munsell's Sons, 1886.

Roberts, John M. ed., "James Collins", *Autobiography of a Revolutionary Soldier.* NY: Arno Press, 1979.

Roberts, Kenneth ed. *March to Quebec: Journals of the Members of Arnold's Expedition*. New York: Country Life Press, 1938.

Roberts, Kenneth Roberts, ed. *Journals of the Members of Arnold's Expedition*. Garden City, NY: Doubleday & Co., 1940.

Rogers, Horatio, ed. *Hadden's Journal and Orderly Book: A Journal Kept in Canada and Upon Burgoyne's Campaign in 1776 and 1777*. Boston: Gregg Press, 1972.

Runge, Beverly H. ed. *The Papers of George Washington, Colonial Series,* Vol. 10. Charlottesville, VA: University Press of Virginia, 1995.

Saffel, W.T.R. *Records of the Revolutionary War, 3rd Ed.* Baltimore: Charles Saffell, 1894.

Scheer, George F. and Hugh F. Rankin, *Rebels & Rodcoats: The American Revolution Through the Eyes of Those Who Fought and Lived It*. Da Capo Press, 1957.

Showman, Richard and Dennis Conrad, eds. *The Papers of General Nathanael Greene*, Vol. 6. Chapel Hill, NC: The University of North Carolina Press, 1991.

Smith, Paul H. ed. *Letters of Delegates to Congress*, Vol. 1. Washington, D.C.: Library of Congress, 1976.

Tarleton, Lieut. Col. Banastre. *A History of the Campaigns of 1780 and 1781 in the Southern Provinces of North America*. North Stratford, NH: Ayer Company Publishers Inc., 1999.

Taylor, Robert J. ed. *The Papers of John Adams*, Vol. 3. Cambridge, MA: Harvard University Press, 1979.

Thacher, James, M.D., *Military Journal of the American Revolution.* Gansevoort, New York: Corner House Historical Publications, 1998.

Thwaites, Reuben Gold and Louise Phelps Kellog, eds., *Documentary History of Dunmore's War : 1774.* Madison, WI: Wisconsin Historical Society, 1905.

Williams, Otho Holland, "A Narrative of the Campaign of 1780, by Otho Holland Williams," *Sketches of the Life and Correspondence of Nathanael Greene,* Vol. 1. edited by William Johnson, Charleston: 1822.

Wilkinson, General James. *Memoirs of My Own Times,* Vol. 1. Philadelphia: Abraham Small, 1816.

Willard, Margaret ed., *Letters on the American Revolution: 1774-1776.* Boston & New York: Houghton Mifflin Co., 1925.

Periodicals

Boyle, Joseph Lee, ed. "From Saratoga to Valley Forge: The Diary of Lt. Samuel Armstrong," *The Pennsylvania Magazine of History and Biograp hy.* Vol. 121 No. 3 July 1997.

Chappelear, Curtis. "The George Carter Tract," *Proceedings of the Clarke County Historical Association*, Vol. 3, (1943

DAR Patriot Index, Vol. 2. Baltimore, MD: Gateway Press, Inc., 2003.

Dawson, Henry B. "General Daniel Morgan, An Autobiography", *The Historical Magazine and Notes and Queries Concerning the Antiquities, History and Biography of America, 2nd Series* Vol. 9. 1871.

Dearborn, Henry. "A Narrative of the Saratoga Campaign – Major General Henry Dearborn, 1815," *The Bulletin of the Fort Ticonderoga Museum.* Vol. 1, No. 5, January, 1929.

Egle, Wm. H. ed., "The Journal of Captain William Hendricks and Captain John Chambers," *Pennsylvania Archives, 2nd Series*, Vol. 15. 1890

Flickinger, B. Floyd ed. "Diary of Lieutenant William Heth while a Prisoner in Quebec, 1776", *Annual Papers of Winchester Virginia Historical Society,* Vol. 1. 1931.

Frederick County Order Book Abstracts, Order Book 15, "10 May, 1771."

Gates, Horatio. "General Gates to Congress, 4 July, 1780," *Magazine of American History*, Vol. 5. New York: A.S. Barnes & Co., 1880.

Joyner, Peggy Shomo, ed., "Allason Papers: Store Day Book, 1761-63,"*Magazine of Virginia Genealogy*, Vol. 34, No. 4, Fall 1996.

LeMoine, J.M. "Col. Caldwell to Gen. James Murray, Spring, 1776," *The Centenary Fete of the Literary and Historical Society of Quebec*, 1876.

Orderly Book of Major William Heth of the Third (sic) Virginia Regiment, May 15 – July 1, 1777. *Virginia Historical Society Collections, New Series, 11.* 1892.

Porterfield, Charles. "Diary of Colonel Charles Porterfield," *Magazine of American History.* Vol. 21. April 1889.

Seymour, William. "Journal of the Southern Expedition, 1780-1783", *The Pennsylvania Magazine of History and Biography,* Vol. 7. 1883.

Strange, Lt. Col. "Historical Notes on the Defence of Quebec in 1775," *The Centenary Fete of the Literary and Historical Society of Quebec.* 1876.

Tyler, Lyon ed. "John Chilton to his brother, 29 June, 1777", *Tyler's Quarterly Historical and Genealogical Magazine,* Vol. 12. Richmond, VA: Richmond Press Inc., 1931.

Waddell, J.A. ed., 'Diary of a Prisoner of War at Quebec, 1776," *The Virginia Magazine of History and Biography,* Vol. 9. Richmond,VA: The Virginia Historical Society, July 1901 no. 1.

Williams W. William, ed., "Robert Magaw to the Carlisle Committee of Correspondence, 13 August, 1775," *Magazine of Western History.* Vol. 4, (May-October, 1886.

Newspapers

Dixon and Hunter. "Extract of a letter from an officer in camp, Dec. 16, 1777," *Virginia Gazette*. 26 December, 1777.

Purdie, Alexander Purdie's *Virginia Gazette*, 7 February, 1777," 1

Purdie & Dixon. "A Meeting of Officers…," *Virginia Gazette*. 22 December, 1774.

Unpublished and Online Sources

"A Return of the 2nd Company of Rangers Commanded by Capt. John Ashby, 21 October, 1755," *George Washington Papers at the Library of Congress, 1741-1799*: Series 4, General Correspondence, 1697-1799.
(Accessed through the Library of Congress website)

"*A Short Biography of the Life of Governor Thomas Posey*," Thomas Posey Papers, Indiana Historical Society Library, Indianapolis, IN.

Bacheller, Nathaniel. Letter, 9 October, 1777. Copy on file at Saratoga National Historical Park.

Berry, Benjamin. "Notes from Benjamin Berry on Daniel Morgan," Virginia Historical Society.

Butler, Richard. "Lt. Col. Richard Butler to Col. James Wilson, 22 January, 1778," Gratz Collection, Case 4, Box 11, Historical Society of Pennsylvania

Gates, Horatio. "Gates, Horatio to Daniel Morgan, 23 June, 1780," Theodorus Bailey Myers Collection, Series 5, #857, NY Public Library

Gates, Horatio. "General Gates to General Smallwood, 3 October, 1780," Letters from Horatio Gates, *Papers of the Continental Congress*, Record Group 360, Item Number 171, National Archives

Hill, William, Reverend. Sketch of Daniel Morgan, Notes and Sermon," Virginia Historical Society.

Morgan, Daniel. "General Morgan to General Washington, 20 September, 1781," Theodorus Bailey Myers Collection, Series 5, # 945, NY Public Library.

Morgan, Daniel. "General Morgan to William Snickers, 26 January 1781," Horatio Gates Papers, NY Historical Society.

Nevill, John, Col. "Colonel John Nevill to Colonel Daniel Morgan, 9 November, 1779" Theodorus Bailey Myers Collection, Series 5, #1000, NY Public Library.

"Report on Virginia Battalions, 17 May, 1777," *George Washington Papers at the Library of Congress, 1741-1799: Series 4,* Image 943
    (Online)

Watts, Garret. "GarretWatts Pension Statement, Revolutionary Pension Roll", in Vol. 14 Sen. Doc. 514, 23rd Cong., 1st sess., 1833-34.

Secondary Sources

Books

Babits, Lawrence E. *A Devil of a Whipping: The Battle of Cowpens*. Chapel Hill : The University of North Carolina Press, 1998.

Boatner III, Mark M. ed., *Encyclopedia of the American Revolution, 3rd. ed.* Stackpole Books, 1994.

Bockstruck, Lloyd D. *Virginia's Colonial Soldiers*. Baltimore, MD: 1990.

Buchanan, John. *The Road to Guilford Courthouse: The American Revolution in the Carolinas*, (New York: John Wiley & Sons, Inc., 1997.

Cecere, Michael. *They Are Indeed a Very Useful Corps*. Heritage Books, 2006.

Cecere, Michael. *They Behaved Like Soldiers: Captain John Chilton and the Third Virginia Regiment*. Heritage Books, 2004.

Clark, Stephen. *Following Their Footsteps: A Travel Guide & History of the 1775 Secret Expedition to Capture Quebec,* 2003.

Dandridge Danske. *Historic Shepherdstown*. Charlottesville, VA: Michie Co., 1910.

Desjardin, Thomas A. *Through A Howling Wilderness: Benedict Arnold's March to Quebec, 1775.* New York: St. Martin's Griffin, 2007.

Draper, Lyman C. *King's Mountain and Its Heroes: History of the Battle of King's Mountain.* Cincinnati :Peter G. Thomson, 1881.

Graham, James. *Life of General Daniel Morgan.* Bloomingburg, NY: Zebrowski: Historical Services Publishing Co., 1993.
    (Originally published in 1856)

Higginbotham, Don. *Daniel Morgan: Revolutionary Rifleman.* Chapel Hill: University of North Carolina Press, 1961.

Ketchum, Richard M. *Saratoga,: Turning Point of America's Revolutionary War.* NY: Holt & Co., 1997.

Lacrosse, Richard B. LaCrosse Jr., *The Frontier Rifleman.* Union City, TN: Pioneer Press, 1989.

Landers, Lt. Col. H.L. *The Battle of Camden, South Carolina: August 16, 1780.* U.S. Printing Officer, 1929.

Luzader, John. *Saratoga: A Military History of the Decisive Campaign of the American Revolution.* New York: Savas Beatie, 2008.

Marshall, John. *The Life of George Washington,* Vol. 3. Fredericksburg, VA: Citizen's Guild of Washington's Boyhood Home, 1926.

Martin, David. *The Philadelphia Campaign, June 1777 – July 1778.* Da Capa Press, 1993.

Maxwell, William, ed., "A Recollection of the American Revolutionary War," *Virginia Historical Register and Literary Companion,* Vol. 6. Richmond: MacFarland & Fergusson, 1853.

McGuire, Thomas. *The Philadelphia Campaign: Germantown and the Roads to Valley Forge*, Vol. 2. Stackpole Books, 2007.

Morissey, Brendan. *Quebec 1775: The American invasion of Canada.* Osprey, 2003.

Piecuch, Jim and John Beakes, *"Cool Deliberate Courage": John Eager Howard in the American Revolution.* Charleston, SC: Nautical and Aviation Publishing, 2009.

Sanchez-Saavedra, E.M. *A Guide to Virginia Military Organizations in the American Revolution, 1774-1787.* Westminster, MD: Willow Bend, 1978.

Stedman, C. *A History of the Origin, Progress, and Termination of the American War*, Vol. 2. London: 1794.

Stewart, Catesby Willis ed. *The Life of Brigadier General William Woodford of the American Revolution,* Vol. 2. Richmond, VA: Whittet & Shepperson, 1973.

Stryker, William. *The Battle of Monmouth.* Princeton: Princeton Univ. Press, 1927.

Periodicals

Flickinger, B. Floyd, "Captain Morgan and His Riflemen," *Winchester-Frederick County Historical Society Journal,* Vol. 14. 2002.

Jordon, John W. ed., "Bethleham During the Revolution," *Pennsylvania Magazine of History and Biography,* Vol. 12. 1888.

Schnitzer, Eric. "Battling for the Saratoga Landscape," *Cultural Landscape Report: Saratoga Battle, Saratoga National Park,* Vol. 1. Boston, MA: Olmsted Center for Landscape Preservation.

Index

2nd Virginia Regiment, 90
3rd Virginia Regiment, 90, 96, 99
7th Regt. Royal Fusiliers, 194
7th Virginia Regiment, 90, 146, 160, 162
9th British Regiment, 106
11th Virginia Regiment, 85-99, 162
15th Virginia Regiment, 90, 162
17th British Dragoons, 194
20th British Regiment, 106
21st British Regiment, 106
47th British Regiment, 105
62nd British Regiment, 106, 111, 113
71st Battalion, 192-193, 208
Abercromby, Robert, Col., 143
Ackland, John, Maj., 125
Adams, John, 4, 23, 30
Albany, NY, 101, 102, 103, 105, 118, 120, 130

Alexandria, VA, 5
Anburey, Thomas, Ensign, 109, 115, 117, 132
Anderson, Capt., 75
Armstrong, Samuel, 106, 108
Arnold, Benedict, 21, 31,
 expedition to Canada, 33-64,
 attack on Quebec, 66-69, 72-73, 77
 mentioned, 80-81, 83, 91, 104,
 at Saratoga, 122-130
Ashby, John, Capt., 6
Balcarres, Alexander, Lt. Col., 120
Balcarress Redoubt, 126-129
Battletown, VA, 7
Bedinger, Henry, 18, 23-24, 26-27
Bemis Heights, NY, 105-106, 118, 120-121
Bennington, Battle of 1777, 104

Berkeley, Co. VA, 17-18
Bethleham, PA, 27
Bigelow, Timothy, Maj., 81
Blackwell, William, Capt., 86-88
Boston, MA, 8, 12, 15, 17, 20, 23-27, 29-30, 32, 82
Bound Brook, NJ, 90, 97
Braddock, Edward, Gen., 5
Brandywine, Battle of 1777, 119, 137, 141, 160
Breymann, Heinrich, Lt. Col., 120
Breymann Redoubt, 126-130

Brian, John Oliver, Rev., 79
British Parliament, 8, 12, 15, 151
Bruin, Peter, 20, 76-77, 85-87, 89
Burgoyne, John, Gen., 97, 100-101, 104-106, 108-109, 111, 113-114, 116-122, 124-126, 130
Burwell, Robert, 4, 6
Burwell, Nathaniel, 223
Butler, Richard, Lt. Col., 110, 123, 129, 138, 165

Calderwood, James, Capt., 86-87
Caldwell, Henry, Maj., 61, 73, 77
Cambridge, MA, 23, 27, 30, 35
Camden, Battle of, 1780, 174-176, 178-179, 184, 186, 193
Carleton, Guy, Governor,, 33, 64, 79-80, 82
Caswell, Richard, Gen., 175
Charleston, SC, 171, 178, 192, 210
Charleston, WV, 4

Charlotte, NC, 178-179, 183, 185, 187, 191
Chesney, Alexander, 191
Chilton, John, Capt., 21, 96, 99
Clevenger, Eden, 87
Clinton, George, Governor, 102-103
Clinton, Henry, Gen., 117-118, 151, 153-155, 159-161, 169, 171, 193, 220
Colburn, Reuben, 34, 37
Collins, James, 206

Continental Congress, 15, 82, 103, 164-169, 171-173, 180-181, 184
Cornwallis, Charles, Lord, 141, 175, 177-178, 180, 183, 188, 191-193, 195-197, 213, 220
Cowpens, Battle of, 1, 191-211
Crawford, William, Maj., 11
Cresep, Michael, Capt., 26
Cumberland Co. VA, 5, 17, 217
Curry, Abigail, 7
Davidson, William, Gen., 197
Dearborn, Henry, Maj., 52, 104, 108, 111, 116-117, 120-125, 129-131
Digby, William, Lt., 105, 108, 112, 114-115, 131-132
Draper, Lyman, 24
Dumfries, VA, 5
Dunmore, John Murray, Earl of,, 8-13, 16, 20, 89-90
Enos, Roger, Lt. Col.,, 41, 51-52
Ewald, Johann, Capt., 141

Fauquier Co., VA, 86, 89
Febiger, Christian, 62, 85, 88-89
Ferguson, Patrick, Maj., 183
Fishkill, NY, 27
Fithian, Philip Rev., 16
Franklin, Benjamin, 4
Fraser, Simon, Gen., 106, 109, 125-126
Frederick, MD, 23
Frederick Co. VA,, 3, 5-9, 15-18, 23-24, 26-27, 86-87, 89, 143, 149, 219-220, 223-224
Fredericksburg, VA, 5, 172
Ft. Cumberland, MD, 5
Ft. Edward, VA, 6
Ft. Gower, VA, 10, 12
Ft. Gower Resolves, 12
Ft. Mercer, 138
Ft. Stanwix, NY, 104
Ft. Ticonderoga, NY, 33, 64, 121, 130
Ft. Washington, NY, 84-86
Ft. Western, ME, 36-38, 41, 51-52
Gallihue, Charles, Capt., 89
Gates, Horatio, Gen.,

at Saratoga, 103-106, 109, 118-122, 130, commands Southern army, 171-181, 184-187

Germain, George,, 116, 142, 179, 215

Germain, Lord George, 116

Germantown, Battle of 1777, 99, 137, 141, 160

Gerry, Elbridge, 23

Goodrich, William, Capt., 81-82

Green Spring, Battle of, 220

Greene, Christopher, Lt. Col., 39, 41, 43, 49, 51-52

Greene, Nathanael, Gen., 94, 137-139, 178, 184-189, commands Southern army, 191-192, 194-197, 205, 207, 209-211, 213-218

Grey, Charles, Gen., 141

Guilford Courthouse, NC, 216, 218

Hackensack, NJ, 98

Hadden, James, Lt., 109, 111-112

Hager, George, Col., 143

Hamilton, Alexander, 106, 111, 137

Hamilton, James, 137

Hamilton, James, Gen., 106, 111, 113-114

Hampshire Co., VA, 218

Hanchet, Oliver, Capt., 51

Hancock, John, 84

Harlem Heights, Battle of, 84

Harrison, Carter, 217

Hartford, CT, 27

Haskell, Caleb, 41

Haverstraw, NY, 98

Height of Land, 52-53

Hendricks, William, Capt., 76

Henry, John Joseph, 46, 49-50, 52-54, 57-58, 62-63, 67-68, 76,

Henry, Patrick, 15, 142

Heth, William,, 20, 21, 79, 85, 91

Hill, William, 1, 69

Hillsborough, NC, 178-181, 185

House of Burgesses, 8

Howard, John, Col., 208

Howe, William, Gen., 82, 84, 90, 94, 96-100, 119,

137, 139, 141-142, 144, 151
Huger, Isaac, Gen., 216
Humphreys, John, Lt., 20, 58, 76
Intolerable Acts, 12, 15
Jaegers, 141, 143
Jefferson, Thomas, 187
Johnson, William, Capt., 89, 178
Kalb, Johann, Baron de, 175-178
King George III, 5, 13, 15
Kings Mountain, Battle of, 183, 194
LaFayette, Marquis de,, 138-139, 153, 219
Lamb, Roger, 112, 127
Lamb, Roger, Cpl., 112, 127
Laurens, John Maj., 142-143, 146,167
Lawson, Robert, Gen., 217
Learned, Ebenezer, Gen.,, 122, 127, 129
Lee, Charles, Gen., 153-155, 157
Lee, Light Horse Harry, 134, 224
Lee, Richard Henry, 21, 23
Leesburg, VA, 5

Lewis, Andrew, Col., 10
Lexington and Concord, MA, Battle of 1775, 15, 17
Litchfield, CT, 27
Livingston, James, Col., 66
Long Island, Battle of, 82, 84, 141
Long, Gabriel, Capt., 86-87
Loudoun Co., VA, 86-87
Louis XVI, King of France, 150
Malvern Hill, VA, 220
Marion, Francis, Col., 178
Marshall, John, Lt., 86, 201
McDonald, Angus,Maj., 9-10
McDowell, Charles, 208
McJunkin, Joseph, 205
Meigs, Return, Maj., 41, 51
Merchant, George, 62
Middlebrook, NJ, 162-163
Mingo Indians, 11
Monmouth, Battle of, 1778, 153-158
Montgomery, Richard, Gen., 63-64, 66-67, 72, 77, 83
Morgan, Abigail, 7
Morgan, Betsy, 7

Morgan, Daniel,
  early life and arrival in VA, 4
  whipped for misconduct, 5
  wounded, 6
  brawls in Battletown, 7
  has children with Abigail, 7
  militia commander, 8
  slave owner, 8
  Dunmore's Expedition against the Shawnee, 1774, 9-14
  Ft. Gower Resolves, 12-13
  returns to Frederick Co., 15
  appointed Capt. of rifle company, 1775, 17-18
  raises rifle company, 18-23
  marches to Boston, 1775, 23-27
  siege of Boston, 1775, 30
  expedition to Quebec, 1775, 33-56
  captures British midshipman, 57-58
  outside Quebec, 60-63
  argument with Arnold, 63
  withdraws from Quebec, 63-64
  attack on Quebec, 1775, 66-77
  captured, 77
  captivity in Quebec, 1776, 79-82
  parole, 1776, 82-85
  commands 11th VA Regt., 1777, 85-91
  commands rifle corps, 1777, 91-100
  ordered to NY, 102
  battle of Saratoga, 1777, 105-134
  battle of Whitemarsh, 1777, 139-144
  Valley Forge, 1778, 145-149
  furlough, 1778, 149
  battle of Monmouth, 1778, 153-158
  leaves rifle corps, 1778, 160
  commands Woodford's brigade, 1778-79, 162-164
  resigns from army, 1779, 164-169

returns to army, 1780, 172
commands light flying army, 1780-81, 180-199
battle of Cowpens, 1781, 199-211
retreats to VA, 213-217
home in VA, 217-223
life after the war, 223-224
Morgan, Nancy, 7
Morgan, Willoughby, 223
Morgan's Rifle Corps, formed, 91
Morris, Joseph, Maj., 109-110, 129, 143, 148
Mud Island, 138
Muhlenburg, Peter, Gen., 168
Neville, John, Col., 169-170
New Providence, NC, 184-186
New York, NY, 82, 84, 96, 97, 98, 100, 101- 103, 105, 108, 118, 137, 151, 153, 159-162, 195, 220
Newburyport, MA, 34-37
Newport, RI, 160
Ninety-Six, SC, 192-193

Norridgewock Falls, ME, 43, 45
Paramus, NJ, 98
Pausch, George, 114
Peekskill, NY, 102
Peters, Richard, 148
Philadelphia, PA, 12, 15, 16, 88, 97, 98, 99, 101, 104, 137, 138, 139, 140, 141, 144, 145, 150, 151
Pickens, Andrew, Col., 197
Piscataway, NJ, 95
Pittston, ME, 37
Point Aux Trembles, Canada, 63-64
Point Pleasant, Battle of, 10
Poor, Enoch, Gen., 111, 122, 125
Porterfield, Charles,, 67-70, 72-73, 75-77, Capt., 81, 85-87, 89, Lt. Col.,175
Portsmouth, VA, 220
Posey, Thomas, Capt., 95, 123, 146, 160
Prince Edward Co., VA, 217
Prince William Co., VA, 86, 87, 89
Putnam, Israel, Gen., 102

Quebec, 1, 21, 31, 33-35, 37, 39, 50, 53, 57-65, 79- 81, 83, 85, 104, 109
  Battle of, 1775, 66-77
Race to the Dan, 217
Radnor, PA, 146
Reed, Joseph, 95
Richmond, VA, 5, 15, 21, 63, 81, 86, 96, 169
Riedesel, Friedrich, Gen., 105, 113, 114
Roxbury, MA, 30
Rugeley, Rowland, Col., 186
Salisbury, NC, 181, 183, 216
Sandy Hook, NJ, 98, 151, 158-160
Saratoga, Battle of, 1777, 1, 101, 135, 137, 150, 164, 171, 223,
  Freeman Farm, 105-114
  Interlude, 114-120
  Bemis Heights, 120-130
  Surrender, 131-134
Savannah, GA, 171
Schuyler, Philip, Gen., 33-34, 63, 97, 100, 101, 102, 103
Scott, Charles, Gen., 153, 168

Senter, Isaac, Dr., 45, 48, 54-55
Seymour, William, 176-177, 181, 206
Shawnee Indians, 9-10, 12
Shepherdstown, WV, 18, 23-24, 26-27
Skowhegan, ME, 43-44
Smallwood, William, Gen., 177, 179-181, 185-186
Smith, Matthew, Capt., 50, 63
Stephenson, Hugh, Capt., 18, 24, 27, 30, 83, 85
Steuben, Friedrich Wilhelm, Gen., 149
Stevens, Edward, Gen., 175, 218
Stirling, Alexander, Gen., 96
Stocking, Abner, 37, 43, 55-56, 75
Stony Point, Battle of, 168-169
Stothard, Thomas, 87
Sumter, Thomas, Gen., 178
Sussex Courthouse, NJ, 27
Tarleton, Banastre, Lt. Col., 1, 179, 183, 191-195, 197, 199-203, 205-211, 215, 220

Thacher, James, Maj., 28
Thayer, Simon, Capt., 43, 52
Trenton, NJ, 90, 99
Valley Forge, PA, 145-150
Van Vechten's Bridge, NJ, 94
Varnum, James Gen., 145
Wallace, Andrew, Capt., 208
Ward, Artemas, Gen., 30
Warren, James, 27, 29, 30
Washington, George, Col., 11
  appointed General of the Continental Army, 17
  siege of Boston, 29-30
  plans Quebec expedition, 33-35, 39-40
  attack on Quebec, 60, 63-64
  comments on Morgan's parole, 82-85
  urges Morgan to march to NJ in 1777, 88-89
  reorganizes army, 90-91
  forms Morgan's Rifle Corps, 91-96
  tour of Jerseys, 97-100
  orders Morgan to NY, 101-103
  requests Morgan's return, 118-120
  at Whitemarsh, PA, 137-144
  at Valley Forge, PA, 145-149
  at Monmouth, NJ, 151-159
  reorganizes army, 1778-79, 160-164
  reacts to Morgan's resignation, 165-167
  appoints Gen. Greene to command Southern army, 184
  at Yorktown, 220-222, 224
Washington, William, Lt. Col., 185-186, 188, 191-192, 194, 203, 206, 208-209, 213
Watts, Garret, 175-176
Wayne, Anthony, Gen., 94, 153-154, 157, 163-165, 167-168, 220
Wetherall, Frederick Lt., 143
Wheeling, WV, 9-10
Wells, Henry, 207
Whiskey Rebellion, 224
White Plains, NY, 159-161

Whitemarsh, PA, 137-138
 Battle of 1777, 139-144
Wilkinson, James, 106, 108-110, 112-113, 117-118, 121, 125-127, 129
Williams, Otho, Col., 177-178, 193, 211, 216
Williamsburg, VA, 16
Winchester, VA, 7, 9, 16, 18, 20, 24, 27, 89, 125, 223-224

Winnsboro, SC, 183, 188, 191-193
Wood, James, Capt., 9
Woodford, William, Gen., 90, 160-162, 168-170
Yorktown, VA, 220, 222
Young, Thomas, 200, 203, 207